1989

Marxism

and the Oppression of

Women

Marxism

and the Oppression of

Women

Toward a Unitary Theory

Lise Vogel

Rutgers University Press
New Brunswick, New Jersey

Library of Congress Cataloging in Publication Data

Vogel, Lise.
Marxism and the oppression of women.
Toward a unitary theory.

Bibliography: p.
Includes index.
1. Women and socialism.
2. Marx, Karl, 1818–1883.
I. Title.
HX546.V63   1983   335.4'088042   82–24047
ISBN 0-8135-1234-4 (pbk.)
British Cataloging-in-Publication information available
Second paperback printing, 1989
First paperback printing, 1987

Previously published material has been adapted and/or incorporated in this work. The author wishes to thank the publishers for permission to use the following:

Excerpts from *The Emancipation of Women* by V. I. Lenin. New York: International Publishers, Inc., 1966.

Excerpts from *The Condition of the Working Class in England* by Friedrich Engels. Translated and edited by W. O. Henderson and W. H. Chaloner. Stanford: Stanford University Press, 1968.

Excerpts from *The Origin of the Family, Private Property and the State* by Frederick Engels. New York: International Publishers, Inc., 1972.

"The Question" from *Robinson on the Woman Question* by Lillian Robinson. Buffalo: Earth's Daughters, 1975.

Portions of "Marxism and Feminism: Unhappy Marriage, Trial Separation or Something Else?" by Lise Vogel in *Women and Revolution: A Discussion of the Unhappy Marriage of Marxism and Feminism*, edited by Lydia Sargent. Boston: South End Press, 1981.

Portions of "Marxism and Socialist-Feminist Theory: A Decade of Debate" by Lise Vogel in *Current Perspectives in Social Theory* 2 (1981): 209–231.

In loving memory of my mother
Ethel Morell Vogel
1907–1958
my aunt
Anna Vogel Colloms
1900–1981
and my father
Sidney Vogel M.D.
1904–1986

Contents

Preface

This project began more than ten years ago. Like that of many other women in the late sixties, my commitment to the emerging women's liberation movement coincided with my discovery of Marxist theory. At first, it seemed to many of us that Marxist theory could simply be extended in order to address our concerns as women's liberationists. Very soon, we recognized that this solution was far too mechanical, and left much to be explained. The Marxist theory we encountered, and the socialist legacy of work on women's oppression, required thorough transformation. With this realization, some turned away entirely from Marxism. Others persisted in the attempt to use Marxist theory, aiming now to develop a "socialist-feminist" synthesis that would transcend the inadequacies of the socialist tradition. While sympathetic to this approach, I continued to pursue the original goal of extending Marxist theory, and quickly came up against the necessity of examining just what Marxist theory is. Additionally, a careful reading of the major nineteenth-century texts pertaining to the so-called woman question made it clear that the theoretical tradition is highly contradictory. In the past several years I have sought to confront these and related problems. This book is the result. Not surprisingly, its order of presentation parallels the development of my own thinking on the issues. That is, the text begins with an evaluation of socialist-feminist theory, moves on to a critical reading of the nineteenth-century writings, and closes with a theoretical treatment of women's oppression that situates it in the context of the overall reproduction of society. In the course of working on the book, my respect for socialist-feminist efforts to address the question of women's op-pression has deepened. Notwithstanding, I remain convinced that the revival of Marxist theory, not the construction of some socialist-feminist synthesis, offers the best chance to provide theoretical guid-ance in the coming battles for the liberation of women.

When I first started work on the problem of women's oppression, a text by Marx caught my attention. He is commenting on the relation-ship between religious ideology and social reality, and uses the Chris-tian holy family as his example: "Once the earthly family is discovered to be the secret of the holy family, the former must then itself be criti-cised in theory and revolutionised in practice."[1] It seemed to me that with these words, Marx had also captured the essence of a historical materialist understanding of family experience. Indeed, socialists have attempted to criticize as well as revolutionize "the earthly family" for more than a century, although with limited effectiveness. The condi-tions that gave rise to today's women's liberation movement have at last, I think, produced the possibility of a more adequate critique and a real revolution. But possibilities are never certainties. As early as 1971, Juliet Mitchell had analyzed the state of the women's liberation move-ment in terms of a potential battle between liberationists with a social-ist analysis and feminists with a radical feminist analysis. The sugges-tion of a way forward she made then remains valid, I believe, today:

> We have to develop our feminist consciousness to the full, and
> at the same time transform it by beginning a scientific socialist
> analysis of our oppression. The two processes must go on si-
> multaneously—feminist consciousness will not "naturally" de-
> velop into socialism, nor should it: the two are coextensive
> and must be worked on together. If we simply develop femi-
> nist consciousness . . . we will get, not political consciousness,
> but the equivalent of national chauvinism among Third World
> nations or economism among working-class organizations;
> simply a self-directed gaze, that sees only the internal work-
> ings of one segment; only this segment's self-interest. Political
> consciousness responds to all forms of oppression.[2]

It is precisely the need to respond to all forms of oppression while simultaneously deciphering the specific character of women's oppres-sion that has motivated my efforts. To the so-called woman question I make, therefore, a clear reply. In the words of Lillian Robinson's poem:[3]

Women?
    Yes.

Several articles came to my attention too late to be incorporated in the text. They are relevant to the arguments I make concerning the limited scope of the concept of patriarchy, and the problems inherent in paralleling sex, race, and class as comparable sources of oppression. Recent work in social history emphasizes that the concept of patriarchy does not suffice to explain the complex linkages among women's oppression, family experience, and social reproduction. Two studies on the family wage and on occupational segregation by sex are especially interesting: Martha May, "The Historical Problem of the Family Wage: The Ford Motor Company and the Five Dollar Day," *Feminist Studies* 8 (1982): 399–424; Ava Baron, "Women and the Making of the American Working Class: A Study of the Proletarianization of Printers," *Review of Radical Political Economics* 14, no. 3 (Fall 1982): 23–42. The problem of the paralleling of different oppressions is raised by several studies that document the history of women of color and analyze the specific consequences of racial and national oppression for women. Jacqueline Jones, for example, shows that slave families on American plantations represented an arena of support, autonomy, and resistance for the slave community, while simultaneously nurturing the seeds of later patriarchal family relations: "'My Mother was Much of a Woman': Black Women, Work, and the Family Under Slavery," *Feminist Studies* 8 (1982): 235–269. Bonnie Thornton Dill analyzes how the history of oppressed groups created barriers to social participation that affect women in these groups today: "Race, Class, and Gender: Prospects for an All-inclusive Sisterhood," *Feminist Studies* 9 (1983): 131–150. Such studies shed light on the reasons underlying black women's general distrust of the contemporary women's movement, for feminist emphasis on the analogy between sex and race oppression and on sisterhood tends to deny the special character of racial and national oppression. By breaking with the simplistic paralleling of sex, race, and class as comparable sources of oppression, Jones, Dill, and others establish the foundation for a strategic orientation that responds to the special concerns of women of color. Feminists and socialists must, in Dill's words, go beyond "the concept of sisterhood as a global construct based on unexamined assumptions about [women's] similarities" if they wish to develop strategies for social transformation that can unite women on a more solid basis.

Acknowledgments

I cannot list here all the friends and coworkers who have provided encouragement and helpful criticism during the years in which I worked on this project. For their warm support I am deeply grateful. As the manuscript took shape in an early version, I benefited from the critical judgment of many. In particular, I am indebted to Lee Austin, Egon Bittner, Ron Blackwell, Ralph Miliband, Molly Nolan, and Charlotte Weissberg for intelligent readings and detailed commentaries on this version. I want also to thank Jeanne Butterfield, Marlene Fried, Sheila Morfield, Susan Okin, Tim Patterson, Rayna Rapp, Carol Robb, and the members of several study groups. As I prepared the manuscript for publication, several people read, and in some cases reread, sizable portions of it: Jill Benderly, Ira Gerstein, Nancy Holmstrom, Beth Lyons, and Susan Reverby. For their thoughtful comments and suggestions, particularly on the theoretical arguments and political ramifications, as well as their generous willingness to come through on short notice, I would like to express a special gratitude. Appreciation also to the staff at Rutgers University Press, and especially to my editor Marlie Wasserman, for her firm support of this project, and to my copyeditor Barbara Westergaard, for her high standards and good sense.

Thanks, finally, to the women throughout the world whose participation in movements for liberation gives this theoretical project meaning. Without them, it would not exist.

1

Introduction

T he 1960s marked the appearance of movements for the liberation of women in virtually every capitalist country, a phenomenon that had not been seen for half a century. Beginning in North America, this second wave of militant feminism spread quickly. Great Britain and the nations of Europe reacted first to the North American stimulus, and a new feminist consciousness emerged as well in such places as Japan, India, Iran, and Latin America. Although reminiscent of earlier feminism, the women's movement of the 1960s and 1970s necessarily constituted a specific response to new social conditions. Not the least of its peculiarities was the existence of a significant trend within it known as socialist feminism or Marxist feminism, which sought to merge the two traditions so self-consciously linked together. Socialist feminism, argued its proponents, represents "a unique politics that addresses the interconnection of patriarchy and capitalism, with the goal of dealing with sexism, class conflict, and racism."[1]

The emergence of a socialist-feminist trend in the late 1960s was an extremely important development. Socialist feminism stood in solidarity with anti-imperialist and progressive struggles both at home and abroad. Simultaneously, it placed itself in opposition to a growing radical feminist tendency that considered male supremacy the root of all human oppression and the main obstacle to female liberation. By the mid-seventies, however, the socialist-feminist movement began to lose some of its momentum and bearings, as anti-imperialist activity receded and as many Marxist women withdrew from socialist-feminist organizations, if not from the women's movement altogether. The

1

theoretical and organizational perspectives of radical feminism now appeared to offer more guidance to socialist feminists than they had before, particularly on the critical questions of sexuality, interpersonal relations, ideology, and the persistence of male domination through-out history. At the same time, women's experience in revolutionary movements and socialist countries seemed more removed from im-mediate socialist-feminist concerns. A certain pessimism regarding the achievements of existing socialist movements and the possibilities of current revolutionary initiatives developed. In this atmosphere, some socialist feminists became persuaded that Marxism could not be trans-formed or extended by means of the application of feminist insight. They suggested, moreover, that such a goal is not only unattainable but betrays women's liberation to the demands of socialism. Whereas socialist feminism had originated in a commitment to the simultane-ous achievement of women's liberation and socialist revolution, that double commitment now threatened to break apart.

This book constitutes an argument *for* the power of Marxism to analyze the issues that face women today in their struggle for libera-tion. It strongly rejects, however, the assumption made by many social-ists that the classical Marxist tradition bequeaths a more or less com-plete analysis of the problem of women's oppression. In this sense, it could be called a socialist-feminist work, although it shares neither the current skepticism among socialist feminists as to the usefulness of Marxist theory, nor their high hopes for radical feminist perspectives. Instead, the text argues that the socialist tradition is deeply flawed, that it has never adequately addressed the question of women, but that Marxism can nevertheless be used to develop a theoretical framework in which to situate the problems of women's oppression and women's liberation.

The force and character of the feminist upsurge of the 1960s and 1970s, and of its socialist-feminist component, owe much to the partic-ular circumstances of the postwar period. Serious transformations in capitalist domination followed the end of World War II, as the structure of power began to undergo profound changes, both within each na-tion and internationally. Women, no matter what their class, soon faced significantly altered tasks, expectations, and contradictions.

During World War II, an emergency mobilization had thrust women into an unprecedented variety of new roles, many of them tra-ditionally the preserve of men. With the war's end and the return of the soldiers, the situation changed dramatically. Men flooded into the labor force, pushing women back down the job ladder or out altogether. In reality, women's participation in the labor force never returned to its prewar level. Within a few years, moreover, statistics revealed a new phenomenon. Whereas before the war the typical woman worker had been young, unmarried, and only temporarily in the labor force, by 1950 large numbers of older married women, often with school-age children, had entered the labor force on a semipermanent basis. The trend was to continue unabated, in flagrant contradiction to the ideal of the nuclear family.

The social impact of these shifts in the character of female labor force participation was blunted by the intensification of the ideology emphasizing women's place in the home. Beginning in the late 1940s, a new emphasis on domesticity projected images of the happy homemaker devoting herself solely to the consumption of goods and services and to the socialization of children in isolated nuclear family households. Women, especially wives, were working in increasing numbers but were supposed to believe that their real identity lay in their family roles. In more intimate fashion, the myth of the nuclear family fostered interpersonal relations characterized by hierarchy, oppression, and isolation, thereby contributing at the psychic level to the postwar reconstruction of stability.

Tensions between the norm of the nuclear family and the reality of women's lives were especially sharp in the United States. In the late 1950s, they reached the breaking point, as more and more women chafed at the bonds of what Betty Friedan was soon to name the feminine mystique. The early sixties witnessed the beginnings of a critique, which took a variety of political, ideological, and organizational forms. Many of these converged in the formation of the National Organization for Women (NOW) by a group of militant middle-class feminists. Founded in 1966, NOW announced its purpose to be "to take action to bring women into full participation in the mainstream of American society *now*, exercising all the privileges and responsibilities thereof in truly equal partnership with men."[2]

To all appearances, the new movement represented a genuine revival of traditional liberal feminism, seeking complete equality for women within capitalist society. Two characteristics distinguished it, however, from older forms of liberal feminism. First, the 1960s feminists began to extend the concept of equality beyond the earlier movement's emphasis on formal equality in the civil and political sphere. NOW, for instance, initially focused on legal redress, but its concerns soon extended to areas of female experience formerly viewed as private, and untouched by traditional feminist programs. It demanded child-care facilities and control over one's own reproductive life as basic rights for all women. Implicit, if not explicit, in the discussion about such rights were the issues of sexuality and the sex division of labor in housework. Furthermore, the feminists of the Kennedy-Johnson years sometimes distinguished among women by economic status, as when NOW argued for the right of poor women to secure job training, housing, and family support. This differentiation marked a break, however unwitting, from the strict emphasis on formal equality that typified nineteenth-century versions of feminism. With its extreme sensitivity to the most subtle aspects of inequality, as well as its occasional forays into questions of sexuality, the sex division of labor in the household, and differential economic oppression, the new movement pushed liberal feminism to its limits.

The second characteristic that distinguished modern feminism from its nineteenth-century predecessor was the political atmosphere out of which it emerged. The women's movement of the nineteenth and early twentieth centuries had ridden the crest of an advancing capitalist world order, demanding, in essence, that the promise of equality held out by the triumphant bourgeoisie be extended to women. While individual feminists argued that women needed more than equal rights, and that bourgeois society itself required transformation, their critiques represented a visionary strain, largely peripheral to the mainstream feminist movement of the time. In sharp contrast, modern feminism drew strength from the critique of capitalism that flourished and deepened following the end of the Second World War. Internationally, capitalism had come under siege, as large portions of the world freed themselves from direct imperialist domination, often turning to socialism. A number of countries began to follow strategies for the achievement of human liberation in a socialist society that differed sharply from policies pursued in the Soviet Union. At the same time, national liberation movements around the world were intensifying their struggles to achieve independence. These developments in the international arena shaped a more thoroughgoing consciousness of the issues of freedom, equality, and personal liberation. It was against this background that a newly militant movement for civil rights emerged in the United States in the fifties, serving, in turn, as an important inspiration for the feminist movement of the early sixties. Both movements demanded equality within the framework of capitalist society, yet pressed the notion of equal rights to the threshold of a vision of liberation.

Not until the mid-1960s did large numbers of people step across that threshold. In the United States, the rise of black liberation movements, highly sensitive to international developments, converged with the intensification of the war in Vietnam. Periodic urban insurrections, an aggressive antiwar movement, and resistance to the war within the military itself shook the country. Meanwhile, a massive resurgence of left activity swept Europe in the wake of the May 1968 events in France. And everywhere, the Chinese Cultural Revolution inspired a new generation of social activists, who rejected all attempts to resolve discontent within the confines of bourgeois society. Drastic social transformation seemed on the immediate agenda. In this atmosphere, a "women's liberation movement" emerged in the United States, its founding members seasoned as (white) activists in the civil rights, community organizing, and antiwar movements. Seemingly independent of all earlier feminist efforts, including the liberal feminism of the early sixties, the new movement initially adopted the form of small groups committed to consciousness raising, local organizing, and, at times, direct action. Unlike the more sober feminism of such organizations as NOW, women's liberation succeeded in tapping and mobilizing the dissatisfaction engendered by the many contradictions in all aspects of women's lives. "Sisterhood is powerful" argued the women's liberation movement, as it rapidly spread throughout the United States, Canada, Europe, and beyond. No sphere of experience could escape attention, moreover, for these feminists recognized that "the personal is political," and put their theories into practice. In a period of social upheaval, the women's liberation movement catapulted the idea of female liberation into public consciousness and laid the groundwork for a mass women's movement.

From the start, activists in the women's liberation movement differed among themselves on the role of women's issues in the process of social change, and developed distinct strategic orientations. Some saw the fight against women's oppression as part of a larger struggle for socialism. For these women, the task became how to resist a traditional socialist tendency to subordinate feminist issues in the course of the struggle for socialism. Others insisted that the issue of women's domination by men was fundamental to any process of social transformation, had a sharply autonomous character, and required a qualitatively distinct struggle. Here, the problem concerned the demarcation of this position from that held by the most militant liberal feminists. As both discussion and practice deepened, a cleavage developed within the women's liberation movement. Radical feminists increasingly emphasized the primacy of sex antagonisms in social development, the critical role of sexuality and sexual preference, and the irredeemable weaknesses of socialist work on women. In opposition, another tendency within the women's liberation movement began to argue that the strengths of radical feminism could in fact be melded with socialist analysis into a new strategy. By the early seventies, this latter tendency—soon dubbed Marxist feminism or socialist feminism—had consolidated into an important force within the women's movement, as well as on the left.[3]

Socialist feminists share a general strategic and organizational perspective. They argue that the participation of women, conscious of their own oppression as a group, is critical to the success of any revolutionary struggle. They assert that the key oppressions of sex, class, and race are interrelated and that the struggles against them must be coordinated—although the precise character of that coordination remains unspecified. In any case, socialist feminists agree on the necessity of an independent movement of women from all sectors of society throughout the revolutionary process: working women; housewives; single women; lesbians; black, brown, and white women; blue-collar and white-collar women, and so on. For socialist feminists, only such an autonomous women's movement can guarantee socialist commitment to women's liberation, particularly in the ideological and interpersonal areas, and in the domestic sphere. Autonomy, they maintain, is a political as well as a tactical principle. Finally, socialist-feminist theorists argue that the movement shares with much of the new left "a totalistic view of the socialist transformation, an emphasis on subjective factors in the revolutionary process, and a rejection of mechanical stage-ism."[4] For most activists, however, the essence and strength of the socialist-feminist movement lie not in its view of socialism but in its tenacious insistence on, and particular interpretation of, the feminist insights that sisterhood is powerful and the personal political.

Theory did not play a large role in the development of the women's liberation movement in its first stages. Indeed, the very ability to exist and grow without firm theoretical or organizational bearings testified to the movement's strength as a real social force. By the early seventies, however, the movement began to reevaluate its practice, and to examine more closely the theoretical framework implicitly guiding its activity. In turning to theoretical work, participants in the women's liberation movement addressed practical issues arising out of their political experience. Nowhere was this new commitment to theory stronger than among socialist feminists. Their interest in theory responded, in large part, to a sense that the already established socialist-feminist strategic orientation needed a more adequate foundation.

Socialist feminists quite naturally looked to the socialist tradition for a theoretical starting point. The issue of women's subordination has a long and relatively distinguished pedigree as an object of concern for socialists. In practice, socialist movements have sought, as best they could, and often with lapses, weaknesses, and deviations, to involve women in social change on a basis of equality. At the theoretical level, socialists have generally conceptualized the problem of women's oppression as "the woman question." The socialist theoretical tradition has been unable, however, to develop adequate or consistent answers to this so-called woman question, as socialist feminists soon discovered. In the gloomy wake of this failure, socialist feminists pose a series of difficult questions that must be confronted more successfully. These questions center on three interrelated areas:

☐   First, all women, not just working-class women, are oppressed in capitalist society. Women occupy a subordinate place, moreover, in all class societies, and some would argue that women are subordinated in every society, including socialist society. What is the root of women's oppression? How can its cross-class and transhistorical character be understood theoretically?

☐   Second, divisions of labor according to sex exist in every known society: women and men do different types of work.[5] In particular, women tend to be responsible for work in the area of child rearing, as well as other types of labor in the household; they may also be involved in production. Generally speaking, sex divisions of labor represent stubborn barriers to women's full participation in every society. What is the relationship of these sex divisions of labor to women's oppression? Given women's childbearing capacity, how is it possible for women to be truly equal? Shouldn't the very notion of equality be discarded or transcended in order for women to be liberated?

☐   Third, women's oppression bears strong analogies to the oppression of racial and national groups, as well as to the exploitation of subordinate classes. Are sex, race, and class parallel oppressions of essentially similar kind? Does female oppression have its own theoretically specific character? What is the relationship of the fight against women's oppression to the struggle for national liberation and for socialism?

Explicitly or implicitly, socialist feminism sets itself the task of developing a better set of answers to these questions than the socialist tradition has been able to offer. But in its haste to define and take up this weighty burden, socialist-feminist theory often leaves behind those elements in the tradition that might actually lighten the load. All too quickly, socialist feminism abandons the socialist tradition's revolutionary Marxist core.

The chapters that follow present a case for the usefulness of Marxist theory in developing a theoretical framework that can encompass the problem of women's oppression. Because the focus throughout is on the material foundations that underpin the oppression of women, certain other aspects must be put to one side for the moment. In particular, the text does not address directly the psychological, interpersonal, and ideological issues that so often form the main subject of writings on the question of women's liberation. Adequate consideration of these crucial issues must be rooted in a materialist theory of women's oppression, and attempts to supply such a theory have been deficient. These deficiencies are noted in the two chapters of Part One, which assess the state of existing theoretical work carried out from a socialist-feminist perspective. Chapter 2 surveys the development of socialist-feminist theory over more than a decade. Chapter 3 sums up its contributions, emphasizing strengths but pointing to certain persistent limitations. Chapter 3 also considers the inadequacy of the Marxist theoretical tradition on the so-called woman question, and suggests that it is in fact very poorly understood. The Marxist theoretical legacy requires serious reevaluation. Parts Two and Three therefore undertake a review of major texts of the tradition that pertain to the issue of women's liberation. In Chapters 4, 5, and 6, the work of Marx and Engels is examined in chronological order, revealing its incomplete and contradictory nature as well as its substantial contribution. Chapters 7 and 8 then discuss the manner in which the efforts of the late nineteenth-century socialist movement to confront the issue of woman's oppression exacerbated the analytical confusion.

With Part Four, the text returns to the problem of developing an adequate theoretical framework. Chapter 9 argues that the Marxist socialist movement failed to establish a stable theoretical foundation for its consideration of the so-called woman question. The chapter points out, furthermore, that the socialist legacy actually represents a contradictory mix of divergent views, never sufficiently clarified, much less elaborated in detail. As a result, Marxist efforts to address the problem of women's liberation have been haunted by a hidden debate between two perspectives, only one of which situates the problem within the framework of Marx's analysis of the processes of overall social reproduction. Chapters 10 and 11 therefore take up the task of elaborating this latter perspective. Chapter 10 develops a theoretical approach that puts childbearing and the oppression of women at the heart of every class mode of production. In Chapter 11, the specific situation of women in capitalist society is addressed theoretically, together with the conditions for women's liberation. Both chapters take as their object of analysis the phenomenon of women's oppression in the context of overall social reproduction. That is, the theoretical focus is shifted away from the vague concept of the woman question, so common in traditional socialist writings. Likewise, the category of "the family," often used by both socialists and socialist feminists, is found to be wanting as an analytical starting point; its deceptive obviousness masks a tangle of conceptual problems. Hence, these theoretical chapters first establish the basis in social reproduction for women's oppression, before considering the institution known as the family. Once the special character of women's oppression in capitalist social reproduction is understood, for example, it becomes possible to analyze families in capitalist societies.

This book constitutes, it should be emphasized, a theoretical undertaking. It seeks to place the problem of women's oppression in a theoretical context. The last two chapters in particular present what may appear to be a fairly abstract set of concepts and analytical framework. This is as it should be. Only in the analysis of an actual situation will abstraction spring to life, for it is history that puts flesh on the bare bones of theory.

Part One

Socialist

Feminism

2

A Decade

of Debate

Socialist-feminist theory, like the movement to which it owes its existence, is far from monolithic. In general, socialist feminists argue that socialist theory must be extended or even entirely transformed by means of the insights offered by feminist theory and practice. A variety of attempts to execute this transformation has been made, although no consensus yet exists on their adequacy. If anything, socialist feminists increasingly recognize the difficulty of the theoretical task. "We have been excessively impatient for finished products, answers, and total theories," comments one group. "We have not allowed for the tremendous amount of work involved in clearing new paths and dealing with new questions."[1] Nonetheless, more than ten years of theoretical efforts in the name of socialist feminism have left their mark. Despite weaknesses, which sometimes function as obstacles to further progress, the socialist-feminist movement has made the most important advances in the development of socialist theory on the question of women since the nineteenth century.

Initial efforts to develop a socialist-feminist theoretical perspective focused on the family unit and the labor of housework and child rearing in contemporary capitalist societies. The opening argument, an article entitled "Women: The Longest Revolution" by Juliet Mitchell, actually appeared well before the development of the socialist-feminist movement proper. First printed in 1966 in *New Left Review*, a British Marxist journal, Mitchell's piece began to circulate widely in the United States two years later. It rapidly became a major theoretical influence on the emerging socialist-feminist trend within the women's liberation movement. The publication in 1971 of Mitchell's book, *Woman's Estate*, based on the earlier article, reinforced the impact of Mitchell's ideas.[2]

Mitchell begins "Women: The Longest Revolution" with an intelligent critique of the classical Marxist literature on the question of women. She comments briefly on the schematic views of women's liberation held by Marx, Engels, Bebel, and Lenin, locating their inadequacies in the absence of an appropriate strategic context. In these texts, "the liberation of women remains a normative ideal, an adjunct to socialist theory, not structurally integrated into it." Even De Beauvoir's *The Second Sex*, while an important contribution, is limited by its attempt to meld "idealist psychological explanation [with] an orthodox economist approach." In sum, "the classical literature on the problem of woman's condition is predominantly economist in emphasis."[3]

For Mitchell, the way out of this impasse is to differentiate woman's condition into four separate structures: production, reproduction, socialization, and sexuality. Each structure develops separately and requires its own analysis; together, they form the "complex unity" of woman's position. Under production, Mitchell includes various activities external to what we might intuitively call the domestic or family sphere, for example, participation in wage labor in capitalist society. Conversely, the remaining three categories, oppressively united in the institution known as the family, encompass woman's existence outside of production, as wife and mother. In an effort to reach general strategic conclusions, Mitchell then surveys the current state of each of the four structures. Production, reproduction, and socialization show little dynamism, she says, and indeed have not for years. The structure of sexuality, by contrast, is currently undergoing severe strain, and represents the strategic weak link—that is, the structure most vulnerable to immediate attack.

While one structure may be the weak link, Mitchell argues that socialist strategy will have to confront all four structures of woman's position in the long run. Furthermore, "economic demands are still primary" in the last instance. In this context, Mitchell makes a number of sensitive strategic observations. The left must reject both reformism and voluntarism on the issue of woman's oppression, for they always lead to inadequate strategic programs. The reformist tendency manifests itself as a set of modest ameliorative demands divorced from any fundamental critique of women's position. The voluntarist approach takes the more belligerent form of maximalist demands concerning the abolition of the family, total sexual freedom, collective child rearing, and the like. Although these demands appear radical, they "merely serve as a substitute for the job of theoretical analysis or practical persuasion. By pitching the whole subject in totally intransigent terms, voluntarism objectively helps to maintain it outside the framework of normal political discussion." In place of such abstract programs, the socialist movement requires a practical set of demands that address all four structures of woman's position. For instance, in the area of wage labor, Mitchell observes that "the most elementary demand is not the right to work or receive equal pay for work—the two traditional reformist demands—but *the right to equal work itself.*" As for the abolition of the family, the strategic concern should rather be the liberation of women and the equality of the sexes. The consequences of this concern are "no less radical, but they are concrete and positive, and can be integrated into the real course of history. The family as it exists at present, is, in fact, incompatible with either women's liberation or the equality of the sexes. But equality will not come from its administrative abolition, but from the historical differentiation of its functions. The revolutionary demand should be for the liberation of these functions from an oppressive monolithic fusion."[4]

Questions about Mitchell's analysis of woman's situation arise in four areas. First, the discussion of the empirical state of the separate structures is extremely weak, a failure that has, or should have, consequences in the realm of strategy. To maintain that "production, reproduction, and socialization are all more or less stationary in the West today in that they have not changed for three or more decades" grossly misrepresents not only postwar history but the evolution of twentieth-century capitalism. Moreover, as Mitchell herself sometimes recognizes, the contradictions produced by rapid movement in all four of her structures form the very context for the emergence of the women's liberation movement. A generally inadequate historical vision accompanies Mitchell's failure to identify contemporary changes in the structures, and her work reveals, overall, a certain disregard for concrete analysis.

Second, Mitchell's view of women's relationship to production is open to serious criticism. She presents production as a structure from which women have been barred since the beginning of class society. Even capitalism has ameliorated this situation but little, for it perpetuates "the exclusion of women from production—social human activity." Like all previous forms of social organization, capitalist society constitutes the family as "a triptych of sexual, reproductive, and socializatory functions (the woman's world) embraced by production (the man's world)."[5] In sum, Mitchell views production as an aspect of experience essentially external to women. Once again she misreads history, for women's participation in production has been a central element of many class societies. Furthermore, Mitchell persistently devalues women's domestic labor as well, and gives it no clear theoretical status.

A third problem in Mitchell's analysis is her treatment of the family. While she mentions the family at every point, Mitchell denies the category "family" any explicit theoretical presence. Its place is taken by the triptych of structures that make up the woman's world: reproduction, socialization, and sexuality. At the same time, the actual content of these three structures has a severe arbitrariness, and Mitchell fails to establish clear lines of demarcation among them. Women are seen as imprisoned in their "confinement to a monolithic condensation of functions in a unity—the family," but that unity has itself no articulated analytical existence.[6]

Finally, Mitchell's manner of establishing a structural framework to analyze the problem of women's oppression requires critical examination. The four structures that make up the "complex unity" of woman's position operate at a level of abstraction that renders social analysis almost impossible. They provide a universal grid on which women—and, implicitly, the family—can be located irrespective of mode of production or class position. Societal variation and class struggle appear, if at all, as afterthoughts rather than central determinants. Furthermore, the manner in which the four structures combine to produce a complex unity remains largely unspecified, as well as abstract and ahistorical. As a result, Mitchell's theoretical approach resembles the functionalism of bourgeois social science, which posits quite similar models of complex interaction among variables. Indeed, the content of her four structures also derives from functionalist hypotheses, specifically, those of George Murdock. Despite her staunchly Marxist intentions, then, Mitchell's theoretical perspective proves inadequate to sustain her analysis.[7]

Even with its problems, easier to recognize at a distance of more than fifteen years, Mitchell's 1966 article played an extremely positive role within the developing socialist-feminist movement. Its differentiation of the content of women's lives into constituent categories helped women's liberationists to articulate their experience and begin to act on it. Its perceptive overview of the classical Marxist literature on women provided a base from which to confront both mechanical versions of Marxism and the growing influence of radical feminism. Its insistence, within a Marxist framework, on the critical importance of social phenomena not easily characterized as economic anticipated the socialist-feminist critique of economic determinism. And the political intelligence of its specific strategic comments set a standard that remains a model. "If socialism is to regain its status as *the* revolutionary politics," Mitchell concluded, "it has to make good its practical sins of commission against women and its huge sin of omission—the absence of an adequate place for them in its theory."[8] In the theoretical arena, Mitchell's central contribution was to legitimate a perspective that recognizes the ultimate primacy of economic phenomena, yet allows for the fact that other aspects of women's situation not only have importance but may play key roles at certain junctures.

By 1969, the North American women's liberation movement had reached a high point of activity, its militance complemented by a flourishing literature, published and unpublished. In this atmosphere, two Canadians, Margaret Benston and Peggy Morton, circulated and then published important essays. Each piece offered an analysis in Marxist terms of the nature of women's unpaid work within the family household and discussed its relationship to existing social contradictions and the possibilities for change.[9]

Benston starts from the problem of specifying the root of women's secondary status in capitalist society. She maintains that this root is "economic" or "material," and can be located in women's unpaid domestic labor. Women undertake a great deal of economic activity— they cook meals, sew buttons on garments, do laundry, care for children, and so forth—but the products and services that result from this work are consumed directly and never reach the marketplace. In Marxist terms, these products and services have use-value but no exchange value. For Benston, then, women have a definite relationship to the means of production, one that is distinct from the one men have. Women constitute the "group of people who are responsible for the production of simple use-values in those activities associated with the home and family." Hence, the family is an economic unit whose primary function is not consumption, as was generally held at the time by feminists, but production. "The family should be seen primarily as a production unit for housework and child-rearing." Moreover, Benston argues, because women's unpaid domestic labor is technologically primitive and outside the money economy, each family household represents an essentially preindustrial and precapitalist entity. While noting that women also participate in wage labor, she regards such production as transient and not central to women's definition as a group. It is women's responsibility for domestic work that provides the material basis for their oppression and enables the capitalist economy to treat them as a massive reserve army of labor. Equal access to jobs outside the home will remain a woefully insufficient precondition for women's liberation if domestic labor continues to be private and technologically backward. Benston's strategic suggestions therefore center on the need to provide a more important precondition by converting work now done in the home into public production. That is, society must move toward the socialization of housework and child care. "When such work is moved into the public sector, then the material basis for discrimination against women will be gone." In this way, Benston revives a traditional socialist theme, not as cliché but as forceful argument made in the context of a developing discussion within the contemporary women's movement.[10]

Peggy Morton's article, published in 1970, one year after Benston's, extended the analysis of the family household as a materially rooted social unit in capitalist society. For Morton, Benston's discussion of how unpaid household labor forms the material basis of women's oppression leaves open a number of questions: Do women form a class? Should women be organized only through their work in the household? How and why has the nature of the family as an economic institution in capitalist society changed? Morton sees the family "as a unit whose function is the *maintenance of and reproduction of labor power*," meaning that "the task of the family is to maintain the present work force and provide the next generation of workers, fitted with the skills and values necessary for them to be productive members of the work force."[11] Using this approach, Morton is able to tie her analysis of the family to the workings of the capitalist mode of production, and to focus on the contradictions experienced by working-class women within the family, in the labor force, and between the two roles. In particular, she shows that as members of the reserve army of labor, women are central, not peripheral, to the economy, for they make possible the functioning of those manufacturing, service, and state sectors in which low wages are a priority. While the strategic outlook in the several versions of Morton's paper bears only a loose relationship to its analysis, and fluctuates from workers' control to revolutionary cadre building, her discussion of the contradictory tendencies in women's situation introduces a dynamic element that had been missing from Benston's approach.

Both Benston's and Morton's articles have a certain simplicity that even at the time invited criticism. In the bright glare of hindsight, their grasp of Marxist theory and their ability to develop an argument appear painfully limited. Benston's facile dismissal of women's participation in wage labor requires correction, as Morton and others quickly pointed out. Moreover, her delineation of women's domestic labor as a remnant from precapitalist modes of production, which had somehow survived into the capitalist present, cannot be sustained theoretically.[12] Morton's position, while analytically more precise, glosses over the question of the special oppression of *all* women as a group, and threatens to convert the issue of women's oppression into a purely working-class concern. None of these problems should obscure, however, the theoretical advances made by Benston and Morton. Taken together, their two articles established the material character of women's unpaid domestic labor in the family household. Each offered an analysis of the way this labor functioned as the material basis for the host of contradictions in women's experience in capitalist society. Morton, in addition, formulated the issues in terms of a concept of the reproduction of labor power, and emphasized the specific nature of contradictions within the working class. These theoretical insights had a lasting impact on subsequent socialist-feminist work, and remain an important contribution. Moreover, they definitively shifted the framework for discussion of women's oppression. Where Mitchell had analyzed women's situation in terms of roles, functions, and structures, Benston and Morton focused on the issue of women's unpaid labor in the household and its relationship to the reproduction of labor power. In this sense, they rooted the problem of women's oppression in the theoretical terrain of materialism.

An article by Mariarosa Dalla Costa, published simultaneously in Italy and the United States in 1972, took the argument several steps further.[13] Agreeing that women constitute a distinct group whose oppression is based on the material character of unpaid household labor, Dalla Costa maintains that on a world level, all women are housewives. Whether or not a woman works outside the home, "it is precisely what is particular to domestic work, not only measured as number of hours and nature of work, but as quality of life and quality of relationships which it generates, that determines a woman's place wherever she is and to whichever class she belongs."[14] At the same time, Dalla Costa concentrates her attention on the working-class housewife, whom she sees as indispensable to capitalist production.

As housewives, working-class women find themselves excluded from capitalist production, isolated in routines of domestic labor that have the technological character of precapitalist labor processes. Dalla Costa disputes the notion that these housewives are mere suppliers of use-values in the home. Polemicizing against both traditional left views and the literature of the women's movement, she argues that housework only appears to be a personal service outside the arena of capitalist production. In reality, it produces not just use-values for direct consumption in the family, but the essential commodity labor power—the capacity of a worker to work. Indeed, she claims, housewives are exploited "productive workers" in the strict Marxist sense, for they produce surplus value. Appropriation of this surplus value is accomplished by the capitalist's payment of a wage to the working-class husband, who thereby becomes the instrument of woman's exploitation. The survival of the working class depends on the working-class family, "but *at the woman's expense against the class itself.* The woman is the slave of a wage slave, and her slavery ensures the slavery of her man. . . . And that is why the struggle of the woman of the working class against the family is crucial."[15]

Since working-class housewives are productive laborers who are peculiarly excluded from the sphere of capitalist production, demystification of domestic work as a "masked form of productive labor" becomes a central task. Dalla Costa proposes two major strategic alternatives. First socialize the struggle—not the work—of the isolated domestic laborer by mobilizing working-class housewives around community issues, the wagelessness of housework, the denial of sexuality, the separation of family from outside world, and the like. "We must discover forms of struggle which immediately break the whole structure of domestic work, rejecting it absolutely, rejecting our role as housewives and the home as the ghetto of our existence, since the problem is not only to stop doing this work, but to smash the entire role of housewife." Second, reject work altogether, especially in a capitalist economy which increasingly draws women into the wage labor force. In opposition to the left's traditional view of this latter tendency as progressive, Dalla Costa maintains that the modern women's movement constitutes a rejection of this alternative. Economic independence achieved through "performing social labor in a socialized structure" is no more than a sham reform. Women have worked enough, and they must "refuse the myth of liberation through work."[16]

The polemical energy and political range of Dalla Costa's article had a substantial impact on the women's movement on both sides of the Atlantic. Unlike Benston, Morton, and other North American activists, Dalla Costa seemed to have a sophisticated grasp of Marxist theory and socialist politics. Her arguments and strategic proposals struck a responsive chord in a movement already committed to viewing women's oppression mainly in terms of their family situation. Few noticed that Dalla Costa, like Morton, talked only of the working class, and never specified the relationship between the oppression of working-class housewives and that of *all* women. What was most important was that Dalla Costa, even more than Benston and Morton, seemed to have situated the question of women's oppression within an analysis of the role of their unpaid domestic labor in the reproduction of capitalist social relations. Moreover, since her article functioned as the theoretical foundation for a small but aggressive movement to demand wages for housework, which flourished briefly in the early 1970s, it acquired an overtly political role denied to most women's liberation theoretical efforts.[17]

Dalla Costa's vigorous insistence that "housework as work is *productive* in the Marxian sense, that is, is producing surplus value" intensified a controversy already simmering within the socialist-feminist movement. The discussion, which became known as the domestic labor debate, revolved around the theoretical status of women's unpaid domestic work and its product.[18] Published contributions, usually appearing in British or North American left journals, established their particular positions by means of intricate arguments in Marxist economic theory—abstract, hard to follow, and in the atmosphere of the period, seemingly remote from practical application. With some justification, many in the women's movement regarded the debate as an obscure exercise in Marxist pedantry. Yet critical issues were at stake, even if they generally went unrecognized.

In the first place, the domestic labor debate attempted to put into theoretical context the contemporary feminist insight that childbearing, child care, and housework are material activities resulting in products, thus pointing to a materialist analysis of the basis for women's oppression. At the same time, the debate focused attention on the issues of women's position as housewives and of domestic labor's contribution to the reproduction of social relations. Various interpretations corresponded, more or less closely, to a variety of political and strategic perspectives on the relationship of women's oppression to class exploitation and to revolutionary struggle, although theorists rarely stated these implications clearly, leaving political and strategic issues unconfronted. Finally, and perhaps most consequential for the development of theory, the domestic labor debate employed categories drawn from *Capital*, thereby displaying confidence that women's oppression could be analyzed within a Marxist framework.

At issue in the domestic labor debate was the problem of how the commodity labor power gets produced and reproduced in capitalist societies. Differences arose over the precise meaning and application of Marxist categories in carrying out an analysis of this problem. In particular, discussion centered on the nature of the product of domestic labor, on its theoretical status as productive or unproductive labor, and on its relationship to the wage and to work done for wages.

Many suggested, following Benston, that domestic labor produces use-values—useful articles that satisfy human wants of some sort—for direct consumption within the household. The consumption of these use-values enables family members to renew themselves and return to work the next day; that is, it contributes to the overall maintenance and renewal of the working class. While various relationships were posited between this process of use-value production and capitalist production as a whole, the linkages remained somewhat vague. Others claimed, along with Dalla Costa, that domestic labor produces not just use-values but the special commodity known as labor power. In this way, they seemed to tie women's unpaid household labor more tightly to the workings of the capitalist mode of production, a position that many found, at first encounter, very attractive.

A particular position on the product of domestic labor naturally had some bearing, in the domestic labor debate, on the view taken of the theoretical character of that labor. The notion that domestic labor creates value as well as use-value suggested to some, for example, that it could be categorized in Marxist terms as either productive or unproductive, meaning productive or unproductive of surplus value for the capitalist class. For those who argued that domestic labor only produces use-values, no obvious Marxist category was at hand. Neither productive nor unproductive, domestic labor had to be something else.

Most of the initial energy expended in the domestic labor debate focused on the question of whether domestic labor is productive or unproductive. Among those who followed the controversy, theoretical underdevelopment combined with a certain moralism and strategic opportunism to create a great deal of confusion. Again and again, the terms productive and unproductive, which Marx used as scientific economic categories, were invested with moral overtones. After all, to label women's work unproductive seemed uncharitable, if not downright sexist. Furthermore, the argument that unpaid labor in the household is productive suggested that women perform a certain amount of surplus labor, which is expropriated from them by men for the benefit of capital. In this sense, women could be said to be exploited, sex contradictions acquire a clear material basis, and housewives occupy the same strategic position in the class struggle as factory workers. For those wishing to reconcile commitments to both Marxism and feminism, this implication acted as a powerful magnet. Few participants in the women's movement or on the left had the theoretical and political ability to grasp, much less propose, a convincing alternative.

Once the domestic labor debate was under way, the problem of the relationship between wages and domestic labor emerged as an issue. For Marx, the wage represents the value of the commodity labor power, a value that corresponds at any given historical moment to a socially established normal level of subsistence. Participants in the domestic labor debate pointed to difficulties created by Marx's formulation, and asked a number of questions about the role of domestic labor and household structure in the establishment of the normal wage level. For example, it was not clear in Marx's work whether the normal wage covers individuals or the entire household supported by a worker. In addition, the functioning of the wage as a type of articulation between domestic labor and the capitalist mode of production required investigation. Those who viewed domestic labor as value producing proposed that the wage is the vehicle by which the value produced by women, and embodied in male wage workers' labor power, is transferred to the capitalist employer. Many also believed that women's unpaid domestic labor enables the capitalist class to pay less than the value of labor power, that is, less than the normal level of subsistence. Some suggested that a nonworking wife cheapens the value of male labor power. Those who maintained that domestic labor produces use-value but not value attempted to identify the role of domestic labor in the reproduction of labor power. Most participants in the debate also explored the possibility that certain tendencies immanent in capitalist development affect the performance of domestic labor and therefore wage levels.

Several years after the domestic labor debate began, certain questions could be said to be settled. As it turned out, it was relatively easy to demonstrate theoretically that domestic labor in capitalist societies does not take the social form of value-producing labor.[19] Benston's original insight that domestic labor produces use-values for direct consumption had been essentially correct. In the scientific sense, then, domestic labor cannot be either productive or unproductive, and women are not exploited as domestic laborers. At the same time, domestic labor is indispensable for the reproduction of capitalist social relations. Just what domestic labor is, rather than what it is not, remained a problem only superficially addressed by participants in the domestic labor debate. Some suggested it constitutes a separate mode of production, outside the capitalist mode of production but subordinate to it. Others implied domestic labor is simply a special form of work within the capitalist mode of production. Most left the question unanswered. The problem of specifying the character of domestic labor, and issues concerning the wage and women's wage work, now represent the central concerns of most theorists working with Marxist economic categories. As for politics and strategy, few today would use their analyses of the material foundation for women's oppression to draw easy conclusions about the role of women in revolutionary struggle.

Benston, Morton, Dalla Costa, and the participants in the domestic labor debate set an important agenda for the study of women's position as housewives and the role of domestic labor in the reproduction of social relations. Their work proceeded, however, within severe limits which were not clearly identified. In the first place, they focused mainly on the capitalist mode of production. Second, they concentrated almost exclusively on domestic labor and women's oppression in the working class. Third, they generally restricted their analysis to the economic level. Fourth, they tended to identify domestic labor with housework and child care, leaving the status of childbearing undefined. Some of these limitations might have been defended as necessary steps in the development of a theoretical argument, but they rarely were. Although the discussion of domestic labor had been launched in response to the need for a materialist theory of women's oppression, its promise remained unfulfilled.

In any case, by the mid-1970s, socialist-feminist theorists were turning their attention to other questions. For example, the domestic labor debate shed little light on the problem of whether housework is analytically the same in different classes within capitalist society, and even less on the theoretical status of domestic labor in noncapitalist societies. Socialist feminists also turned their attention to the childbearing and child-rearing components of domestic labor, and investigated the problem of why domestic labor generally falls to women. Since women's oppression is not specific to capitalist societies, furthermore, many wondered how to reconcile its particular contemporary character with the fact that women have been subordinated for thousands of years. Similarly, they asked whether women are liberated in socialist countries, and if not, what obstacles hold them back. Finally, the relationship between the material processes of domestic labor and the range of phenomena that make up women's oppression, especially those of an ideological and psychological nature, became a key issue. In general, these questions spoke more directly than the issues of the domestic labor debate to the experience and political tasks of activists in the women's movement, and they quickly became the focus of socialist-feminist theorizing.

While Juliet Mitchell had advised that "we should ask the feminist questions, but try to come up with some Marxist answers," many socialist feminists began to disagree. They argued that the quest for Marxist answers to their questions led down a blind alley, where the feminist struggle became submerged in the socialist struggle against capitalism. Marxist theory, they believed, was incapable of incorporating the phenomenon of sex differences. To move forward, then, socialist feminism had to take on the task of constructing an alternative framework using other theoretical categories. As Heidi Hartmann put it, "if we think Marxism alone inadequate, and radical feminism itself insufficient, then we need to develop new categories."[20]

Socialist feminists turned first to the radical feminism of the late sixties for a conceptual orientation that could address the depth and pervasiveness of women's oppression in all societies. Radical feminists typically considered male supremacy and the struggle between the sexes to be universal, constituting indeed, the essential dynamic underlying all social development. At the same time, some radical feminist writings seemed to be extensions or deepenings of the insights offered by Marx and Engels. Shulamith Firestone's *Dialectic of Sex*, for instance, claimed to go beyond the merely economic level addressed by Marx and Engels, in order to uncover the more fundamental problem of sex oppression. "The class analysis is a beautiful piece of work," Firestone wrote, "but limited." In proposing a dialectic of sex, she hoped "to take the class analysis one step further to its roots in the biological division of the sexes. We have not thrown out the insights of the socialists; on the contrary, radical feminism can enlarge their analysis, granting it an even deeper basis in objective conditions and thereby explaining many of its insolubles." Similarly, Kate Millett's *Sexual Politics* acknowledged Engels as a major theorist, but her presentation of Engels's work transformed it almost beyond recognition into a subordinate contribution to what she called the sexual revolution. The limitation of Marxist theory, she maintained, was that it "failed to supply a sufficient ideological base for a sexual revolution, and was remarkably naive as to the historical and psychological strength of patriarchy." In broad strokes, Millett depicted Nazi Germany, the Soviet Union, and Freudian psychology as comparable instances of reactionary patriarchal policy and ideology, arguing that patriarchy will survive so long as psychic structures remain untouched by social programs. For Millett, the sexual revolution requires not only an understanding of sexual politics but the development of a comprehensive theory of patriarchy.[21]

Firestone's and Millett's books, both published in 1970, had a tremendous impact on the emerging socialist-feminist trend within the women's movement. Their focus on sexuality, on psychological and ideological phenomena, and on the stubborn persistence of social practices oppressive to women struck a responsive chord. The concept of patriarchy entered socialist-feminist discourse virtually without objection. Those few critiques framed within a more orthodox Marxist perspective, such as Juliet Mitchell's, went unheard. Although acknowledging the limitations of radical feminism, many socialist feminists, particularly in the United States, simply assumed that "the synthesis of radical feminism and Marxist analysis is a necessary first step in formulating a cohesive socialist feminist political theory, one that does not merely add together these two theories of power but sees them as interrelated through the sexual division of labor."[22] No longer was the problem one of using Marxist categories to build a theoretical framework for the analysis of women's oppression. Like the radical feminists, these socialist feminists took Marxism more or less as a given, and did not seek to elaborate or deepen it.

The task, then, was to develop the synthesis that is socialist feminism—or, as one writer put it, to dissolve the hyphen. To accomplish this task, socialist feminists explored two related concepts: patriarchy and reproduction. The notion of patriarchy, taken over from radical feminism, required appropriate transformation. Millett had used the term to indicate a universal system of political, economic, ideological, and above all, psychological structures through which men subordinate women. Socialist feminists had to develop a concept of patriarchy capable of being linked with the theory of class struggle, which posits each mode of production as a specific system of structures through which one class exploits and subordinates another. In general, socialist feminists suggested, as Heidi Hartmann and Amy Bridges put it, that "Marxist categories, like capital itself, are sex-blind; the categories of patriarchy as used by radical feminists are blind to history." From this point of view, the concept of patriarchy provided a means for discussing social phenomena that seem to escape Marxist categories. Some suggested that a theory of patriarchy could explain why certain individuals, men as well as women, are in particular subordinate or dominant places within the social structure of a given society. Others believed that issues of interpersonal dominance and subordination could best be addressed by a theory of patriarchy. Socialist-feminist theorists were not in agreement, moreover, on the meaning of the concept patriarchy. For some, it represented a primarily ideological force or system. Many argued that it has a major material foundation in men's ability to control women's labor, access to resources, and sexuality. "Patriarchal authority," wrote Sheila Rowbotham, for example, "is based on male control over the woman's productive capacity, and over her person." Different approaches emerged also to the problems of the origin of divisions of labor by sex, and of the relationship between patriarchy and the workings of a particular mode of production.[23]

The concept of reproduction was invoked as a means of linking theoretically women's oppression and the Marxist analysis of production and the class struggle. Socialist-feminist theorists analyzed processes of reproduction as comparable to, but relatively autonomous from, the production that characterizes a given society. Often, they talked in terms of a mode of reproduction, analogous to the mode of production. As with the concept of patriarchy, there was little agreement on the substantive meaning of the term reproduction. Some simply identified reproduction with what appear to be the obvious functions of the family. Despite the empiricism of this approach, it clarified the analytical tasks that socialist feminists confronted. In Renate Bridenthal's words, "the relationship between production and reproduction is a dialectic within a larger historical dialectic. That is, changes in the mode of production give rise to changes in the mode of reproduction," and this dialectic must be analyzed. Several participants in the domestic labor debate postulated the existence of a "housework" or "family" mode of production alongside the capitalist mode of production, but subordinate to it. The concept of a mode of reproduction converged, moreover, with suggestions by Marxist anthropologists that families act as a perpetual source of cheap labor power in both third-world and advanced capitalist countries. A similar concept of the mode of reproduction was often implicit in the work of socialist feminists who studied the relationship between imperialism and the family.[24]

Recent socialist-feminist discussion has challenged the use of the notions of patriarchy and reproduction, arguing that existing theoretical efforts have failed to develop satisfactory ways of conceptualizing either.[25] In the first place, neither patriarchy nor reproduction has been defined with any consistency. The concept of patriarchy often remains embedded in its radical feminist origins as an essentially ideological and psychological system. Where it is used in a more materialist sense, it has not been adequately integrated into a Marxist account of productive relations. Problems in defining the concept of reproduction derive from its wide range of potential meanings. Felicity Edholm,

Olivia Harris, and Kate Young suggest that three levels of analysis might be distinguished: social reproduction, or the reproduction of the conditions of production; reproduction of the labor force; and human or biological reproduction.[26] While the suggestion has been helpful, the issue of the relationship among the different aspects remains.

A second theme in recent critiques is the problem of dualism. Again and again, theorists using the concepts of patriarchy and reproduction analyze women's oppression in terms of two separate structures; for example, capitalism and patriarchy, the mode of production and the mode of reproduction, the class system and the gender system. These "dual systems theories," as Iris Young terms them, imply that "women's oppression arises from two distinct and relatively autonomous systems." Because they fail to relate the systems in a coherent nonmechanical way, dual systems theories present a mysterious coexistence of disjunct explanations of social development. The duality generally recapitulates the opposition between feminism and Marxism that socialist-feminist theory had attempted to transcend. Veronica Beechey argues, for instance, that "the separation of reproduction or patriarchy from other aspects of the mode of production has tended to leave the Marxist analysis of production untouched and uncriticized by feminist thinking." Similarly, Young suggests that "dual systems theory has not succeeded in confronting and revising traditional Marxist theory enough, because it allows Marxism to retain in basically unchanged form its theory of economic and social relations, to which it merely grafts on a theory of gender relations."[27]

The problem is not just dualism, furthermore. Socialist-feminist theory has focused on the relationship between feminism and socialism, and between sex and class oppression, largely to the exclusion of issues of racial or national oppression. At most, sex, race, and class are described as comparable sources of oppression, whose parallel manifestations harm their victims more or less equally. Strategically, socialist feminists call for sisterhood and a women's movement that unites women from all sectors of society. Nonetheless, their sisters of color often express distrust of the contemporary women's movement and generally remain committed to activity in their own communities. The socialist-feminist movement has been unable to confront this phenomenon either theoretically or practically.

In short, despite the vitality of debate, socialist-feminist theorists have not yet been able to achieve their goal of developing a unified dialectical materialist perspective on women's liberation.

3

Socialist Feminism

and the

Woman Question

A review of the theoretical work produced in the context of the socialist-feminist movement reveals many significant themes. Taken together, they indicate the important contribution made by socialist feminism to the development of theory on the question of women.

Socialist-feminist theory starts from an insistence that beneath the serious social, psychological, and ideological phenomena of women's oppression lies a material root. It points out that Marxism has never adequately analyzed the nature and location of that root. And it hypothesizes that the family constitutes a major if not the major terrain that nourishes it. With this position, socialist feminism implicitly rejects two fallacious, as well as contradictory, currents in the legacy of socialist theory and practice on the question of women. First, the socialist-feminist emphasis on the material root of oppression counters an idealist tendency within the left, which trivializes the issue of women's oppression as a mere matter of lack of rights and ideological chauvinism. Second, socialist feminists' special concern with psychological and ideological issues, especially those arising within the family, stands opposed to the crudities of an economic determinist interpretation of women's position, also common within the socialist movement. These perspectives—which make up the implicit theoretical content of the slogan "the personal is political"—establish guidelines for the socialist-feminist consideration of women's oppression and women's liberation.

Socialist feminists recognize the inadequacies as well as the contributions of Engels's discussion of the family and property relations in *The Origin of the Family, Private Property and the State*. Like Engels, they locate the oppression of women within the dynamic of social development, but they seek to establish a more dialectical phenomenon as its basis than Engels was able to identify. Such a phenomenon must satisfy several implicit criteria. It must be a material process that is specific to a particular mode of production. Its identification should nevertheless suggest why women are oppressed in all class societies—or, for some socialist feminists, in all known societies. Most important, it must offer a better understanding of women's oppression in subordinate as well as ruling classes than does Engels's critique of property. Socialist-feminist analyses share the view that childbearing, child raising, and housework fit these criteria, although they offer a wide variety of theoretical interpretations of the relationship between these activities and women's oppression.

Some socialist feminists try to situate domestic labor within broader concepts covering the processes of maintenance and reproduction of labor power. They suggest that these processes have a material character, and that they can be analyzed, furthermore, in terms of social reproduction as a whole. For elaboration of this position, which shifts the immediate theoretical focus away from women's oppression per se, and on to wider social phenomena, they turn to Marx's writings, and especially to *Capital*. At the same time, they resist, as best they can, the contradictory pulls of economic determinism and idealism inherited from the socialist tradition.

The relationship between the capitalist wage and the household it supports represents yet another major theme. Socialist feminists point out that Marxism has never been clear on the question of whom the wage covers. The concept of the historical subsistence level of wages refers, at times, to individuals, and at other times, to the worker "and his family." Recognition of this ambiguity has inspired a series of attempts to reformulate and answer questions concerning divisions of labor according to sex in both the family and wage labor. While some such efforts stress concepts of authority and patriarchy, others focus on questions involving the determination of wage levels, competition in the labor market, and the structure of the industrial reserve army. Whatever the approach, the identification of the problem in itself constitutes a significant theoretical step forward.

Socialist-feminist theory also emphasizes that women in capitalist society have a double relation to wage labor, as both paid and unpaid workers. It generally regards women's activity as consumers and unpaid domestic laborers as the dominant factor shaping every woman's consciousness, whether or not she participates in wage labor. An important strategic orientation accompanies this view. Socialist feminists maintain, against some opinions on the left, that women can be successfully organized, and they emphasize the need for organizations that include women from all sectors of society. In support of their position, they point to the long history of militant activity by women in the labor movement, in communities, and in social revolution. They observe, moreover, that mobilization demands a special sensitivity to women's experience as women, and they assert the legitimacy and importance of organizations comprised of women only. It is precisely the specific character of women's situation that requires their separate organization. Here, socialist feminists frequently find themselves in opposition to much of the tradition of socialist theory and practice. Socialist-feminist theory takes on the essential task of developing a framework that can guide the process of organizing women from different classes and sectors into an autonomous women's movement.

Finally, socialist-feminist theory links its theoretical outlook to a passage from Engels's preface to the *Origin*:

> According to the materialistic conception, the determining factor in history is, in the final instance, the production and reproduction of immediate life. This, again, is of a twofold character: on the one side, the production of the means of existence, of food, clothing and shelter and the tools necessary for that production; on the other side, the production of human beings themselves, the propagation of the species. The social organization under which the people of a particular historical epoch and a particular country live is determined by both kinds of production: by the stage of development of labor on the one hand and of the family on the other.[1]

The citation of these sentences, in article after article, accomplishes several purposes. It affirms the socialist-feminist commitment to the Marxist tradition. It suggests that Marx and Engels had more to say about the question of women than the later socialist movement was able to hear. It seems to situate the problem of women's oppression in the context of a theory of general social reproduction. It emphasizes the material essence of the social processes for which women hold major responsibility. And it implies that the production of human beings constitutes a process that has not only an autonomous character, but a theoretical weight equal to that of the production of the means of existence. In short, Engels's remarks appear to offer authoritative Marxist backing for the socialist-feminist movement's focus on the family, sex divisions of labor, and unpaid domestic work, as well as for its theoretical dualism and its strategic commitment to the autonomous organization of women. Yet the passage actually reflects Engels at his theoretical weakest. Socialist-feminist insights into the role of women in social reproduction need a more solid basis.

Despite the strengths, richness, and real contributions of socialist-feminist theoretical work, its development has been constrained by its practitioners' insufficient grasp of Marxist theory. With their roots in a practical commitment to women's liberation and to the development of a broad-based autonomous women's movement, participants in the socialist-feminist movement have only recently begun to explore their relationship to trends and controversies within the left. At the theoretical level, the exploration has taken the form of several waves of publications seeking, on the one hand, to delineate the substance of socialist feminism more clearly, and on the other, to situate women's oppression more precisely within, rather than alongside, a Marxist theory of social reproduction.[2] These efforts are important, although they continue to suffer from an inadequate theoretical orientation. Socialist-feminist theory has not yet overcome its tendency to analyze women's oppression in dualistic terms as a phenomenon that is independent of class, race, and mode of production. Nor has socialist-feminist theory moved far enough away from its overemphasis on women's position within the family, and within ideological and psychological relations. The links, that is, between women's oppression, social production, and overall societal reproduction have yet to be established on a materialist basis. Most important, socialist-feminist theory has not been able to develop the theoretical underpinning for its strategic commitment to uniting women across such differences as class, race, age, and sexual preference.

Socialist-feminist efforts to build on the socialist theoretical tradition have been hampered by the lack of an adequate foundation for the project. The socialist movement has left a perplexing and contradictory legacy. Even the writings of Marx and Engels, to which many socialist feminists turn for theoretical guidance, remain frustratingly opaque. A core of theoretical insight into the problem of women's oppression lies embedded, nonetheless, within the socialist tradition.

To the extent that the socialist movement directly addressed the issue of women's oppression, it focused on what it called "the woman question." Originating in the nineteenth century, the term is extremely vague, and covers an assortment of important problems situated at distinct theoretical levels. Most generally, it has been used by socialists to refer to the issue of women's subordination in all historical societies. At times this subordination is specified in terms of women's differential role in the family, or in production. Most socialist considerations of the so-called woman question focus on women's oppression and inequality in capitalist society, and the fight for equal rights. The term may also include, finally, personal relations between the sexes and among family members, and sometimes extends to personal and non-work relations of all sorts. In short, the woman question is not a precise analytical category, but a tangled knot of disparate strands. Three major strands have dominated theoretical work on the so-called woman question: the family, women's work, and women's equality. Socialist theory has been unable, however, to weave these strands into a coherent perspective on the problem of women's liberation.[3]

Socialist feminists have subjected the socialist tradition of work on the woman question to critical examination, seeking the kernels of serious theoretical and practical import stored within it. From this point of view, a major contribution of the socialist-feminist movement has been its insistence that those who use traditional categories of Marxist theory must make their case adequately. The questions that socialist feminists raise—concerning the roots of women's oppression, the persistence of sex divisions of labor in all areas of social life, the meaning of women's liberation, and the organization of the struggle against sexism and for socialism—require answers that go beyond what socialist theory has so far been able to provide. All indications suggest, furthermore, that the socialist theoretical legacy is not only unfinished but seriously flawed. An important task, then, is a rigorous reexamination of the texts of the socialist movement, starting with the work of Marx and Engels.

Modern students of the socialist movement often suggest that Marx and Engels produced virtually nothing of real usefulness about the oppression and liberation of women. Even less, it is implied, did they put their convictions concerning women's emancipation into practice. Yet these claims, whether openly stated or merely insinuated, are generally not firmly based in research. Indeed, they are often more the expressions of particular theoretical and political perspectives than they are serious considerations of the actual work of either Marx or Engels. Such statements reveal, therefore, the range and character of the widely held assumption that a theory of women's liberation cannot be based on Marxist categories.

Some take the lack of an important tradition of Marxist work on women's oppression to be entirely obvious. Mark Poster, a scholar of Marxism, laments, for instance, that "Marx himself wrote almost nothing on the family," and that Marx and Engels "relegated the family to the backwaters of the superstructure." More circumspectly, Richard Evans, a meticulous and sympathetic historian of the feminist and socialist movements, comments that "Marx and his collaborator Engels had little to say about the emancipation of women. . . . For them it was a marginal question; Marx himself barely alluded to it except to repeat, in a slightly modified form, Fourier's critique of marriage in an early unpublished manuscript and in the *Communist Manifesto*. There is also a brief passage on women in *Capital*, much quoted because it is all there is."[4] The carelessness of these statements, made by otherwise scrupulous scholars, is surprising. Masked by the current interest in a feminist reinterpretation of Marxism, it suggests a certain prejudice against Marxism itself.

On a different tack, the observation that Marx and Engels were imprisoned within the limited and sexist horizons of their period provides a somewhat more secure basis for pessimism concerning their commitment to the liberation of women. Marx was, after all, not only a man but a Victorian husband and father with traditionally patriarchal attitudes in his own family life. Engels, while more unconventional in his personal relationships, could hardly escape the sex-typed presumptions of nineteenth-century society. Both men participated in the largely all-male socialist and working-class movements of their time. These facts have led many, particularly activists in the women's movement, to conclude that Marx and Engels could never have transcended their male chauvinist blinders to say or do anything useful on the woman question. Marlene Dixon, for example, an influential militant in the women's movement and on the left for more than ten years, has argued that the circumstance that Marx and Engels were men living in a particular historical context irrevocably blocked their ability to implement good intentions with respect to the woman question. Moreover, she contends, nineteenth- and early twentieth-century Marxists never adequately challenged their own bourgeois and sexist ideas concerning women, much less those of the (male) proletariat. As a result, the sexist bias in Marxism, originating with Marx himself, actually reinforced the oppression of socialist women and contributed to the growth of distortions of theory and strategy within the socialist movement. Although Dixon herself might not go so far, the logical implication of this line of reasoning is that socialists who today seek to develop theory, strategy, and program for women's liberation waste their time when they study Marx and Engels.

Despite its obvious limitations, many socialist feminists have searched the work of Marx and Engels for insights into the problem of women's subordination. They expect, not unreasonably, that the founders of the modern socialist tradition were able at least to suggest some general orientation. These efforts often end, nonetheless, in frustration and disappointment. Reluctantly, those who had hoped for more concrete theoretical and practical guidance conclude that Marx and Engels could only do so much. Charnie Guettel expresses the views of many in her pamphlet *Marxism and Feminism*. "Just as Marx and Engels had no theoretical work on racism, a phenomenon that has become a central brake on progress in the working class movement in the stage of imperialism, so did they lack a developed critique of sexism under capitalism. Their class analysis of society still provides us with the best tools for analyzing both forms of oppression, although concerning women it is very underdeveloped."[6]

The indisputable failure of Marx and Engels to develop adequate tools and a comprehensive theory on women represents only part of the problem. The frustration many socialist feminists experience derives also from the fact that Marx and Engels did not say what these modern critics of the so-called woman question want to hear. Or, to put it another way, today's questioners often ask, and try to answer, a different set of woman questions.

Marx and Engels approached the issue of women's subordination and liberation from the point of view of an evolving socialist movement. They sought to situate the question within a theory of the essential mechanisms of social development as a whole, and therefore paid special attention to social relations of production. By contrast, contemporary socialist-feminist theorists and activists usually approach it from within the framework of the women's movement. They seek a theoretical perspective that will encompass both an understanding of how female persons come to be oppressed women and a comprehensive analysis of the elements required for women's total liberation. Despite its commitment to socialism, socialist feminism's different starting point often leads to a theoretical emphasis divergent from that of Marx and Engels.

While Marx and Engels focused on the oppression of women within given social relations of production, contemporary socialist-feminist theorists frequently try to disengage the issue of women's oppression from the study of the family and social reproduction. Juliet Mitchell complains, for example, that "what is striking in [Marx's] later comments on the family is that the problem of women becomes submerged in the analysis of the family—women, as such, are not even mentioned!" At the same time, she finds the analysis of Marx and Engels too narrow, and too dependent on what she sees as simplistic economic explanation. "The position of women, then, in the work of Marx and Engels remains dissociated from, or subsidiary to, a discussion of the family, which is in its turn subordinated as merely a precondition of private property."[7] These statements, originally formulated in 1966, reflect two widely held assumptions within the socialist-feminist movement: first, that women and the family constitute the sole possible objects of analysis, and that the category of woman, rather than the family, represents the appropriate object for women's liberationists; and second, that an adequate Marxist approach to the problem of women's oppression cannot be developed, even conditionally, at the level of relations of production.

Not surprisingly, it proves impossible to speak of women's oppression without some discussion of the family, and many socialist feminists focus on questions of gender development and on relations between the sexes in the family, or, more generally, in society. These are often conceptualized in terms of interpersonal dynamics, ideology, and power relations, while productive relations and issues of class tend to recede into the background. Then, when the works of Marx and Engels are studied for their contribution, they are found to be wanting. Contemporary theorists offer various explanations for the gaps, and move on quickly to alternative versions of a Marxist theory of the family and women's subordination. Yet, what they have actually done is to substitute their own concerns and categories—a primary focus on psychology, on ideology, and on relations of hierarchy and authority—for those of Marx and Engels.

In sum, because they are asking different questions, however important, those socialist-feminist theorists and activists who today chide Marx and Engels for their failings often cannot hear what they actually said. And yet a substantial amount of the material is there, waiting to be developed. As a matter of fact, Marx and Engels had a great deal more to say of relevance to resolving the so-called woman question than either socialists or women's liberationists have noticed. More precisely, Marx and Engels had a great deal to say, even if it was, nonetheless, nowhere near enough.

Before proceeding, it is important to consider the kinds of things a comprehensive approach to the problem of women's oppression ought to include. First, it must start from a firm commitment to the liberation of women and to the real social equality of all human beings. Second, it must make a concrete analysis of the current situation for women, as well as study how it arose. Third, it must present a theory of the position of women in society. That is, in addition to a *history* of women's position, it must also have a *theory*. Fourth, a comprehensive discussion of the situation of women must be informed by a vision of women's liberation in a future society that is consistent with its theory and history of women's subordination in past and present societies. Finally, and almost by definition, to ask the so-called woman question is also to demand an answer, in terms of practical program and strategy.

In their work, Marx and Engels addressed, at least partially, each of these aspects. The next three chapters review this work from a theoretical perspective that situates the problem of women's oppression in terms of the reproduction of labor power and the process of social reproduction. Thus, each text is examined not only for its discussion of women, the family, or divisions of labor according to sex, but also for its consideration of problems and concepts associated with the reproduction of labor power. From this point of view, certain concepts play an especially important role, and their development is followed carefully: individual consumption, the value of labor power, the determination of wage levels, surplus population, and the industrial reserve army. Over the years, furthermore, involvement in the working-class movements and political struggles of their time enabled Marx and Engels to modify and extend their positions in crucial ways. The writings are surveyed, therefore, in chronological order.

Part Two

Marx and

Engels

4

Early Views

Karl Marx and Friedrich Engels arrived at a commitment to socialist politics, and to women's liberation as they understood it, by quite different routes. Marx, son of a lawyer, descendant of rabbis, and educated for a professional career, began from the perspective of a student of philosophy. By contrast, Engels, who was born into a securely established bourgeois family, started from his own experience as a clerk in the family textile firm in Manchester, England, where he served the apprenticeship expected of a future German industrialist. Having set out separately, each man initially approached the problem of women's oppression in a distinctive way.

Marx's earliest comments on the question of women have a decidedly philosophical and symbolic tone. At the university, he had moved quickly from a youthful romanticism through Hegelianism to the more philosophical position taken by the group known as the Young Hegelians, intellectuals who sought to draw revolutionary socialist conclusions out of Hegel's work. Not until somewhat later, after he began his collaboration with Engels, did Marx study economics seriously. Thus, like many nineteenth-century socialists, Marx at first does not so much confront the issue of women's actual subordination in social life as use it to symbolize the state of society in general.

In *On the Jewish Question*, published in 1843 when Marx was twenty-five, and in the unpublished "Economic and Philosophic Manuscripts" written in 1844, Marx discusses the relationship between man and woman as representative of the level of social development. Where relations of private property and possession dominate, "the species-

41

relation itself, the relation between man and woman, etc., becomes an object of trade! The woman is bought and sold." More generally, the relation of man to woman constitutes the "direct, natural, and necessary relation of person to person. . . . In this relationship, therefore, is *sensuously manifested*, reduced to an observable *fact*, the extent to which the human essence has become nature to man, or to which nature to him has become the human essence of man. From this relationship one can therefore judge man's whole level of development." The relationship of man to woman reveals man's progress beyond a natural state, for it shows "the extent to which . . . the *other* person as a person has become for him a need—the extent to which he in his individual existence is at the same time a social being." In a society based on private property, this relationship takes alienated forms, but a communist society will witness "the return of man from religion, family, state, etc., to his *human*, i.e. *social* existence."[1] In these remarks, Marx's focus is on the individual "man" (*Mensch*)—on the one hand standing generically for all human beings, but on the other bearing an unmistakable gender identity. To the extent that she appears, woman, the other, reflects and is acted upon by man.

In *The Holy Family*, written shortly after the "Economic and Philosophic Manuscripts" in 1844 and published in 1845, Marx adopts the standpoint of Feuerbachian materialism in order now to argue against the radical idealism of the Young Hegelians. Despite the book's title, which refers ironically to the group, its dense and lengthy polemic does not touch on the issue of the family. However, in a few relevant passages, Marx significantly transforms his previous emphasis on the relation of man to woman. Freely paraphrasing Fourier, he observes that "the change in a historical epoch can always be determined by women's progress toward freedom, because here, in the relation of woman to man, of the weak to the strong, the victory of human nature over brutality is most evident. The degree of emancipation of woman is the natural measure of general emancipation."[2] The focus in these remarks is now on woman's relation to man, and on women in general. As his new index of social development, Marx takes the position of woman, rather than the abstract relation of man to nature. Moreover, in *The Holy Family*, women's oppression becomes somewhat more than a symbolic representation in the realm of ideas. It is also a reality, and one that Marx contrasts, in scathing prose, to the hypocrisy of contemporary bourgeois notions about women. Indeed, he specifies that under current conditions "the general position of woman in modern society is inhuman."[3]

The nature of the tension between social reality and its ideological representation became a central concern for Marx less than a year later, as he developed a severely critical stance with respect to Feuerbachian materialism itself. In a set of "notes hurriedly scribbled down for later elaboration, absolutely not intended for publication," Marx sketched his new perspective. According to Engels, who published these 1845 notes in 1888 as *Theses on Feuerbach*, "they are invaluable as the first document in which is deposited the brilliant germ of the new world outlook."[4] Here it is of interest that Marx uses the family and its contradictory internal relations to illustrate one of the theses: "That the secular basis lifts off from itself and establishes itself as an independent realm in the clouds can only be explained by the inner strife and intrinsic contradictoriness of this secular basis. The latter must, therefore, itself be both understood in its contradiction and revolutionized in practice. Thus, for instance, once the earthly family is discovered to be the secret of the holy family, the former must then itself be destroyed in theory and in practice." Almost accidentally, then, this thesis reveals Marx's initial programmatic orientation toward the family: it must "be both understood in its contradiction and revolutionized in practice. . . . [It must] be destroyed in theory and in practice."[5]

Engels's first examination of woman's position in society appears in his book *The Condition of the Working Class in England*, written in late 1844 and early 1845, and published in May 1845. In contrast to the highly abstract approach taken during this period by Marx, Engels's orientation is largely descriptive and historical. He focuses on the actual experience of working-class women, members of the small but growing industrial and agricultural proletariat. He insists that it is not the invention of machines but capitalism itself, with its drive for accumulation and profit, that makes the cheap labor of women and children attractive to employers. Methodically surveying the development and present state of various spheres of production, he documents the details of the lives of working-class women—as workers and as wives, mothers, and daughters. At the same time, his remarks offer a general overview of the situation of working-class women, as well as some insights of an essentially theoretical character.

To Engels, the most obvious effects of factory work on women are physical and moral. Long hours and ghastly working and living conditions render women workers vulnerable to severe bone deformations and diseases. Women workers have a high rate of miscarriages. Childbirth is exceptionally difficult. Fear of loss of wages or dismissal forces pregnant workers to stay at their jobs to the last moment. "It is quite common for women to be working in the evening and for the child to be delivered the following morning, and it is by no means uncommon for babies to be born in the factory itself among the machinery." For the same reasons, few are able to stay home after the birth of a child for more than a week or two. "It is often only two or three days after confinement that a woman returns to the factory, and of course, she cannot take the baby with her. When there is a break in the factory routine she has to rush home to feed the infant and get her own meal." As might be expected, the babies are weak; perhaps fifty percent of working-class children never reach their fifth birthday. In general, children in the factory districts tend to be "pale and scrofulous," "weak and stunted." Menstruation often begins late, or not at all.[6]

Such conditions are, according to Engels, literally demoralizing. In nineteenth-century fashion, he castigates the moral evils of factory work, where "members of both sexes of all ages work together in a single room." While we may smile at his relatively archaic standards of morality, Engels nevertheless points to real problems: seduction of girls by employers under threat of dismissal, unwanted pregnancy, drunkenness and alcoholism, suicide, general lack of education, and a high level of crime and interpersonal brutality. Moreover, widespread prostitution accompanied the "appalling degree of demoralization" characteristic of the working class Engels describes.[7]

The enormous surge of prostitution in the nineteenth century drew the attention of moral reformers and utopian socialists of every stripe, who repeatedly pointed to it as a shocking cultural symbol of modern social degradation. Marx himself follows this tradition when, in a footnote in the "Economic and Philosophic Manuscripts," he reduces prostitution to a rhetorical metaphor of exploitation. "Prostitution is only a *specific* expression of the *general* prostitution of the *laborer*, and since it is a relationship in which falls not the prostitute alone, but also the one who prostitutes—and the latter's abomination is still greater—the capitalist, etc., also comes under this head."[8] Marx's denunciation, in *The Holy Family*, of liberal philanthropic notions of reform and redemption treats prostitution only a little more specifically, as the paradigm of bourgeois ideological hypocrisy.[9] But it is Engels, in *The Condition of the Working Class in England*, who analyzes the reality and the social roots of that particular hypocrisy. Despite a certain Victorian ring, his indictment of the bourgeoisie reveals a fine comprehension of both social forces and individual options:

> While burdening the workers with numerous hardships the
> middle classes have left them only the two pleasures of drink

and sexual intercourse. The result is that the workers, in order to get something out of life, are passionately devoted to these two pleasures and indulge in them to excess and in the grossest fashion. If people are relegated to the position of animals, they are left with the alternatives of revolting or sinking into bestiality. Moreover the middle classes are themselves in no small degree responsible for the extent to which prostitution exists—how many of the 40,000 prostitutes who fill the streets of London every evening are dependent for their livelihood on the virtuous bourgeoisie? How many of them were first seduced by a member of the middle classes, so that they now have to sell their persons to passers-by in order to live? Truly, the middle classes are least entitled to accuse the workers of sexual licence.[10]

From all this, Engels draws the stark conclusion that "family life for the worker is almost impossible under the existing social system." Again and again he looks at prevailing conditions and finds "the dissolution of family ties," and "the universal decadence of family life among the workers." Again and again he notes that "these faults are due entirely to existing social conditions." More specifically, Engels points to the employment of married women in factory work. "If a married woman works in a factory family life is inevitably destroyed and in the present state of society, which is based upon family life, its dissolution has the most demoralizing consequences both for parents and children." The problem is not just the work itself. Long hours and terrible living, as well as working, conditions, take a heavy toll in "endless domestic troubles and family quarrels." Moreover, "if a woman works for twelve or thirteen hours a day in a factory and her husband is employed either in the same establishment or in some other works, what is the fate of the children?" So far as Engels could see in England in 1844, capitalism, unless blocked by the united action of the working class, promised a succession of generations faced with the same conditions: "Pregnant women working until the hour of their confinement, lack of skill as housewives, the neglect of household duties, the neglect of the children, indifference to—even hostility towards—family life, and general social demoralization."[11]

Women sometimes became the main earner in working-class households, and this epitomized, to Engels, the apparent tendency toward family dissolution. Confused as well as struck by this trend, he experienced it as a "complete reversal of normal social relationships," and therefore a betrayal of the "normal structure of the family." In shocked tones he observes that "very often the fact that a married woman is working does not lead to the complete disruption of the home but to a reversal of the normal division of labour within the family. The wife is the breadwinner while her husband stays at home to look after the children and do the cleaning and cooking. . . . Family relationships are reversed, although other social conditions remain unchanged." Such a situation "deprives the husband of his manhood and the wife of all womanly qualities. . . . It is a state of affairs shameful and degrading to the human attributes of the sexes." In the same vein, Engels lists among child-labor's "evil consequences" the possibility that "the children become emancipated and regard their parents' house merely as lodgings, and quite often, if they feel like it, they leave home and take lodgings elsewhere."[12]

Engels's comments on the dissolution of the family, which emphasize the supposedly natural character of divisions of labor and authority according to sex or age, and misconstrue the effects of their reversal, reflect conventional nineteenth-century assumptions. Engels fails, at this point, to recognize the possibility of a contemporary form of family life other than that established by the bourgeoisie, and therefore declares the working-class family to be in a state of disintegration. He senses the contradictory character of his remarks, however, and seeks to root them in historical development. If the present state of the working-class family seems to be unnatural, it must result from "some radical error in the original relationship between men and women. If the rule of the wife over her husband—a natural consequence of the factory system—is unnatural, then the former rule of the husband over the wife must also have been unnatural." Indeed, these observations permit Engels a glimpse not only into the past but into the future as well. "Such a state of affairs shows clearly that there is no rational or sensible principle at the root of our ideas concerning family income and property. If the family as it exists in our present-day society comes to an end then its disappearance will prove that the real bond holding the family together was not affection but merely self-interest engendered by the false concept of family property."[13]

In *The Condition of the Working Class in England*, Engels also makes three genuine theoretical contributions to an understanding of the situation of women, each, as he later observed, in embryonic form.[14] First, he implicitly recognizes that neither individuals nor the family exist as ahistorical abstractions. Focusing throughout the book on working-class people and the working-class family, he often contrasts their experience with bourgeois expectations and relationships.

Furthermore, he links, however vaguely and inconsistently, the nature of relations between the sexes in the family to social forms of property holding. In short, Engels suggests that women's oppression and the family must be conceptualized in terms of specific modes of production and specific classes.

Second, Engels considers the determination and structure of the wage—the means by which individual and family ensure their own reproduction. He argues that two types of competition affect the level of the wage. Exceptionally, in periods of full employment or even job surplus, employers must compete among themselves for labor, and wages of course rise. More normally, competition among workers for available jobs tends to force wages down. Nevertheless, there are limits in the play of these forces of labor supply and demand. Different categories of workers require different living standards and therefore command different wages, under even the severest competition. Wages must be "high enough to maintain the living standards of the worker at a level appropriate to the job." Moreover, wages must be high enough for workers to replace themselves, although again within definite limits. In the case of factory labor, for example, it is "in the interests of the middle classes that factory wages should be high enough to enable the workers to bring up their children, who will in due course be fit for regular industrial employment. On the other hand, the worker's wages must be low enough to force him to send his children to the factory rather than encourage them to improve their lot by training for something better than mere factory labor."[15]

The number of earners in a household affects the level of the wage. "When an entire family is working the wages of the individual can be cut down." In this way, the greedy bourgeoisie has "craftily succeeded in depressing men's wages" by requiring the work of wives and children in factories. In practice, Engels observes, wage rates have to correspond to some assumption about the average number of earners within the household. In general, however, wages cannot fall below the "something a little more than nothing" defined by Engels as the "minimum" required for physical subsistence. From here, Engels attempts to determine the relationship between this "minimum" wage and the "average" wage in normal times, that is, when there is no unusual competition among either workers or capitalists. "In such a state of equilibrium wages will be a little more than the 'minimum.' The extent to which the level of the 'average' wage is above that of the 'minimum' wage depends upon the standard of living and the level of culture of the workers." Although this formulation takes a hypothetical physical minimum as a standard, it broadly anticipates Marx's later emphasis in *Capital* that "a historical and moral element" plays a critical part in the determination of all wage levels. In these passages, Engels has sketched, then, the outlines of a theory of the relationship between wages and the working-class family: the level of wages is as much a social as a physical issue; wages cover the reproduction of the working class by supporting households, not individuals; capitalists can therefore force wages down by drawing more household members into wage labor; such a depreciation of the value of an individual's work may require a significant alteration in what Engels terms "the standard of living and the level of culture of the workers."[16]

Engels's third theoretical insight concerns the overall reproduction of the working class, specifically, the relationship between population and capitalism. He observes that the cyclical nature of capitalist development regulates the size of the total work force at any given moment. "English industry must always have a reserve of unemployed workers." Ordinarily, this massive "superfluous population" competes for the available jobs. At the peak of a boom, however, the existing population suddenly appears insufficient, and must be supplemented. Laborers from outlying agricultural districts and even from Ireland, as well as women and young people, enter the work force. "These groups of workers differ from the main body inasmuch as it is only at times of exceptionally good trade that they realize that they are in fact part of the reserve army of labor." In opposition to Malthus, then, Engels emphasizes the structural necessity of a so-called surplus population for industrial expansion. Malthus "was wrong when he expressed the view that more people existed than could be fed from available resources. The real reason for the existence of the superfluous population is the competition of the workers among themselves." Engels thereby links the phenomenon of surplus population to the same processes that regulate wages and the length of the working day. The difference is simply that they take place "on a much larger scale [and] in the country as a whole."[17]

By 1845, Marx and Engels had arrived, on different paths, at a provisional understanding of what was to become known as the materialist theory of history, or historical materialism. Between November 1845 and August 1846, they produced a long manuscript entitled "The German Ideology." As Marx later recalled, they "decided to set forth together our conception as opposed to the ideological one of German philosophy, in fact to settle accounts with our former philosophical conscience." The intention was carried out in the form of a critique of post-Hegelian philosophy. Although never published in full, the manuscript "achieved our main purpose—self-clarification."[18] "The German Ideology" marks a turning point in the development of Marx and Engels's work. It also contains their first comprehensive formulation of a theory and history of the family.

In "The German Ideology," Marx and Engels take the opportunity to explore several aspects of the relationships among family, ideology, and social reproduction. They call attention to the contradiction between ideological conceptions of the family and the actual historical experience of families in different classes. In the bourgeoisie, the family acts as a property-transmitting unit whose existence "is made necessary by its connection with the mode of production." The bourgeoisie develops an idealized concept of the family which it nevertheless betrays in its every action. In the bourgeois family, "boredom and money are the binding link, [yet] its dirty existence has its counterpart in the holy concept of it in official phraseology and universal hypocrisy." Marx and Engels claim that, in contrast, the family is "*actually* abolished" in the proletariat, where "the concept of the family does not exist at all, but here and there family affection based on extremely real relations is certainly to be found." In sum, Marx and Engels draw the explicit theoretical lesson that "one cannot speak at all of the family '*as such.*'"[19]

How then can one speak of the family? Marx and Engels view it as a social form rooted in relations of production, for "life involves before everything else eating and drinking, housing, clothing and various other things." They identify three simultaneous aspects of social activity that respond to these requirements. First, people produce means to satisfy basic needs. Second, this very act leads to the creation of new needs. And third, "men, who daily re-create their own life, begin to make other men, to propagate their kind: the relation between man and woman, parents and children, the *family*." In this section of "The German Ideology," the family has the theoretical status of a site of reproduction of individuals whose essential characteristic is that they participate in social labor. The relationship between the biological or "natural," and the social on this site—that is, in the family—remains highly ambiguous. For instance, a well-known passage in "The German Ideology" asserts that "the production of life, both of one's own in labor and of fresh life in procreation, now appears as a twofold relation: on the one hand as a natural, on the other as a social relation—social in the sense that it denotes the co-operation of several individuals, no matter under what conditions, in what manner and to what end."[20]

Using the concept of the division of labor—which often plays the role, in "The German Ideology," of a motivating force—Marx and Engels sketch the outlines of a history of the family in social development. The division of labor "was originally nothing but the division of labor in the sexual act." Out of it arises the "natural" division of labor in the family. Stages in the development of the division of labor correspond, moreover, to different forms of property. At first, in the stage of tribal property, the division of labor is "still very elementary and is confined to a further extension of the natural division of labor existing in the family." Initially the family "is the only social relation," but in the long run, as "increased needs create new social relations and the increased population new needs, [it becomes] a subordinate one."[21]

In "The German Ideology," Marx and Engels also comment briefly on the family in communist society. They are examining the relationship between forms of social organization and the state of development of productive forces. Early agricultural societies, they note, were characterized by "individual economy" and could not develop along communal lines. "The abolition [*Aufhebung*] of individual economy, which is inseparable from the abolition of private property, was impossible for the simple reason that the material conditions required were not present." Then, almost as an afterthought, they note that it is obvious that "the supersession [*Aufhebung*] of individual economy is inseparable from the supersession of the family."[22] For the first time in their work, Marx and Engels here touch on the utopian socialist theme of the abolition of the family.

Marx and Engels now had the firm beginnings of both a theory and a history of the issues involved in the problem of women's subordination. Marx summed up the general theoretical insight in a letter to the Russian liberal Annenkov. "Assume particular stages of development in production, commerce and consumption and you will have a corresponding social constitution, a corresponding organization of the family, of orders or of classes, in a word, a corresponding civil society."[23] From a theoretical point of view, in other words, all social relations can ultimately be rooted in the relations of production dominant in a given society. As for empirical material concerning the history of women and the family, it was still quite scarce, but Marx and Engels had already been able to piece together a fair sketch of the historical development.

With the "new world outlook" consolidated in the writings of 1845–1846, Marx and Engels found themselves confronting new tasks. A wave of reawakened democratic aspirations and intensified political activity was sweeping across Europe, triggered by the economic crisis of 1847 and culminating in the revolutions of 1848–1850. Practical organizational work, first with the Communist Correspondence Committee and then with the Communist League, became paramount. When the newly formed Communist League required a theoretical and practical platform, Marx and Engels were asked to draft it. Two preparatory versions, both by Engels, survive. An initial "Draft of a Communist Confession of Faith," written in the question and answer format commonly used at the time by workers' organizations, was discussed at the First Congress of the Communist League in London in June 1847. In late October, Engels produced an improved version, the "Principles of Communism," also in the form of a revolutionary catechism. By November 1847 it was clear that the question and answer format conflicted with the historical approach, and Engels suggested to Marx that they drop the catechism form.[24] The result, *The Manifesto of the Communist Party,* was written between December 1847 and January 1848, on the instructions of the Second Congress of the Communist League. In its pages, as well as in the drafts, Marx and Engels recast their views on the issue of women's subordination into a more programmatic, and frequently quite striking, form.

Having grasped the mechanisms underlying historical development, Marx and Engels were able to link past, present, and future phenomena with a new, if still rather unsubtle, clarity. Thus Engels observes in the "Confession of Faith" that "the family relationship has been modified in the course of history by the property relationship and by periods of development, and . . . consequently the ending of private property will also have a most important influence on it." More dramatically, the *Manifesto* delineates the relationship between family and property in capitalist society. The bourgeois family is based "on capital, on private gain. In its completely developed form this family exists only among the bourgeoisie. But this state of things finds its complement in the practical absence of the family among the proletarians, and in public prostitution." Since the working class lacks property, the proletarian's "relation to his wife and children has no longer anything in common with bourgeois family relations." At the ideological level, the *Manifesto* claims, with a dramatic flourish, that "the bourgeoisie has torn away from the family its sentimental veil, and has reduced the family relation to a mere money relation."[25]

Communists argued that such relations within families, as well as prostitution, are natural products of bourgeois society. In addition, they had to respond to the bourgeois accusation that they intended to collectivize women, that is, turn them into prostitutes. In the "Principles of Communism," Engels is terse and analytic. "Community of women is a relationship that belongs altogether to bourgeois society and is completely realized today in prostitution. But prostitution is rooted in private property and falls with it. Thus instead of introducing the community of women, communist organization puts an end to it." Still, no issue so inflamed and frightened the nineteenth-century bourgeoisie, for, as Sheila Rowbotham compellingly argues, "the prostitute became the symbol of [its] class and sex guilt." The question of prostitution takes a much greater place in *The Communist Manifesto* than in the two preparatory drafts. In passionate terms, Marx and Engels denounce the bourgeoisie's small-minded ignorance and ideological hypocrisy:

> But you Communists would introduce community of women, screams the whole bourgeoisie in chorus.
>
> The bourgeois sees in his wife a mere instrument of production. He hears that the instruments of production are to be exploited in common, and, naturally, can come to no other conclusion than that the lot of being common to all will likewise fall to the women.
>
> He has not even a suspicion that the real point aimed at is to do away with the status of women as mere instruments of production.
>
> For the rest, nothing is more ridiculous than the virtuous indignation of our bourgeois at the community of women which, they pretend, is to be openly and officially established by the Communists. The Communists have no need to introduce community of women; it has existed almost from time immemorial.[26]

The *Manifesto* also situates the future of marriage and of relations between the sexes with respect to the prevailing mode of production. "The abolition of the present system of production must bring with it the abolition of the community of women springing from that system, i.e., of prostitution both public and private." More specifically, "the bourgeois family will vanish as a matter of course when its complement [public prostitution and the disintegrating working-class family] vanishes, and both will vanish with the vanishing of capital." In contrast to these fairly cryptic remarks, Engels's draft versions are in places more explicit. The "Confession of Faith," for example, argues that communist society would be able, if necessary, to "interfere in the personal relationship between men and women or with the family in general to the extent that the maintenance of the existing institution would disturb the new social order." In "Principles of Communism," Engels revises this position:

> *Question 21*: What influence will the communist order of society have upon the family?
> *Answer*: It will make the relation between the sexes a purely private relation which concerns only the persons involved, and in which society has no call to interfere. It is able to do this because it abolishes private property and educates children communally, thus destroying the twin foundation of hitherto existing marriage—the dependence through private property of the wife upon the husband and of the children upon the parents.

What seems here to be an about-face may in fact be a clarification. Engels now differentiates among types of societal intervention. Abolition of private property and communal education beginning at the earliest possible age strike at the heart of capitalist society. Having thus drastically intervened, a communist society can, Engels feels, safely leave other relations between the sexes alone.[27]

These draft formulations recall typical nineteenth-century socialist positions concerning the abolition of the family. While their omission from the *Manifesto* leaves the issue frustratingly open, Marx and Engels evidently concluded that a more precise and less utopian statement referring to the abolition of *both* the bourgeois and the proletarian family better represented their position. In this way, to the bourgeoisie's charge that communists seek the destruction of "the family '*as such*,'" they quite properly replied that communists fight for the abolition of classes as embodied in the specific institutions—here, the bourgeois and the working-class family—of class society.

Marx and Engels also refer very briefly, in the *Manifesto*, to the problem of the structure of the wage with respect to the household. In an analytic mode they observe that "the less the skill and exertion of strength implied in manual labor, in other words, the more modern industry becomes developed, the more is the labor of men superseded by that of women. Differences of age and sex have no longer any distinctive social validity for the working class. All are instruments of labor, more or less expensive to use, according to their age and sex." This foundation laid, they proclaim dramatically that "all family ties among the proletarians are torn asunder, and their children transformed into simple articles of commerce and instruments of labor."[28]

Marx addressed the theoretical questions surrounding the wage more directly in a set of lectures delivered at the time of the writing of the *Manifesto*, and published sixteen months later as *Wage Labor and Capital*. He observes that with the development of capitalism, competition increases and wages fall. Furthermore, the introduction of machinery has the effect of "replacing skilled workers by unskilled, men by women, adults by children," thereby generally depreciating the value of labor power and changing the structure of the household's income. When, for example, the factory employs three children and a woman in place of a man discharged because of the machine, "now four times as many workers' lives are used up in order to gain a livelihood for *one* worker's family." At the same time, Marx confronts the difficult question of the determination of wage levels. Wages, or the "wage minimum," are the price of "the cost of existence and reproduction of the worker." Marx cautions, however, that the concept of a wage minimum pertains to the working class as a whole. "This wage minimum, like the determination of the price of commodities by the cost of production in general, does not hold good for the *single individual* but for the *species*. Individual workers, millions of workers, do not get enough to be able to exist and reproduce themselves; *but the wages of the whole working class* level down, within their fluctuations, to this minimum." While still holding to the notion of a hypothetical minimum wage, Marx recognizes its essentially aggregate and social character.[29]

In their early writings, Marx and Engels evidence a commitment to the importance of the problem of the oppression of women. They dissect, to the extent the available empirical material allowed, the hard facts of women's subordination in past and present society. Against this ugly picture they counterpose a serious, if somewhat simplistic vision of women's liberation in the future, and of the abolition of the family as it exists in class society. Although their strategic approach hardly matches the scope of this vision, its programmatic weakness reflects the level of development of the working-class movement at the time. In their theoretical views, Marx and Engels begin to distinguish their position on the question of women from the imprecision and utopianism of earlier socialist opinions.

In the next decades, both Marx and Engels sought to elaborate the theoretical, as well as the programmatic, aspects of their perspective. Insofar as they continued their emphasis on the division of labor according to sex, on the oppression of proletarian women at work, and on the supposed dissolution of the working-class family, they set the terms within which the so-called woman question was to be discussed and acted upon by socialists for the next hundred years. At the same time, they deepened their understanding of women's oppression as a structural element of the overall reproduction of the working class and of general social reproduction. In this sense, they began to move toward a broader theoretical and practical approach to achieving the goal of women's liberation.

5

Marx:

The Mature Years

By 1850, the series of insurrections that had inspired democratic and revolutionary hopes across the European continent was checked. Encouraged by an upward turn in the economic cycle, counterrevolutionary regimes sought to reassert the power of the propertied. Marx and Engels, the leading spokesmen of the Communist League, soon became major targets of reactionary governmental ire. Hounded from the continent, they took refuge in England: Engels to Manchester, where he took a position in his father's textile firm, and Marx to London, where he remained for the rest of his life.

Marx now began his economic studies anew, deciding "to start again from the very beginning and to work carefully through the new material."[1] Between 1857 and 1858 he consolidated his notes in a manuscript known today as the *Grundrisse*. While many formulations in the *Grundrisse* remain incorrect or imprecise from the point of view of the works later prepared for actual publication, the manuscript shows how far Marx's studies had brought him. It presents his first mature attempt "to lay bare," as he was to phrase it ten years later in the preface to *Capital*, "the economic law of motion of modern society." And it includes some comments broadly relevant to the issues of women's subordination and liberation.

Because Marx strives to understand the capitalist mode of production as a whole, he returns again and again in the *Grundrisse* to the problem of the relationships among production, distribution, exchange, and consumption. In this way he addresses the issue of the

56

reproduction, within definite relations, of individuals by means of the consumption of products. "Consumption reproduces the individual himself in a specific mode of being, not only in his immediate quality of being alive, and in specific social relations. So that the ultimate appropriation by individuals taking place in the consumption process reproduces them in the original relations in which they move within the production process and towards each other; reproduces them in their social being, and hence reproduces their social being—society— which appears as much the subject as the result of this great total process."[2] This very general statement underscores the inseparability of the reproduction of individuals from overall social reproduction, even if it lacks specificity with respect to class membership.

Elsewhere in the *Grundrisse*, Marx focuses on the reproduction of individuals as direct producers in the capitalist mode of production, that is, as members of the working class. The individual worker possesses a commodity, the capacity to labor, that the capitalist needs to set the production process in motion. On the market, the worker exchanges this commodity "for money, for the general form of wealth, but only in order to exchange this again for commodities, considered as the objects of his immediate consumption, as the means of satisfying his needs."[3] The wages paid to the worker by the capitalist represent the amount of labor embodied in these commodities bought for immediate consumption.

Wage levels fluctuate. In general, they correspond to "the objectified labor necessary bodily to maintain not only the general substance in which [the worker's] labor power exists, i.e. the worker himself, but also that required to modify this general substance so as to develop its particular capacity." When business is good, needs and consumption—the worker's "share of civilization"—expand. In the long run, capital's drive for accumulation has the tendency to permit the worker to augment and replace "natural" needs with "historically created" ones. It is this element of flexibility that distinguishes the wage worker from the serf or slave, for "he is neither bound to particular objects, nor to a particular manner of satisfaction. The sphere of his consumption is not qualitatively restricted, only quantitatively."[4]

So long as Marx examines the immediate production process, as in these remarks on wages, he treats the worker as a sort of "perennial subject and not yet as a mortal individual of the working species." At this level, "we are not yet dealing with the working class, i.e. the replacement for wear and tear so that it can maintain itself as a class."[5] Once the analysis turns to capital accumulation, however, the problem of the aggregate reproduction of the working class comes into clearer focus. Marx approaches it by means of a critique of Malthus's theory of overpopulation.

Malthus makes two serious errors, according to Marx. First, he fails to recognize that the determination of population proceeds according to qualitative and quantitative relations specific to a given mode of production. "He transforms the immanent, historically changing limits of the human reproduction process into *outer barriers*; and the *outer barriers* to natural reproduction into *immanent limits* or *natural laws* of reproduction." Second, Malthus argues that a fixed quantity of necessaries can sustain only a given number of people, when he should have analyzed the social relations enabling individuals to acquire means of subsistence. In capitalist societies, for example, a person must have employment to obtain money to buy necessaries. More generally, the question is the "*social mediation* as such, through which the individual gains access to the means of his reproduction and creates them."[6]

Overpopulation therefore has a characteristic form in the capitalist mode of production. The surplus population represents a surplus of "labor capacities," and is made up of workers rather than non-workers. In general, the absolute size of the working class tends to grow as capital accumulates. At the same time, capital's need to develop the productive forces causes a continual decrease in the proportion of necessary to surplus labor which "appears as increase of the relatively superfluous laboring capacities—i.e. as the positing of surplus population." To the extent that a portion of this surplus population is sustained as a "reserve for later use," all classes pay the costs. In this way, "Mr. Capitalist . . . shifts a part of the reproduction costs of the working class off his own shoulders and thus pauperizes a part of the remaining population for his own profit."[7]

Far from embodying an abstract law of nature, overpopulation in the form of a relative surplus of workers—what Engels had called the reserve army of labor—is inherent in capitalist relations of production. Its actual character at any given time responds to the contradictory tendencies of capital to both increase the laboring population absolutely and render a growing portion of it relatively superfluous. In short, "all the contradictions which modern population theory expresses as such, but does not grasp," emerge from the phenomenon of surplus value.[8] With these observations, Marx suggests an intimate theoretical linkage between the reproduction of the working class and the workings of the capitalist mode of production.

As for family and household, Marx only mentions them in the *Grundrisse* when considering precapitalist forms of production. Speaking of various preindustrial or non-European societies, he consistently represents the family household by its individual, presumed male, head. Thus, for example, the aim of work in such societies is "sustenance of the individual proprietor and of his family, as well as of the total community." Moreover, Marx assumes the universality of a natural sex division of labor when he puts production of certain goods in brackets as a "domestic side occupation of wives and daughters (spinning and weaving)." Marx's surprisingly uncritical stance in these remarks in part owes its existence to the weakness of his sources.[9] It is more deeply rooted, as we shall see in the next section, in the relatively broad and unexplored conceptual boundaries accorded the sphere of "the natural" in nineteenth-century thought.

The *Grundrisse* was the first in a series of manuscripts culminating in the publication of *Capital*. Only Volume 1 of *Capital*, which first appeared in 1867, was edited by Marx himself. After Marx's death, Engels used the various drafts produced by Marx in the sixties to edit versions of Volumes 2 and 3 for publication. Volume 4, known today as *Theories of Surplus Value*, was assembled and published by Karl Kautsky. Considerable portions of the manuscripts Marx drafted between 1857 and 1870 remain unpublished.[10]

Scattered through the pages of *Capital*, Marx's comments on women's situation, on the family, on divisions of labor according to sex and age, and on the reproduction of the working class have never been sufficiently appreciated by students of the so-called woman question. A systematic review of the three volumes discloses a great deal of important material.

Marx considers the actual situation of working-class women, as well as children, in the context of his description of capitalist development, focusing on the impact of the introduction of machinery. Machinery notably lessens the importance of physical strength in the labor process. Under capitalist conditions, machinery therefore enables the employer to hire women and children, paying lower wages than male workers ordinarily command. Employment of women and children has specific physical, moral, and intellectual consequences, which Marx describes in a manner reminiscent of Engels's account, twenty years earlier, in *The Condition of the Working Class in England*.[11] He emphasizes how the introduction of machinery also has a severe impact on branches of production not yet mechanized. Here, employers shift to "cheap labor," that is, to a work force composed of women, children, and the unskilled. The exploitation of these workers is merciless, for "the technical foundation of the factory system, namely, the substitution of machines for muscular power, and the light character of the labor, is almost entirely absent in Manufacture, and at the same time women and over-young children are subjected, in a most unconscionable way, to the influence of poisonous or injurious substances." In such sweatshops, mines, and huts, even more than in the mechanized factories, the capitalist mode of production "shows its antagonistic and murderous side."[12]

The evolution of capitalism has the general effect of continually altering the composition of the labor force with respect to sex and age, as well as size. The introduction of machinery, for example, throws many people out of work, but may draw in others, among them women and children. In numerous branches of production, women and children replace men as the principal element in the work force. Moreover, the extraordinary productivity of capitalist mechanized industry permits the number of domestic servants, ninety percent of them women, to increase greatly. Despite constant capitalist expansion, which to some extent offsets the impact of mechanization on employment, crises periodically cripple production, force wages down, and cause mass unemployment. "The workpeople are thus continually both repelled and attracted, hustled from pillar to post, while, at the same time, constant changes take place in the sex, age, and skill of the levies."[13]

Next to the rich picture of social conditions under capitalism, the descriptive material in *Capital* on noncapitalist past societies is quite sparse. Nothing specifically relevant to the experience of women per se appears, and Marx concentrates instead on the family. Alluding to the variety of family forms in history, he observes that no single form is "absolute and final." Moreover, "taken together [they] form a series in historical development."[14] He is most interested in the self-supporting peasant family, for it represents the family form just preceding that of capitalist society. The peasant family is an elementary unit of production, an "individual direct producer," which unites "agricultural activity and the rural home industries connected with it" in an "indispensable combination." Characterizing the peasant household as "an isolated laborer with his family," Marx is minimally concerned with the division of labor inside it. Rather, he focuses on the peasant family as a producing unit that may itself dispose of some surplus labor, because it is here, in the distribution of this "combined agricultural and industrial family labor," that he locates the mechanism for social reproduction in the feudal system.[15]

Marx explicitly discusses divisions of labor by sex or age in several places in *Capital*. The peasant family "possesses a spontaneously developed system of division of labor. The distribution of the work within the family, and the regulation of the labor-time of the several members, depend as well upon differences of age and sex as upon natural conditions varying with the seasons." Machinery sweeps away the importance of skill: "In the place of the artificially produced distinctions between specialized workers, step the natural differences of age and sex." When early industrial capitalists tried to extend working hours beyond any possible endurance, "all bounds of morals and nature, age and sex, day and night, were broken down."[16] These natural distinctions have their historical root in biology. At the beginning of time, "there springs up naturally a division of labor, caused by differences of sex and age, a division that is consequently based on a purely physiological foundation."[17]

Marx's view of the natural character of divisions of labor by sex and age leads him to the corollary that servile relations naturally constitute the internal organization of all families in class society. Along with most of his contemporaries, including Engels, he assumes that a single male adult, the husband and father of subordinate family members, ordinarily and naturally heads the family household in all societies. Hence, he observes, "in private property of every type the *slavery* of the members of the family at least is always implicit since they are made use of and exploited by the head of the family."[18] As early as "The German Ideology," Marx and Engels had used the notion of "latent slavery" to represent internal relations in the family. Like the division of labor itself, "the slavery latent in the family only develops gradually with the increase of population, the growth of wants, and with the extension of external intercourse, both of war and of barter." Indeed, it is clear that "latent slavery in the family, though still very crude, is the first form of property."[19] In his mature work, Marx returns to the theme when he argues that the development of capitalist machine industry transforms parents into "slave-holders, sellers of their own children." Formerly, "the workman sold his own labor-power, which he disposed of nominally as a free agent. Now he sells wife and child. He has become a slave-dealer."[20] The image of slavery in these statements flows, in part, from assumptions about the natural character of the division of labor within the family, and tends to present a picture of women and children as passive victims rather than historical actors. Behind such formulations, which are more metaphorical than scientific, lurks a series of nineteenth-century ideological notions never sufficiently challenged.

Nineteenth-century social commentators often claimed a permanence based on nature for social relations that are actually specific to the capitalist mode of production. Such claims constituted a ready target for socialist polemics. In the *Manifesto*, for instance, Marx and Engels observe how a "selfish misconception" on the part of the bourgeoisie leads it to "transform into eternal laws of nature and of reason, the social forms springing from [the] present mode of production and form of property—historical relations that rise and disappear in the progress of production."[21] But Marx and Engels were not equally capable of demystifying bourgeois notions regarding the natural status of historical divisions of labor according to sex and age, much less of replacing them with more appropriate concepts. Indeed, in this area, they come perilously close to a position that holds biology to be destiny. A quite damaging specter of "the natural" haunts their work, from the earliest writings to the most mature. It stamps their concept of a wage minimum by assuming the obviousness of the division between mere physical subsistence and some more socially determined standard of living that might, for example, include generational reproduction or a family household. It obscures their understanding of relationships within the working-class household, particularly where the wife is also a wage laborer. And it undercuts their investigations of historical development by tying it to an unquestioned assumption of a natural division of labor between the sexes, originating in the biology of the sexual act. In the course of their work, Marx and Engels managed to soften some of the worst effects of these assumptions, often by postulating additional "social" phenomena that outweigh the supposedly natural facts, but they never entirely overcame them. Only with the development of feminist perspectives in modern anthropology, and more especially of an approach in the social sciences that is simultaneously Marxist and feminist, have the boundaries of "the natural" in this area begun to be seriously questioned.[22]

The existence of divisions of labor according to age and sex has definite political ramifications, to which Marx briefly alludes in *Capital*. In the early period of capitalist development, "the habits and the resistance of the male laborers" successfully block the entry of women and children into the wage labor force. The introduction of machinery, however, "at last breaks down the resistance which the male operatives in the manufacturing period continued to oppose to the despotism of capital."[23] Thereafter, capital tends to equalize all work, while "the technical subordination of the workman to the uniform motion of the instruments of labor, and the peculiar composition of the body of workpeople, consisting as it does of individuals of both sexes and of all ages, gives rise to a barrack discipline."[24] This process of economic and social equalization meets a barrier, however, in the dependent and subordinate status of women, and especially of children, who are also highly vulnerable to the assaults of large-scale industrial capitalism. Marx argues the necessity of protective legislation, and sketches its history. The development of capitalism overturned "the economic foundation on which was based the traditional family, and the family labor corresponding to it," and thus tended to dissolve traditional family relationships. "The rights of the children had to be proclaimed." [25] A long struggle ensued to force the state to formulate, officially recognize, and promulgate regulations protecting children and women. The passage of such protective legislation—limiting hours, forbidding night work, providing meal periods, and so forth—represented the outcome "of a protracted civil war, more or less dissembled, between the capitalist class and the working-class." [26]

Marx does more, in *Capital*, than comment descriptively on the situation of women, the family, and sex divisions of labor in past and present society. He makes a major contribution toward the development of the theory required to illuminate such historical developments. To the extent that the object of the so-called woman question actually lies in the sphere of the reproduction of labor power and the working class, Marx's economic writings constitute an essential starting point. From this perspective, the Marx of *Capital* had more to say of relevance to the issue of women's liberation than either he or his socialist followers ever realized. Three concepts are key: individual consumption, the value of labor power, and the industrial reserve army.

Individual consumption is a concept that Marx develops in opposition to productive consumption. While both productive and individual consumption pertain to labor processes in which human beings use up, that is, consume, products, the distinction is critical. Productive consumption refers, broadly speaking, to the bringing together of means of production—raw materials, tools or machines, auxiliary substances—and producers in a specific labor process whose outcome is new products, either means of production or means of subsistence. By contrast, individual consumption refers to the processes by which producers consume means of subsistence—food, housing, clothing, and the like—with the result that they maintain themselves. "The product, therefore, of individual consumption, is the consumer himself; the result of productive consumption is a product distinct from the consumer." [27]

In the most general sense, individual and productive consumption are processes that must take place in some form in any society, if it is to reproduce itself from day to day and year to year. Marx is, of course, especially interested in the workings of the capitalist mode of production, and focuses on the particular forms taken by individual and productive consumption under its dominance. Here, the process of individual consumption is mediated by the wage paid to the worker by the capitalist for the use of his or her capacity to work, and the distinction between productive and individual consumption takes a specific dual form. "The laborer consumes in a two-fold way. While producing he consumes by his labor the means of production, and converts them into products with a higher value than that of the capital advanced. This is his productive consumption. . . . On the other hand, the laborer turns the money paid to him for his labor-power into means of subsistence: this is his individual consumption." [28]

Most of Marx's remarks on the individual consumption of the worker present it as a process that takes place alone and in the abstract. Obviously, this is not enough. "Taking the working class as a whole, a portion of [the] means of subsistence is consumed by members of the family who either do not yet work, or have ceased to do so." Marx implies here a concept that would cover the maintenance not only of present wage workers but of future and past wage workers (e.g. children, aged and disabled persons, the unemployed), including those who are not currently wage workers but take part in the process of individual consumption (e.g. housewives). This concept would operate at the level of class relations and social reproduction as a whole. Such a concept of the reproduction of the working class in fact lies just below the surface of Marx's discussion of individual consumption. From the point of view of "capitalist production in full swing, and on its actual social scale," the working class's individual consumption is "the reconversion of the means of subsistence given by capital in exchange for labor-power, into fresh labor-power at the disposal of capital for exploitation. It is the production and reproduction of that means of production so indispensable to the capitalist: the laborer himself." [29] At the level of social reproduction, the problem of the renewal of the working class becomes critical. "The labor-power withdrawn from the market by wear and tear and death, must be continually replaced by, at the very least, an equal amount of fresh labor power." While Marx himself never developed a comprehensive and rigorous view of the reproduction of labor power, he recognized its importance for a theory of the capitalist mode of production whenever he pointed out that "the maintenance and reproduction of the working-class is, and must ever be, a necessary condition to the reproduction of capital." [30]

In the capitalist mode of production, the processes of individual consumption enable the worker to return to the market, ready to sell his or her labor power to the capitalist. But what, exactly, is labor power, and how is its value determined?

Marx defines labor power as "the aggregate of those mental and physical capabilities existing in a human being, which he exercises whenever he produces a use-value of any description." In the capitalist mode of production, labor power takes the form of a commodity, that is, a thing that has both use-value and value. It is labor power's use-value that so endears it to the capitalist, for unlike any other commodity, it "possesses the peculiar property of being a source of value." When put to use—consumed—in the capitalist labor process, labor power creates more value than was originally invested. Surplus value originates, then, in the productive consumption of this unique and wonderful commodity.[31] But before labor power can be consumed in the production process, the capitalist must acquire it in the market by exchanging for it an equivalent value.

According to Marx, the value of the commodity labor power is determined in the same way as the value of any other commodity. That is, the value of labor power represents the socially necessary labor required for the production of labor power. For a given individual, then, "the production of labor power consists in his reproduction of himself or his maintenance. For his maintenance he requires a given quantity of the means of subsistence. Therefore the labor-time requisite for the production of labor power reduces itself to that necessary for the production of those means of subsistence; in other words, the value of labor power is the value of the means of subsistence necessary for the maintenance of the laborer." Nonetheless, there is something quite special about the value of labor power, for "the number and extent of [man's] so-called necessary wants, as also the modes of satisfying them, are themselves the product of historical development." Into the determination of the value of labor power enters, therefore, a "historical and moral element."[32]

Marx developed this point at greater length in a series of lectures entitled "Wages, Price, and Profit," delivered two years before the publication of *Capital*. Here Marx distinguishes two components of the value of labor power, "the one merely physical, the other historical or social." The physical element determines the ultimate lower limit, although Marx observes that this limit is extremely elastic. Thus, "a quick succession of unhealthy and short-lived generations will keep the labor market as well supplied as a series of vigorous and long-lived generations." The value of labor power "is in every country determined by a *traditional standard of life*. It is not mere physical life, but it is the satisfaction of certain wants springing from the social conditions in which people are placed and reared up." Marx retains, in this discussion, the concept of a more or less natural physical subsistence level, but emphasizes the wide latitude for expansion and contraction in the "historical or social" component. In *Capital*, even this small concession to the notion of a natural physical minimum has all but disappeared, and the "historical and moral element" plays the principal role. Nevertheless, Marx insists that the value of labor power can be established, for "in a given country, at a given period, the average quantity of the means of subsistence necessary for the laborer is practically known."[33]

As with every commodity, the price of labor power does not ordinarily coincide with its value, but rather fluctuates around it. At times, the price will rise above the value of labor power, with a consequent easing of "the length and weight of the golden chain" of capitalist exploitation. More ominously, the price of labor power may fall substantially below its value, to the point that sectors of existing labor power are not renewed in the next generation.[34]

The existence of fluctuations in the price of labor power, and their impact on working people's lives, had already been discussed several times by Marx and Engels. With *Capital*, Marx roots these fluctuations in a theory of the value of labor power, and thereby goes beyond the surface phenomena of supply, demand, and capitalist avarice. Thus, for example, he offers a clear, if all too brief, analysis of the structure of the value of labor power with respect to the household, focusing, as in earlier texts, on the effects of the increasing entry of women and children into the wage labor force. Marx assumes a situation in which the value of labor power is such that the wage of a single adult male worker suffices to support an entire family household. While this assumption is questionable from a historical perspective, it provides a theoretical base line against which to examine variations in the value of labor power. An innovation such as the introduction of machinery, "by throwing every member of [the worker's] family on to the labor market, spreads the value of the man's labor power over his whole family. It thus depreciates his labor power." The value of the individual worker's labor power falls because it now takes the wage work of several household members to obtain the original quantity of means of subsistence. Marx amplifies this observation in several ways. Most important, the entry of additional household members into wage labor means, other things being equal, an intensification of the rate of exploitation. Further, the fact that several family members work where only one did before may require the purchase of more means of subsistence, and thus raise somewhat the total value of the household's labor power. For example, "domestic work, such as sewing and mending, must be replaced by the purchase of ready-made articles. Hence the diminished expenditure of labor in the house is accompanied by an increased expenditure of money. The cost of keeping the family increases, and balances the greater income."[35]

It is perfectly possible for the value of the labor power expended by an entire household to rise substantially, accompanied by a real shift upward in its "standard of life," while at the same time the value of the labor power of the individuals comprising the household falls and the rate of exploitation increases. In general, "the capitalist may pay *higher wages* and still lower the *value of labor* [power], if the rise of wages does not correspond to the greater amount of labor extracted, and the quicker decay of the laboring power thus caused." Marx gives a strikingly familiar example of how bourgeois ideology interprets this phenomenon: "Your middle class statisticians will tell you . . . that the average wages of factory families in Lancashire have risen. They forget that instead of the labor of the man, the head of the family, his wife and perhaps three or four children are now thrown under the Juggernaut wheels of capital, and that the rise of the aggregate wages does not correspond to the aggregate surplus labor extracted from the family."[36]

The subject of the industrial reserve army, which Marx characterizes as the principal manifestation of capitalism's impact on the working class, takes up an entire chapter of Volume 1 of *Capital*. In general, "the greater the social wealth, the functioning capital, the extent and energy of its growth, and, therefore, also the absolute mass of the proletariat and the productiveness of its labor, the greater is the industrial reserve army. . . . *This is the absolute general law of capitalist accumulation.*"[37] More clearly than in the *Grundrisse*, Marx ties the existence, size, and form of a surplus population to the processes of capital accumulation.

As capital grows, it demands progressively more labor. Workers must work harder and for longer hours, and more workers must be hired. "Accumulation of capital is, therefore, increase of the proletariat." This tendency to swell the number of wage workers absolutely is opposed by a second, and far more powerful, mechanism also inherent in capital accumulation. The drive for surplus value forces capitalists constantly to augment productivity, chiefly through the introduction of machinery. An ever-growing quantity of means of production requires less and less human labor to be set in motion in the production process. As a result, demand for labor falls relatively, and a surplus population of wage workers emerges. This relative surplus population constitutes "a condition of existence of the capitalist mode of production. It forms a disposable industrial reserve army. . . . Independently of the limits of the actual increase of population, it creates, for the changing needs of the self-expansion of capital, a mass of human material always ready for exploitation."[38]

The industrial reserve army fluctuates in size according to the cruel whims of the capitalist accumulation cycle. At all times, moreover, relative surplus population takes several distinct forms. The floating reserve is made up of workers who move in and out of employment according to the needs of the constantly changing capitalist labor process. The latent reserve consists of those thrust out of work by the extension of capitalism into noncapitalist sectors. The stagnant reserve is formed by chronically underemployed workers, who are condemned to terrible poverty and always willing to work for the lowest wages in the worst conditions. Below these three categories of reserves, paupers make up the bottom layer of the surplus population. "Pauperism," Marx observes, "is the hospital of the active labor army and the dead weight of the industrial reserve army."[39] While he is never entirely clear in his formulations, Marx seems to regard the industrial reserve army as included in, rather than coextensive with, the relative surplus population.

At once the product of capital accumulation and the lever for its further extension, the industrial reserve army embodies a "law of population" specific to capitalism. In this sense, Marx puts the reproduction of the working class at the heart of the capital accumulation process. "The reproduction of a mass of labor power, which must incessantly re-incorporate itself with capital for that capital's self-expansion; which cannot get free from capital, and whose enslavement to capital is only concealed by the variety of individual capitalists to whom it sells itself; this reproduction of labor power forms, in fact, an essential of the reproduction of capital itself."[40]

In Volume 3 of *Capital*, Marx returns to the concepts of relative surplus population and the industrial reserve army, this time looking at them in the context of total social reproduction. At this level, the capitalist accumulation process itself gives rise to the tendency of the average rate of profit to fall. Among the factors potentially counteracting this tendency, Marx names the relative surplus population. Members of the industrial reserve army form a pool of available cheap labor. Some capitalists hire them at extremely low wages, and forgo the advances in productivity that lead eventually to a falling average rate of profit. In these branches of production, the rate and mass of surplus value are unusually high, producing a counterbalance to those branches in which the rates have fallen. It may even be that the industrial reserve army "more or less paralyzes" the tendency of the average rate of profit to fall. Once again, the reproduction of the working class stands at the center of the process of capitalist production, now considered as a whole.[41]

Marx's discussion of individual consumption, the value of labor power, and the industrial reserve army is tantalizingly incomplete. In particular, the treatment of three issues remains vague and requires clarification. First, it is never obvious whether the concept of the value of labor power covers the maintenance and replacement of the individual worker alone or includes that of other persons as well, for example, family members supported by a worker's wage. Second, Marx scarcely mentions the unpaid domestic labor performed as part of the tasks that result in the reproduction of the worker, and accords it no clear theoretical status. Third, the critical question of the relationship between the concept of the industrial reserve army, which appears in the context of discussions of capital accumulation, and the more limited concept of individual consumption is never really addressed.[42] Despite these ambiguities, and the generally schematic and unfinished character of Marx's remarks on the reproduction of labor power and the working class, his work provides the foundation for a theory of the relationship of women and the family to social reproduction in general and the capitalist mode of production in particular.

Consistent with his achievement, in *Capital*, of the rudiments of a scientific perspective on the reproduction of labor power and the working class, Marx's brief comments on the future of the family and relations between the sexes place them in the context of social reproduction as a whole. The development of capitalism creates "a new economic foundation for a higher form of the family and of the relations between the sexes." In its present, capitalist, guise, large-scale industry brings workers together in a "brutal" labor process, which "becomes a pestiferous source of corruption and slavery," where "the laborer exists for the process of production, and not the process of production for the laborer." Nonetheless, it is precisely this phenomenon that Marx identifies as the potential basis for new family relations, inasmuch as it assigns "an important part in the process of production, outside the domestic sphere, to women, to young persons, and to children of both sexes." In sum, "the fact of the collective working group being composed of individuals of both sexes and all ages must necessarily, under suitable conditions, become a source of humane development." As to what form that development might take in terms of the family and sexual relations in a future communist society, Marx cautiously refrains from speculating.[43]

In these years, Marx seized, once again, the opportunity to engage in practical political work. After a period of relative inactivity, the working classes of Europe recovered from the defeats of 1848–1850, and began a process of reorganization which took its most advanced form in the International Working Men's Association. Founded in 1864 on the initiative of working-class militants, the International represented an uneasy coalition of English trade union leaders, whose chief political aim was suffrage, and French utopian socialists, bent on establishing producers' cooperatives and opposed to both strikes and political action. It fell largely to Marx and Engels to attempt the shaping of this amalgam into an adequate force for socialism. For a decade, until the International collapsed in the wake of the Paris Commune, they committed themselves to the delicate task.

As its name suggests, the International was an organization composed almost exclusively of men. In this it reflected the general character of the working-class movement, if not the working class, of the time. Not only was the working-class movement a largely male province, it ordinarily espoused a decidedly backward view of women and of women's work. Throughout the nineteenth century, male workers and their organizations argued for the abolition of female wage labor, refused to admit women into labor organizations, opposed female suffrage, and promoted an idealized image of woman's proper place at the family hearth. Although the horrible conditions in which women worked and their desperate misery struck everyone, the arguments to exclude them from wage labor were unrealistic as well as pragmatically unwise. Such reasoning denied the fact that sizable sectors of working-class women were already permanent members of the wage labor force. And it enabled employers to perpetuate division and competition within the working class. In this atmosphere, Marx put forth positions that upheld the rights of women and protected, to the best of his understanding, the interests and future of all members of the working class. At the same time, a nineteenth-century view of the social meaning of physiological differences between the sexes influenced his programmatic suggestions.

The critical theoretical insight that backed Marx's positions on women's and children's wage labor was his distinction between the labor process and the particular form it takes under capitalist conditions. "I do not say it is wrong that women and children should participate in our social production," he observed at one meeting of the International's General Council. Rather, the issue is "the way in which they are made to work under existing circumstances."[44] Given this situation, what was the working-class movement to do? Women, and especially children, should be protected by legislation against the worst assaults of capitalist exploitation. "The laborers must put their heads together, and, as a class, compel the passing of a law, an all-powerful social barrier that shall prevent the very workers from selling, by voluntary contract with capital, themselves and their families into slavery and death."[45] Children need time to grow and learn. Women must be excluded "from branches of industry that are specifically unhealthy for the female body or are objectionable morally for the female sex."[46] The necessity for such protective legislation arises from the contradictory position of women and children within capitalist society. On the one hand, the drawing of women and children out of social isolation and patriarchal oppression in the peasant family to "cooperate in the great work of social production [is] a progressive, sound and legitimate tendency." On the other, "under capital it was distorted into an abomination."[47]

"The woman has thus become an active agent in our social production," Marx observed. It followed that women must be incorporated as active participants in political work. "Anybody who knows anything of history," he wrote to his friend Dr. Kugelmann, "knows that major social transformations are impossible without ferment among women."[48] In 1871, Marx initiated and the International adopted a new rule recommending the establishment of female branches, without excluding the possibility of branches composed of both sexes.[49] Effective implementation of the recommendation depended, above all, on its being taken seriously by men at every level of leadership. In view of the history of the nineteenth-century working-class movement, prospects for such a general commitment were quite poor, and in any case, the International was nearing the end of its organizational existence. Nonetheless, Marx's recommendation left an important legacy by establishing, at least in principle, the legitimacy of autonomous women's organizations within the mass movement.

After the collapse of the first International, Marx and Engels served as theoretical and tactical advisers to the emerging working-class parties that were later to form the Second International. Thus, delegates from the new French Workers' party consulted them on the party's program for the 1880 elections. Discussed and drawn up in London, the program included an introduction by Marx in which, as he later put it, "the communist goal is defined in a few words." The opening sentence of the introduction specifically asserts that "the emancipation of the producing class involves all human beings without distinction of sex or race."[50] These two issues—which, in the form of the so-called woman and national questions, were to constitute central problems for revolutionaries in the coming decades—had already become a pressing concern in socialist theory and practice. At the threshold of the epoch of imperialist domination and world revolution, but at the close of his own life, Marx was still very much in step.

Taken as a whole, Marx's mature writings offer the rudiments of a theoretical foundation for analyzing the situation of women from the point of view of social reproduction. Marx himself did not, however, develop such an analysis, nor did he leave significant notes on the subject. Subsequent attempts by late nineteenth-century socialists, including Engels, to use Marx's theory of social development to examine women's situation fell rather short of the mark. As the years passed, moreover, and the problem of women's oppression became codified in the form of the so-called woman question, the very possibility of taking the perspective suggested in Marx's mature work diminished. Recent socialist-feminist efforts to situate women in terms of a concept of the reproduction of labor power therefore constitute the first sustained attempt to develop an understanding of women's oppression based on Marx's theory of social reproduction.

6

Engels: A Defective Formulation

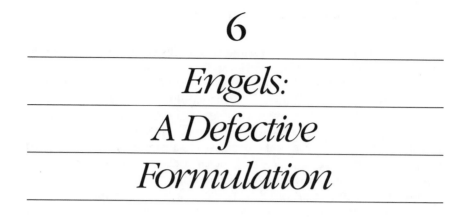

Having arrived in 1850 as an exile from the political storms on the continent, Engels remained in Manchester for two decades, employed in the family textile firm. A secure and growing income enabled him to assist Marx, continually in financial difficulty during these years. In 1870, on the eve of the Paris Commune, and with developments in the International quickening, Engels liquidated his partnership in the business and moved to London, where he could more fully participate in political life. Until Marx's death in 1883, the two friends worked side by side in the socialist movement, daily discussing every aspect of their political and theoretical work. With Marx, Engels sat on the General Council of the International, and worked to unify the various trends within the socialist movement. And like Marx, he played the part of dean and adviser to the movement after the International's collapse, continuing in this function up to his death in 1895.

During these last twenty years of his life, Engels also embarked on a wide-ranging program of research and writing. Among his published works, two well-known and extremely popular books touch on the problem of women's oppression. Together with *The Communist Manifesto* these texts acted as fundamental guides for the emerging generation of socialists.

Engels produced the work that became known as *Anti-Dühring* in 1878 as a polemic against the views of the socialist Eugen Dühring. The book presents a comprehensive exposition of what Engels saw as "the communist world outlook fought for by Marx and myself." Naturally enough, that outlook included some comments on women, the family, and the reproduction of the working class, which generally recapitulate his own and Marx's earlier analyses and positions. In a survey of pre-Marxist socialist thinkers, for instance, Engels approves Fourier's critique of the relations between the sexes and of women's position in capitalist society, and asserts, following Marx's free paraphrase of Fourier in *The Holy Family*, that the utopian socialist was the first to regard woman's position as an index of general social development.[1] Engels also reviews a number of themes discussed in previous works: the determination of the value of labor power, the effects of machinery on the working-class family, the emergence of an industrial reserve army, the character of bourgeois marriage as a legal form of prostitution, and the progressive dissolution of traditional family bonds, including "patriarchal subordination," with the advance of capitalism.[2] Looking at the family in earlier societies, Engels speaks of "the natural division of labor within the family," and with some qualification, subsumes all members of a household under its male head.[3] Finally, Engels insists that family forms are rooted in social relations, and thus that the family can change if society is transformed. In this context, he draws a critical programmatic corollary from Marx's statement in *Capital* that capitalism creates the foundation for such changes. What is necessary is not only "the free association of men," but "the transformation of private domestic work into a public industry." This is the first formulation within the classical Marxist tradition of a position later to become a central tenet of socialist strategy.[4]

Engels's other major book from this period is the famous *The Origin of the Family, Private Property and the State*, written between March and May of 1884, published that October, and instantaneously accorded the place of a socialist classic.

The circumstances of Engels's startlingly rapid production of the *Origin* remain somewhat mysterious. The book is based, as its subtitle ("In the Light of the Researches of Lewis H. Morgan") indicates, on Morgan's *Ancient Society*, which had appeared in 1877 and immediately engaged Marx's interest. Writing to the German socialist Kautsky on February 16, 1884, Engels described the late Marx's enthusiasm for Morgan's book, adding "if I had the time I would work up the material, with Marx's notes, . . . but I cannot even think of it." Yet by late March he was already at work on the *Origin* and by the end of April close to finishing.[5] The full explanation of the reasons for Engels's change in plan, which is especially striking in view of the fact that he was already immersed in the editing of Marx's unfinished volumes of *Capital*, must await further research. It seems likely that the context was political. In 1879, the German socialist leader August Bebel had published *Woman in the Past, Present and Future*, which appeared in a revised version late in 1883. Tremendously popular from the start, Bebel's *Woman* bore the influence of utopian socialism throughout; in addition, it reflected emerging tendencies toward reformism within the socialist movement. Engels's decision to write the *Origin* surely reflected a recognition of the weaknesses in Bebel's work. The socialist movement's commitment to the liberation of women urgently required an adequate theoretical foundation. Understood as an implicit polemic within the movement, the *Origin* represented Engels's attempt to provide one.[6]

The socialist tradition has treated the *Origin* as the definitive Marxist pronouncement on the family and therefore on the so-called woman question. Further, the tradition holds that the book accurately reflects the views of Marx as well as Engels. Neither assertion fairly measures the work's status. In the first place, the subject covered in the *Origin*, as its title indicates, is the development not only of the family but of private property and the state. The observation is important, for it suggests the book's limited goals with respect to the issue of women's subordination. Rather than provide a comprehensive analysis of women, the family, and the reproduction of the working class, the *Origin* seeks simply to situate certain aspects of the question securely in a historical and theoretical context. In the second place, the *Origin* bears the scars of its hasty genesis throughout. Far from the work of either Marx or Engels at his best, it constitutes, in Engels' words, a "meagre substitute for what my departed friend no longer had the time to do."[7]

In drafting the *Origin*, Engels relied not just on Morgan's *Ancient Society*, but on a series of notebooks in which Marx had entered passages from various authors' writings concerning primitive society. These "Ethnological Notebooks," composed in 1880–1881, include a lengthy abstract of Morgan's book. It is not at all clear what Marx intended to do with the material he was collecting, and Engels altered the framework established in the "Notebooks" to some extent. To grasp the structure and meaning of Engels's book, it is therefore necessary to examine the contents, theoretical assumptions, and weaknesses of Morgan's *Ancient Society*.[8]

In *Ancient Society* Morgan, an American anthropologist living in northern New York State, seeks to demonstrate the strikingly parallel evolution of what he saw as four essential characteristics of human society: inventions and discoveries, government, family, and property. The book organizes a vast array of ethnographic data into sections corresponding to these four characteristics, labeled by Morgan "Lines of Human Progress from Savagery through Barbarism to Civilisation." Part 1, a short survey entitled "Growth of Intelligence through Inventions and Discoveries," grounds Morgan's evolutionary periodization in three major stages of the development of the arts of subsistence. At the most primitive level of human social organization, peoples in the stage of "savagery"—what anthropologists today call hunting and gathering, or foraging, cultures—obtain subsistence by gathering wild plants, fishing, and hunting. The second period, "barbarism," is characterized by food production, as opposed to the food gathering typical of savagery. Cultures at the lower levels of barbarism practice horticulture, a simple type of plant domestication. In the upper stages of barbarism, animals are domesticated, and a more sophisticated agriculture, which includes the use of the plow and irrigation, develops. Finally, in the period of "civilization," societies base themselves on these advanced agricultural methods, to which they add writing and the keeping of records. Morgan divides such societies into two broad types, ancient and modern. With this sequence of stages, Morgan rests all human history on a materialist foundation, but one whose essence is technological, not social.

Morgan devotes nearly two-thirds of *Ancient Society* to Part 2, "Growth of the Idea of Government." Here he presents a theory of the evolution of social organization from early kin-based forms to fully developed political governance. The social organization of the most primitive peoples is based simply on broadly defined "classes" of persons permitted to marry one another. As the circle of possible marriage partners narrows, the "gens," or clan, develops. A clan consists of persons related through one parental line only. In a "gentile" society—that is, one organized on the basis of clans—an individual belongs to the clan of either mother or father, not to both. Marriage must ordinarily be to someone outside one's own clan. Where property exists, it is retained within the clan upon the death of a member. The fundamental social unit is therefore the clan, either matrilineal or patrilineal. The couple bond cannot have the central structural role it later acquires, for it links persons whose major allegiances are to distinct clans. Morgan shows that the gentile, or clan, system provides the foundation for quite complex types of social organization. Clans may be grouped in larger units, called phratries, and these in turn may join to form tribes. In the clan system's most developed form, which Morgan believed he had observed among the Iroquois Indians, several tribes constitute a confederacy, or nation, able to include thousands of members over a vast geographical area, yet lacking formal political institutions and still based on personal ties.

In the latest stages of barbarism, technological advances in productivity render society so complex that clan organization must give way. The city develops, bringing heightened requirements at the level of governance not solvable by the clan system. Property, while not a new phenomenon, attains a dominant role. "Henceforth the creation and protection of property became the primary objects of the government."[9] In place of the clan system step the institutions of political organization, for government can no longer rest on personal relations. Morgan sketches the early evolution of the state, which organizes people, now distributed in property classes, on a territorial basis. Taking Rome as his example, he cites three principal changes that mark the shift from gentile to political society. First, a system of classes based on property replaces the clan organization. Second, instead of government by means of a democratic tribal council, an assembly dominated by the propertied classes holds, and soon extends, political power. Third, territorial areas, rather than kin-based clans, phratries, or tribes, become the units of government.

Even before the emergence of developed political organization, a critical change occurred within the clan system. At a certain point, matrilineal clan organization succumbed to the principle of patrilineality, under the impetus of the development of property. According to Morgan, descent through the female line was the original form of clan organization, because of its biological certainty. However, as soon as property in cattle and land emerged, two facts, entirely self-evident in Morgan's view, meant that "descent in the female line was certain of overthrow, and the substitution of the male line equally assured."[10] First, men naturally became the owners of the property; second, they developed a natural wish to transmit it to their own children. Hence, in the middle stages of barbarism, the accumulation of property has the consequence that the patrilineal clan becomes the basic unit of the gentile social system.

Part 3, entitled "Growth of the Idea of the Family," makes up roughly one-quarter of *Ancient Society*. Emphasizing that the form of the family is highly variable, Morgan traces its evolution through five stages. Progressive restriction of permissible marriage partners constitutes the basis of the development. In the first type of family, the "consanguine," sisters and female cousins are married, as a group, to their brothers and male cousins. The next family type, the "punaluan," modifies the first by prohibiting marriage between own brothers and sisters. These two forms of group marriage, which suggest an even earlier stage of promiscuous intercourse, represent conjectural forms, reconstructed by Morgan on the basis of his understanding of kin terminology, and broadly corresponding to the stages of savagery and early barbarism.

The third form, the "syndyasmian" or "pairing" family, is founded on marriage between single pairs, who live within communal households and whose bond may be dissolved at the will of either partner. The pairing family constitutes the family type associated with clan-based societies. Lineage ties remain primary to each partner, for the clan is the basic social unit and takes final responsibility for its members. Morgan notes the measure of collective security provided to individuals by this system, as well as its relative egalitarianism when compared with subsequent family forms.

The last two family types reflect the influence of the development of property. The "patriarchal" family organizes a group of persons— slave, servant, and free—under a male head who exercises supreme authority. The "monogamian" family is based on the marriage of a single couple which, with its children, composes an independent household. Morgan conceptualizes both family types as institutions whose primary purpose is to hold property and transmit it exclusively to their offspring. To ensure the children's paternity, strict fidelity is required of women. Paternal power is more or less absolute, and only death can break the marriage bond. The patriarchal and monogamian families therefore stand in total opposition to clan organization. They are forms more appropriate for political society, and they appear in the last stages of barbarism and continue into the period of civilization.

Morgan argues that the patriarchal and monogamian families represent a social advance, for they permit a heightened individuality of persons. At the same time, he recognizes that in practice, such individuality was available to men only. Women, as well as children, were generally subordinated to the paternal power of the family head. By contrast, the pairing family of clan society had provided women with a certain level of relative equality and power, particularly before the transition to patrilineal descent. So long as children remained in their mother's clan, the pairing family was embedded in the matrilineal clan household, and Morgan thought it likely that the woman, rather than the man, functioned as the family's center. With the shift to descent in the male line, the pairing family became part of the patrilineal clan household, and the woman was more isolated from her gentile kin. This change "operated powerfully to lower her position and arrest her progress in the social scale," but the woman was still a member of her own clan and thus retained a substantial measure of independent social standing.[11] The advent of paternal power in the patriarchal and monogamian families opens the way to a much more profound degradation of women's position. Here, the cruel subordination of women and children belies Morgan's optimistic notions of evolutionary development. He presents the material honestly, however, heartened by a faith that monogamy is, in principle at least, the highest and most egalitarian form of the family. Nevertheless, the empirical evidence stands in contradiction to Morgan's own commitment to a progressivist theory of evolution.[12] It fell to Engels, in the *Origin*, to suggest a more adequate theoretical framework.

Ancient Society closes with Part 4, entitled "Growth of the Idea of Property," in which Morgan summarizes his understanding of social development. He distinguishes three stages in the development of property, generally corresponding to the three major evolutionary periods. Among the most primitive peoples, those at the level of savagery, property scarcely exists. Lands are held in common, as is housing, and Morgan speculates that the germ of property lies in a developing right to inherit personal articles. Property in land, houses, and livestock emerges in the stage of barbarism. The rules of inheritance at first conform to clan organization: property reverts to the clan of the deceased, not to his or her spouse. Eventually, individual ownership through the monogamian family prevails, with property inherited by the deceased owner's children. The period of civilization has arrived.

In conclusion, Morgan offers the observation that in his own time, property has become an "unmanageable power." Society is on a collision course, and its disintegration is the logical consequence "of a career of which property is the end and aim; because such a career contains the elements of self-destruction." Nevertheless, Morgan holds out hope for society's reconstruction on "the next higher plane," where it will appear as "a revival, in a higher form, of the liberty, equality and fraternity" of ancient clan society.[13]

Ancient Society is a monumental work. In it, Morgan solved the puzzle of clan organization, described the sequence of social institutions in evolutionary terms, and attempted to analyze the basis for their development. Published in 1877, the book became the foundation for all subsequent research on the history of early human societies, despite its many factual and interpretive errors. These shortcomings, as well as Morgan's substantial contributions, have been much discussed.[14] Here, the emphasis will be on Morgan's understanding of the mechanisms of social change.

Morgan presents his material in parallel form, as four kinds of phenomena "which extend themselves in parallel lines along the pathways of human progress from savagery to civilization." Very much the pragmatic scholar, he sticks close to the data and permits himself to generalize but not to theorize. Thus, each line constitutes "a natural as well as necessary sequence of progress," but the source of this necessity remains mysterious. Moreover, Morgan's discussion of the evolution of the family presupposes a grasp of the development of clan organization and vice versa. The extremely repetitive organization of *Ancient Society* reveals its author's inability to establish a clear theoretical relationship among the "four classes of facts." A theory of social development lies implicit, nonetheless, in Morgan's work. Frequently observing that "the experience of mankind has run in nearly uniform channels," he proposes that the placement of the major markers in these channels is determined by the evolution of the arts of subsistence—that is, by the types of inventions and discoveries used to acquire or produce the means of subsistence. In short, human progress ultimately rests on technological advances in the mode of material life.[15]

Morgan acknowledges the critical role played by the development of property. "It is impossible to overestimate the influence of property in the civilization of mankind." The need to transmit property to heirs underlay, in his view, the shift from matrilineal to patrilineal clan organization. Similarly, "property, as it increased in variety and amount, exercised a steady and constantly augmenting influence in the direction of monogamy." And it was the rise of new "complicated wants," growing out of an accelerated accumulation of property, that brought about the dissolution of clan organization and its replacement by political society. But what is property and why is it a motivating force in social development? In Morgan's account, property consists of things, the objects of subsistence, but it is not embedded in any determinate network of social relations. Once the idea of property has germinated, it simply grows automatically, extending itself in both magnitude and complexity while nurturing the sequence of stages in the arts of subsistence. "Commencing at zero in savagery, the passion for the possession of property, as the representative of accumulated subsistence, has now become dominant over the human mind in civilized races." For Morgan, a passion in the minds of men—namely, greed—leads naturally to the evolution of property and, consequently, to social development in general.[16]

In the extracts of *Ancient Society* he made in the "Ethnological

Notebooks," Marx revised Morgan's sequence of presentation.[17] Morgan had begun with the evolution of the arts of subsistence, and then surveyed the parallel development of government, family, and property. Marx moved Morgan's long section on government to the end of his notes and altered the relative amount of space given to each part. He reduced by half the discussion of the arts of subsistence, and by a third the section on the family. At the same time, he extended, proportionately, the space given by Morgan to the consideration of property and government. In sum, Marx's notes rearrange Morgan's material as follows: arts of subsistence (reduced); family (reduced); property (expanded); government (slightly expanded). Through this reorganization Marx perhaps sought to put Morgan's findings in a theoretically more coherent order.

To the extent that Engels incorporated the material in *Ancient Society* into his *Origin of the Family, Private Property and the State*, he adopted the organization of Marx's excerpts in the "Ethnological Notebooks"—making, however, several important structural changes. He did not devote a separate chapter to the subject of property. He greatly enlarged the relative importance of the chapter on the family, giving it almost as much space as he assigned to the chapters on the state. And he shifted the focus to the transition between barbarism and civilization, in accordance with his and Marx's interest in the emergence of the state. In this way, Engels converted Morgan's four "lines of human progress" into three sections, which make up the bulk of the *Origin*.

Substantively, Engels followed Morgan quite closely. He pruned the wealth of ethnographic evidence, even replacing it where his own studies offered more relevant data. He emphasized the points that most tellingly exposed the revised theoretical foundation he was seeking to establish. And he employed a more readable, and often engagingly chatty, literary style. In general, the *Origin* seems to be a shorter, as well as a more focused and accessible version of *Ancient Society*. A closer examination of the ways in which Engels's presentation of the material differs from Morgan's reveals both the contributions and the limitations of the *Origin*.

In a short opening chapter, "Stages in Prehistoric Culture," Engels succinctly recapitulates Morgan's account of the evolution of three stages in the arts of subsistence. Emphasizing the richness and accuracy of the account, he also acknowledges a certain weakness. "My sketch will seem flat and feeble compared with the picture to be unrolled at the end of our travels."[18] Engels refers, here, to his plan to deepen Morgan's work by recasting it in the light of Marx's theory of social development. As it turns out, the *Origin* remains far closer to *Ancient Society* than Engels intended.

Chapter 2, "The Family," constituting about one-third of the *Origin*, presents a reworked and augmented version of Morgan's sequence of family types. Engels underscores the importance of Morgan's discovery of this history and takes the opportunity to situate Morgan's work in the context of eighteenth- and nineteenth-century speculations concerning primate evolution, early human social behavior, and the possibility of a primitive state of promiscuous sexual intercourse. Concluding these half-dozen pages with the observation that bourgeois moral standards cannot be used to interpret primitive societies, he quickly summarizes and comments on Morgan's discussion of the two hypothetical forms of group marriage.[19] Like Morgan, he believes that natural selection, through the innate mechanisms of jealousy and incest taboos, triggered the succession of family types. In addition, the logic behind the change Marx had made in Morgan's sequence of presentation now becomes clear, for Engels is able to explain the origin of the clan system in the course of his description of the punaluan family.

Having disposed of group marriage and the genesis of the clan, Engels turns to the pairing and patriarchal families. He selectively summarizes Morgan's findings, at the same time integrating material Morgan had covered in his chapter on property. Along with Morgan, Bachofen, and others, Engels assumes that supremacy of women characterized primitive societies, but he argues that it rested on the material foundation of a natural sex division of labor within the primitive communistic household. Only if "new, *social* forces" caused that natural material foundation to take a different form could women lose their position of independence.[20] And this occurred when society began to produce a sizable surplus, making it possible for wealth to amass and eventually pass into the private possession of families. Like Morgan, Engels sees the development of productivity as an automatically evolving process, but he makes a distinction, however vaguely, between wealth, a given accumulation of things, and private property, a social relation.

Once wealth is held privately, its accumulation becomes a central social issue. "Mother right," that is, descent in the female line and, along with it, the supremacy of women in the communal household, now constitutes a barrier to social development. Earlier, the supposedly natural division of labor between women and men placed women in charge of the household while men had the task of providing food. In a society at a low level of productivity, therefore, women possessed the household goods, and men the instruments necessary to hunt, fish, cultivate plants, and the like. With increasing productivity and the development of private property in land, cattle, and slaves, this historical accident, as it were, has the grim consequence that men, the former possessors of the instruments of gathering and producing food, now own the wealth. Mother right makes it impossible, however, for men to transmit the newly evolved private property to their children. "Mother right, therefore, had to be overthrown, and overthrown it was."[21]

Engels regards the shift to the patrilineal clan system as pivotal in its impact on society and on women's position. It marks the establishment of a set of social relations conducive to the further evolution not only of private property but of full-scale class society. More dramatically, "the overthrow of mother right was the *world historic defeat of the female sex*. The man took command in the home also; the woman was degraded and reduced to servitude; she became the slave of his lust and a mere instrument for the production of children."[22] The patriarchal family, with its incorporation of slaves and servants under the supreme authority of the male head, now emerges as a form intermediate between the pairing family and monogamy. Engels offers specific historical examples of this transition stage, emphasizing the relationship between land tenure and social structure, as well as the brutality of the patriarch toward women in the household.

In discussing the monogamous family, Engels again follows Morgan while simultaneously incorporating a clearer analysis of property relations and focusing on the question of woman's position. The monogamous family appears toward the end of the second stage in the development of the arts of subsistence—that is, at the threshold of civilization—and represents a perfected form for the transmission of private property from father to children. Engels emphasizes the origin of the monogamous family in economic conditions and its function as a property-holding institution. "It was the first form of the family to be based not on natural but on economic conditions—on the victory of private property over primitive, natural communal property."[23] Although Engels never states it unambiguously, the implication is that the form of the monogamous, as well as the patriarchal, family constitutes a product of the rise of class society.

Engels has no illusions about the position of women in the monogamous family. Monogamy is a standard enforced on the woman only, and exists solely to guarantee the paternity of the offspring, not for any reasons of love or affection. Men remain free to live by a different standard. At the same time, the phenomenon of the neglected wife begets its own consequences. Thus, side by side with the institution of so-called monogamous marriage flourishes all manner of adultery and prostitution. Furthermore, "monogamous marriage comes on the scene as the subjugation of the one sex by the other; it announces a struggle between the sexes unknown throughout the whole previous prehistoric period." In Engels's formulation, this struggle between the sexes appears simultaneously with class relations. "The first class opposition that appears in history coincides with the development of the antagonism between man and woman in monogamous marriage, and the first class oppression coincides with that of the female sex by the male." Contrary to a common misinterpretation of these remarks, Engels does not assert that the sex struggle antedates class conflict. Neither, however, does he clearly argue that it is rooted in the emergence of class society. He simply treats the two developments as parallel, skirting the difficult problems of historical origins and theoretical relationships.[24]

With the basic character of monogamous marriage established, Engels turns briefly to a number of topics not addressed by Morgan. To start, he presents a quick history of the monogamous family's development in the period of civilization, with emphasis on the extent to which it fostered "individual sex love." According to Engels, love-based marriages were impossible prior to the great "moral advance" constituted by the monogamous family. Moreover, in all ruling classes, even after the rise of the monogamous family, expedience rather than love governed the choice of marriage partner. After a brief glance at the medieval ruling-class family, Engels focuses on marriage in capitalist society. Among the bourgeoisie, marriage is a matter of convenience, generally arranged by parents to further their property interests. By contrast, the proletariat has the opportunity to truly experience individual sex love. Among the proletariat, "all the foundations of typical monogamy are cleared away. Here there is no property, for the preservation and inheritance of which monogamy and male supremacy were established; hence there is no incentive to make this male supremacy effective. . . . Here quite other personal and social conditions decide." Moreover, Engels believes that with the increasing employment of women in wage labor, and women's accompanying independence, no basis survives for any kind of male supremacy in the working-class household, "except, perhaps, for something of the brutality toward women that has spread since the introduction of monogamy."[25] Engels's optimism, shared by Marx and the socialist movement of the period, is problematic on three counts. First, it misses the significance of the working-class household as an essential social unit, not for the holding of property but for the reproduction of the working class itself. Second, it overlooks the ways in which a material basis for male supremacy is constituted within the proletarian household. And third, it vastly underestimates the variety of ideological and psychological factors that provide a continuing foundation for male supremacy in the working-class family.

Most of Engels's brief discussion of the situation of women within the family in capitalist society is framed in terms of the gap between formal and substantive equality.[26] He begins with an analogy between the marriage contract and the labor contract. Both are freely entered into, juridically speaking, thereby making the partners equal on paper. This formal equality disguises, in the case of the labor contract, the differences in class position between the worker and the employer. The marriage contract involves a similar mystification since, in the case of a propertied family, parents actually determine the choice of children's marriage partners. In fact, the legal equality of the partners in a marriage is in sharp contrast with their actual inequality. The issue here concerns the nature of the wife's labor within the household. The development of the patriarchal and monogamous families converts such family labor into a private service. As Engels puts it, "the wife became the head servant, excluded from all participation in social production." Her work loses the public or socially necessary place it had held in earlier societies. Both excluded and, later, economically dependent, she therefore becomes subordinate. Only with large-scale capitalist industry, and only for the proletarian woman, does the possibility appear for reentry into production. Yet this opportunity has a contradictory character so long as capitalist relations endure. If the proletarian wife "carries out her duties in the private service of her family, she remains excluded from public production and unable to earn; and if she wants to take part in public production and earn independently, she cannot carry out family duties."[27]

Engels's conclusions regarding the conditions for women's liberation, summarized in a few paragraphs, generally converge with the equally brief remarks on the subject made by Marx in *Capital*. Like Marx, Engels underscores the progressive role that participation in the collective labor process can potentially play, and its crucial importance as a condition for human liberation. Whereas Marx had embedded his comments in an analysis of the historical impact of capitalist large-scale industry, Engels places his observations in the context of a discussion of political rights. He again draws an analogy between workers and women, arguing that both groups must have legal equality if they

are to understand the character of their respective fights for "real social equality." "The democratic republic does not do away with the opposition of [the proletariat and the capitalist class]; on the contrary, it
provides the clear field on which the fight can be fought out. And in
the same way, the peculiar character of the supremacy of the husband
over the wife in the modern family, the necessity of creating real social equality between them and the way to do it, will only be seen in
the clear light of day when both possess legally complete equality of
rights." [28]

Although generally consistent with Marx's sketch of the reproduction of labor power, Engels's consideration of women's oppression is
flawed or incomplete in several critical respects. In the first place, he
assumes that it is natural for "family duties" to be the exclusive province of women, and that therefore they always will be. Furthermore,
he does not clearly link the development of a special sphere associated with the reproduction of labor power to the emergence of class,
or, perhaps, capitalist society. For precapitalist class societies, he fails
to specify the nature of women's subordination in different classes. Finally, Engels's emphasis on the strategic importance of democratic
rights leaves open the question of the relationship between socialist
revolution, women's liberation, and the struggle for equal rights. The
result is ambiguous, potentially suggesting that the socialist program
for women's liberation consists of two discrete objectives: equal rights
with men in the still-capitalist short term; and full liberation on the
basis of a higher form of the family in the far distant revolutionary
millennium.

Engels closes the chapter on the family with a long look to the
future. [29] These pages trace, yet again, the development of monogamy
on the basis of private property, and attempt a sketch of family experience in a society in which the means of production have been converted into social property. True monogamy, that is, monogamy for the
man as well as the woman, will now be possible, along with wide development of that highest of intimate emotions, individual sex love.
Exactly what relations between the sexes will look like cannot be predicted, for it is up to a new generation of women and men born and
raised in socialist society. "When these people are in the world, they
will care precious little what anybody today thinks they ought to do;
they will make their own practice and their corresponding public
opinion about the practice of each individual—and that will be the
end of it." Engels's focus on the emotional and sexual content of interpersonal relations within the family household reflected a common
view that they represent the essence of the so-called woman ques-

tion.[30] Only at one point in this section does he dwell on the implications of the future abolition of the family's economic functions, observing that with the means of production held in common, "the single family ceases to be the economic unit of society. Private housekeeping is transformed into a social industry." Moreover, "the care and education of the children becomes a public affair."[31] These brief hints offer the barest programmatic guidance, and do not differ, in substance, from nineteenth-century communitarian proposals. In short, Engels's chapter on the family in the *Origin* remains an unintegrated mix of Morgan's dry materialism and a radical view of sexual liberation—seasoned with genuine insights into the nature of property and social relations, and liberally sprinkled with Engels's warmth and wit.

In Chapters 3–8 of the *Origin*, corresponding to the section on government in Morgan's *Ancient Society*, Engels examines the nature of clan society and traces the rise of the state. As in Chapter 2 on the family, he follows Morgan's general line of argument, while at the same time focusing it and integrating the material on property. In Engels's words, the changes "in form" between the institutions of the gentile constitution and those of the state "have been outlined by Morgan, but their economic content and cause must largely be added by myself."[32] The resulting discussion suffers from defects similar to those already observed in Engels's account of the family. Moreover, it becomes more obvious in these chapters that Engels identifies private property and the market exchange of commodities as the pivotal social developments in history. Nowhere, however, does he clearly discuss these phenomena in terms of the social relations that constitute the mode of production in which they originate.

In these chapters, a critique of property takes the place of a critique of class relations. Property, not exploitation—the appropriation of the surplus labor of the producing class by another class—becomes the implicit object of class struggle. From the point of view of Marx's theory of social reproduction, however, both private property and commodity exchange only represent specific manifestations of particular types of class society. In such societies, a given set of relations of exploitation always dominates, constituting the basis for specific social relations and forms of private property, the market, the state, and so forth. The difference between this formulation and that in the *Origin* is crucial, and not simply a matter of style or manner of exposition. It reveals that the arguments put forth by Engels in the *Origin* generally remain within the theoretical framework of a utopian critique of property. Marx's comments about his favorite utopian socialist target, Proudhon, would apply equally to Engels: he should have analyzed "*property relations* as a whole, not in their *legal* expression as *relations of volition* but in their real form, that is, as *relations of production.* [Instead,] he has entangled the whole of these economic relations in the general juristic conception of *'property.'*" Furthermore, Engels has confused the circumstance that the products of labor are exchanged in a society, with the presence of capitalist, or at least class, relations of production.[33]

In the *Origin*'s closing Chapter 9, "Barbarism and Civilization," Engels examines the "general economic conditions" behind the developments presented in previous chapters. "Here," he observes, "we shall need Marx's *Capital* as much as Morgan's book."[34] Unfortunately, it is already far too late, for the analytical weaknesses encountered throughout the *Origin* permeate this highly repetitive chapter.

Engels restates his account of social evolution in the period of the decline of clan society and the emergence of civilization, this time pointing out a series of major milestones. In the middle stages of barbarism, the separation of pastoral tribes from the mass of other peoples marks the "first great social division of labor." These tribes tame animals and develop agriculture; as a result they soon find themselves with products that make regular exchange possible. Inevitably and automatically, the increasing exchange leads to higher productivity, more wealth, and a society in which the harnessing of surplus labor becomes feasible. Hence, slavery appears. "From the first great social division of labor arose the first great cleavage of society into two classes: masters and slaves, exploiters and exploited." Engels reminds the reader that the change in the division of labor also has consequences for relations between the sexes in the family. Because the pre-existing division of labor had supposedly assigned the task of procuring subsistence to men, men become the holders of the new wealth, and women find themselves subordinated and confined to private domestic labor. A "second great division of labor" occurs at the close of the period of barbarism, when handicraft separates from agriculture. On this basis, a new cleavage of society into classes develops, the opposition between rich and poor. Inequalities of property among individual male heads of families now lead to the break up of the communal household, and the pairing marriage dissolves into the monogamous single family, even more oppressive to women. Finally, a third division of labor emerges in the period of civilization: a class of merchants arises, parasites whose nefarious activities lead to periodic trade crises. In the meantime, the rise of class cleavages has necessitated replacement of the gentile constitution with a third force, powerful but apparently above the class struggle—namely, the state.[35]

In sum, the concluding chapter of the *Origin* argues that civilization results from the continual evolution of the division of labor, which in turn gives rise to exchange, commodity production, class cleavages, the subordination of women, the single family as the economic unit of society, and the state. What is wrong with this picture is that Engels has once again simply listed phenomena without rooting them in social relations and the workings of a dominant mode of production. Moreover, he awards the leading role to the technical division of labor in the labor process—what Morgan had considered under the rubric "arts of subsistence." The development of class cleavages, that is, of exploitative social relations, simply follows automatically, once a certain level of material productivity is reached. In other words, the state of the forces of production mechanistically determines the nature of the relations of production. The emphasis on the technical division of labor in this chapter constitutes a new element, tending somewhat to replace the focus in earlier chapters on the rise of private property as the prime mover of social change. At the same time, Engels, like Morgan, often invokes innate human greed and competitiveness to explain historical development.[36] All in all, the scattered analysis of social development presented in this final chapter represents some of the weakest reasoning in the *Origin*.

Not surprisingly, the *Origin*'s summary comments in this chapter on the emancipation of women exhibit similar ambiguities. Engels emphasizes, yet again, the crushing impact made by the "first great social division of labor" on women's position, and then leaps to a supposedly self-evident conclusion.

> We can already see from this that to emancipate women and make her the equal of the man is and remains an impossibility so long as the woman is shut out from social productive labor and restricted to private domestic labor. The emancipation of woman will only be possible when woman can take part in production on a large, social scale, and domestic work no longer claims anything but an insignificant amount of her time. And only now has that become possible through modern large-scale industry, which does not merely permit the employment of female labor over a wide range, but positively demands it, while it also tends toward ending private domestic labor by changing it more and more into a public industry.[37]

As in the chapter on the family, Engels here assumes that domestic labor is purely women's work, does not locate his statement with respect to a specific class society, and blurs the relationship between women's eventual liberation in communist society and immediate strategic goals.

Engels formulates the relationship between social transformation and women's equality more specifically in a letter written in 1885: "It is my conviction that real equality of women and men can come true only when the exploitation of either by capital has been abolished and private housework has been transformed into a public industry." In the meantime, protective legislation is necessary. "That the working woman needs special protection against capitalist exploitation because of her special physiological functions seems obvious to me. . . . I admit I am more interested in the health of the future generations than in the absolute formal equality of the sexes during the last years of the capitalist mode of production."[38] Once again, Engels wrestles with the problem of distinguishing juridical equality from real social equality.

Engels made one argument in the *Origin* that the socialist movement later refused to endorse, but which has recently been taken up by theorists of the contemporary women's liberation movement. In a frequently cited passage from the 1884 preface to the *Origin*, Engels spoke of two types of production proceeding in parallel: on the one hand, the production of the means of subsistence, and on the other, the production of human beings. The dualistic formulation strikingly recalls the never published "German Ideology" of 1846, in which Marx and Engels had suggested a similar characterization of the dual essence of social reproduction: "The production of life, both of one's own in labor and of fresh life in procreation, . . . appears as a twofold relation: on the one hand as a natural, on the other as a social relation."[39]

The dependence of the *Origin* on the forty-year-old "German Ideology" is not limited to this dramatic linguistic parallel. Engels drew quite heavily on the forgotten manuscript of his and Marx's youth, which he had just rediscovered among Marx's papers.[40] Thus, both texts make a relatively sharp distinction between natural and social phenomena, emphasizing the purely biological or animallike character of procreation. Furthermore, "The German Ideology" assigns, as does the *Origin*, a central motivating role in social development to the continual evolution of the division of labor. According to "The German Ideology," society develops in stages, beginning from the simplest forms, in which the only division of labor is natural, and rooted in the sexual act. With the growth of the division of labor, social relations distinguish themselves from natural ones, and the "family relation" becomes subordinate. Both "The German Ideology" and the *Origin* refer to the development, at this point in history, of a relationship of latent slavery within the family, representing "the first form of property."[41] Finally, both texts put forth an equivocal image of the family as a germ or nucleus within which larger social contradictions originate or are reflected, and which itself constitutes the fundamental building block of society.[42]

Engels's extensive reliance on "The German Ideology" has the effect of importing into the *Origin* many of the theoretical weaknesses of the earlier manuscript. In 1846, when Marx and Engels composed "The German Ideology," they had been on the threshold of two lifetimes of profound contributions to the socialist movement. The manuscript bears, nonetheless, the marks of its very early place in their development. Thus when Engels, in the preface to the *Origin*, echoes the dichotomy suggested in "The German Ideology" by positing two separate systems of production of material life, he simply takes a very primitive distinction between natural and social phenomena to its logical conclusion. His return to this dichotomy, long after he, and even more so, Marx, had generally transcended it in subsequent work, epitomizes the theoretical ambiguity found throughout the *Origin*. Socialists at the turn of the century found the preface's assertion concerning the duality of social reproduction "very remarkable," indeed, "almost incomprehensible." Soviet commentators eventually settled on the view that Engels was mistaken, and that the statement can only refer to the very earliest period of human history, when people were supposedly so much a part of nature that social relations of production could not be said to exist.[43] What disturbed these theorists was the implication that the family represents an autonomous, if not wholly independent, center of social development. And it is precisely this implication that has caught the imagination of contemporary socialist feminists, often tempting them into a quite cavalier reading of the *Origin*.

Engels's purpose in writing the *Origin* was "to present the results of Morgan's researches in the light of the conclusions of [Marx's] materialist examination of history, and thus to make clear their full significance."[44] Engels's treatment of the material falls short, however, of this goal, for he only partially transforms Morgan's crude materialism. The *Origin* is marred throughout by Engels's failure to base the discussion on an adequate exposition of Marx's theory of social development. Instead, Engels relies, quite erratically, on several theoretical frameworks in addition to his understanding of Marx's work: the technological determinism implicit in Morgan's *Ancient Society*, his main source of data; "The German Ideology's" early version of historical materialism; and a generally utopian critique of property and view of the socialist future. While the *Origin* manages, in places, to rise above this eclecticism, its theoretical weaknesses and omissions were to have serious consequences. The *Origin* constituted a defective text whose ambiguous theoretical and political formulations nevertheless became an integral part of the socialist legacy.

Part Three

The Socialist

Movement

7

The Second

International

In the quarter-century that preceded the First World War, a powerful working-class movement, represented by trade unions and socialist parties, arose in virtually every European country. The new working-class parties shared a commitment, however abstract, to the eventual transformation of capitalist society into classless communism. At the same time, they fought for the extension of suffrage to workers and sometimes to women, ran impressive and often quite successful electoral campaigns, and pushed legislation to better working conditions and insure working people against sickness, disability, and unemployment. Above all, they encouraged the organization of workers into trade unions to bargain directly with employers and, if necessary, strike. Chief among the socialist parties stood the German Social Democratic party, the SPD—presumed heir to the mantle of Marx and Engels, leader of the German trade union movement, and able, at its height, to boast of 4.5 million votes and over 1 million party members.

By 1889, the foundation had been laid for the Second International, a body that sought to coordinate discussion among and action by the various national parties. In theory, socialism and the goal of a classless communist society constituted supremely international tasks, the more so as capitalism developed into a full-scale imperialist system. In practice, the individual working-class movements and their parties responded to conditions of an essentially national character, and generally trod along separate, if parallel paths. When war broke out in 1914, these paths diverged. With a few important exceptions, the International splintered along the lines of opposing armies.

For the socialist movement, the problem of women's oppression was, in principle, an inseparable part of what was called the "social question." Socialist parties took up the so-called woman question in party newspapers, and also produced a modest amount of theoretical and agitational literature. With some reluctance, they incorporated women's political rights in their programs, sought to build mass women's movements, and encouraged trade unions to organize women workers. Despite weaknesses, the socialist movement offered the most sustained and thoroughgoing support then available to the struggle for sex equality and women's liberation. At the same time, examination of some examples of party literature on the woman question suggests that for the most part, the Second International failed to clarify, much less extend, the incomplete legacy of theoretical work left by Marx and Engels. Moreover, by codifying and in some measure sanctifying this legacy, the socialist movement actually hampered its ability to move beyond inherited ambiguities.

Among party and trade union militants able to find time to read socialist books, *Woman and Socialism*, by the German Social Democratic leader August Bebel, ranked first in popularity. Originally published in 1879, by 1895 it had gone through twenty-five editions, and by 1910, fifty, not to mention numerous foreign translations. For years, *Woman and Socialism* was the book most borrowed from workers' libraries in Germany, and it continued to serve as a major socialist primer into the first decades of the twentieth century.

What was it that so persistently drew workers and socialists to a book nearly 500 pages long? In the first place, *Woman*, as the German movement dubbed the book, was virtually the only work in the Marxist literature of the period that spoke to people's desire for a detailed and specific picture of the socialist future. Scanning the oppressive past and dissecting the capitalist present, the book also devoted whole sections to sketching the general outlines of what life in the socialist society to come might be like. "It is quite safe to say," observed a library journal in 1910, "that it was from this book that the proletarian masses derived their socialism." And years later, a party activist reminisced that "for us young socialists Bebel's book was not just a programme, it was a gospel." Until the Bolshevik revolution opened up the possibility of a real-life example, *Woman* offered the most developed vision of what socialists were fighting for.[1]

But the book was not just about socialism, it was also about women —*Woman in the Past, Present and Future*, as the title of the second edition announced. For some readers, it documented the anguish of their own experience as women, inspiring "hope and joy to live and fight." With these words, Ottilie Baader, a working-class woman, recalled the impact the book had on her when she encountered it in 1887 at the age of forty, living "resigned and without hope" under the burden of "life's bitter needs, overwork, and bourgeois family morality."

> Although I was not a Social Democrat I had friends who belonged to the party. Through them I got the precious work. I read it nights through. It was my own fate and that of thousands of my sisters. Neither in the family nor in public life had I ever heard of all the pain the woman must endure. One ignored her life. Bebel's book courageously broke with the old secretiveness. . . . I read the book not once but ten times. Because everything was so new, it took considerable effort to come to grips with Bebel's views. I had to break with so many things that I had previously regarded as correct.

Baader went on to join the party and take an active role in its political life.[2]

For certain militants within the German Social Democratic party, the publication of *Woman and Socialism* had a further meaning. Clara Zetkin, for instance, observed in 1896 that Bebel's book, irrespective of any defects, "must be judged by the time at which it appeared. And it was then more than a book, it was an event, a deed," for it provided party members with a demonstration of the relationship between the subordination of women and the development of society. Zetkin interpreted the publication of Bebel's work as a symbol of the party's practical commitment to developing women as socialist activists. "For the first time," she noted, "from this book issued the watchword: We can conquer the future only if we win the women as co-fighters."[3]

As *Woman* progressed through edition after edition, Bebel continually revised and enlarged its text. The first edition, totaling only 180 pages and not subdivided into chapters, appeared just after the German government attempted to crack down on the growing socialist movement by banning the SPD and instituting severe censorship. Despite the book's illegal status, it sold out in a matter of months. Not until 1883 was Bebel to locate another publisher willing to produce the book, as well as find time to expand and revise it. In an unsuccessful attempt to get around the antisocialist laws, he retitled the 220-page second edition *Woman in the Past, Present and Future*, a change corresponding to the new chapter structure. Although the authorities nevertheless banned the book, it was once again an immediate success and quickly sold out, as did six subsequent editions in the following years. In 1890, the antisocialist laws were lifted, and Bebel prepared a substantially reworked ninth edition, which appeared early in 1891. Rechristened *Woman and Socialism*, and expanded to 384 pages, the ninth edition also incorporated, for the first time, parts of Engels's analysis from the *Origin*. It was this version of *Woman*, repeatedly reprinted, and in 1895 further extended to 472 pages for its twenty-fifth edition, that became the socialist classic.

The German-speaking socialist movement thus had the distinction of producing two major works on the question of women's oppression within a span of only a few years: the first, Bebel's *Woman and Socialism*, by a major leader of the powerful German socialist party, the second, Engels's *Origin*, published in 1884, by Marx's collaborator, now a tremendously respected but somewhat isolated figure, living in political exile. Given the convergence of subject matter and politics in the two books, one would expect the voluminous correspondence between the authors to include a substantial exchange of views on the issues. Instead, a strange silence reigns, punctured by a few casual comments. On January 18, 1884, Engels thanks Bebel for sending him a copy of the second edition of *Woman*. "I have read it with great interest," he notes, "it contains much valuable material. Especially lucid and fine is what you say about the development of industry in Germany." On June 6, he mentions the forthcoming publication of the *Origin*, and promises to send Bebel a copy. On May 1–2, 1891, he notes his desire to prepare a new edition of the *Origin*, which he did that June. Bebel's letters to Engels mention his own book only in the context of problems arising with the English translation, and do not refer to the *Origin* at all. Engels's letters to other correspondents document the *Origin*'s conception, writing, and preparation for publication during the first five months of 1884, but say nothing about his opinion of Bebel's work. The impression remains of a silent polemic between differing views. Despite his special relationship to the socialist movement, Engels probably judged it tactically unwise to do more than publish the *Origin*, and hope it would be recognized as the more accurate approach to the issue of women's oppression.[4]

Bebel divides *Woman and Socialism* into three major sections, "Woman in the Past," "Woman in the Present," and "Woman in the Future." Most of the constant textual revision in successive printings consists of changes of a factual nature, made to deepen and update the arguments. Only the publication of Engels's *Origin* required Bebel to make substantial modifications, which he largely confined to the first section. In the early version of "Woman in the Past," he had presented an abundance of ethnographic evidence in rather disorganized fashion, under the assumption that "although the forms of [woman's] oppression have varied, the oppression has always remained the same."

Engels's work made him realize the inaccuracy of this statement, and, as he later put it, enabled him to place the historical material on a correct foundation. Bebel entirely recast the section in order to argue that relations between the sexes, like all social relations, "have materially changed in the previous course of human development . . . in even step with the existing systems of production, on the one hand, and of the distribution of the products of labor, on the other." With the aid of the *Origin*, he was now able to present the ethnographic material in the context of a more systematic sketch of the history of the development of the family, private property, the state, and capitalism. These changes hardly affected, however, Bebel's analysis in the rest of the book.[5]

The section "Woman in the Present" makes up the bulk of *Woman and Socialism*. It includes two long chapters on the current crisis of capitalism and on the nature of socialist society ("The State and Society" and "The Socialization of Society"). These chapters, as well as the four sections that close the book—"Woman in the Future," "Internationality," "Population and Over-Population," and "Conclusion"—barely touch on the situation of women. In other words, despite its title and chapter headings, over a third of *Woman and Socialism* focuses on the larger "social question." No wonder so many socialists read the book more as a sort of inspirational general text than as a specific study on the question of women.

The strengths of *Woman and Socialism* lie precisely in its powerful indictment of capitalist society, and the contrasting image it presents of a socialist future. As detail follows detail and compelling anecdotes multiply, Bebel assembles a mass of information on virtually every aspect of women's subordination and the social question in general. In capitalist society, marriage and sexuality have acquired a distorted, unnatural character. "The marriage founded upon bourgeois property relations, is more or less a marriage by compulsion, which leads numerous ills in its train." Sexual repression results in mental illness and suicide. Sex without love is also damaging, for "man is no animal. Mere physical satisfaction does not suffice." Where "the blending of the sexes is a purely mechanical act: such a marriage is immoral." The counterpart to loveless marriages based on economic constraint is prostitution, which "becomes a social institution in the capitalist world, the same as the police, standing armies, the Church, and wage-mastership."[6] Women's presumed natural calling as mothers, wives, and sexual providers results in discrimination against them as workers. Given the widespread employment of women, often under the most arduous conditions, it is easy for Bebel to document the hypocrisy of such prejudice. "The men of the upper classes look down upon the lower; and so does almost the whole sex upon woman. The majority of men see in woman only an article of profit and pleasure; to acknowledge her an equal runs against the grain of their prejudices. . . . What absurdity, is it not, to speak of the 'equality of all' and yet seek to keep one-half of the human race outside of the pale!" Bebel insists, moreover, that industrial development tends to free women. In general, *"the whole trend of society is to lead woman out of the narrow sphere of strictly domestic life to a full participation in the public life of the people."* But so long as capitalism survives, woman "suffers both as a social and a sex entity, and it is hard to say in which of the two respects she suffers more."[7]

Bebel portrays socialism as a happy paradise, free of the conflicts that typify capitalist society, and only concerned with the welfare of the people. His comments are far more concrete and programmatic than anything suggested by Marx and Engels. He envisions a society in which everyone works and all are equal. Democratic administrative bodies replace the organized class power of the state. Marriages based on free choice prevail, offering both partners supportive intimacy, time to enjoy their children, and opportunities for wider participation in social and political life. Sexuality develops freely, for "the individual shall himself oversee the satisfaction of his own instincts. *The satisfaction of the sexual instinct is as much a private concern as the satisfaction of any other natural instinct."* Amenities presently available only to the privileged few are extended to the working class. Education and health care are assured, as well as pleasant working and living conditions. Domestic labor is socialized, as far as possible, by means of large, hotellike apartment buildings, with central heating and plumbing, and electric power. Central kitchens, laundries, and cleaning services make individual facilities obsolete. After all, "the small private kitchen is, just like the workshop of the small master mechanic, a transition stage, an arrangement by which time, power and material are senselessly squandered and wasted."[8] At the same time, the darker aspects of capitalist society disappear: sexual repression, prostitution, deteriorating family life, dangerous working conditions, inefficient productive methods, goods of low quality, divisions between mental and manual labor and between city and country, and so forth. Above all the individual has an abundance of free choice and develops himself or herself to the fullest in all possible areas: work, leisure, sexuality, and love.

Throughout *Woman and Socialism*, Bebel challenges the assumption that existing sex divisions of labor represent natural phenomena. What is natural, he says, is the sexual instinct itself. Indeed, "of all the natural impulses human beings are instinct with, along with that of eating and drinking, the sexual impulse is the strongest." Despite a fairly simplistic view of instinct, Bebel's lengthy attack on the notion of eternally fixed sex divisions of labor stands out as an important political contribution to the socialist movement. For once a socialist leader confronted the ideological character of claims about the social consequences of physiological sex differences.[9]

With all its strengths, *Woman and Socialism* nevertheless suffers from a seriously impoverished theoretical apparatus, as well as various political defects. Bebel's theoretical perspective actually consists of an eclectic mix of two major trends within the socialist tradition, trends against which Marx himself had often struggled. On the one hand, *Woman and Socialism* reflects a utopian socialist outlook reminiscent of Fourier and other early nineteenth-century socialists, particularly in its view of individual development within a communitarian context. And on the other, the book exhibits a mechanical and incipiently reformist interpretation of Marxism, thus heralding the severe reformism that overran most parties in the Second International by the turn of the century. Lacking an adequate theoretical foundation, Bebel's discussion of women's oppression and liberation follows an erratic and sometimes contradictory course. From the start, he conceptualizes the issues in terms of the free development of the female individual. "The so-called 'Woman Question' . . . concerns the position that woman should occupy in our social organism; how she may unfold her powers and faculties in all directions, to the end that she become a complete and useful member of human society, enjoying equal rights with all." In the present, capitalist society stamps every facet of women's experience with oppression and inequality. "The mass of the female sex suffers in two respects: On the one side woman suffers from economic and social dependence upon man. True enough, this dependence may be alleviated by formally placing her upon an equality before the law, and in point of rights; but the dependence is not removed. On the other side, woman suffers from the economic dependence that woman in general, the working-woman in particular, finds herself in, along with the workingman." Equality and liberation are thus always social as well as individual issues, and Bebel hastens to add that the "solution of the Woman Question coincides completely with the solution of the Social Question"—incidentally putting the final resolution of the question into the far future.[10] Meanwhile, the working class, and not the bourgeois feminist movement, constitutes women's natural strategic ally in the struggle. Moreover, participation in the revolutionary movement enables "more favorable relations between husband and wife [to] spring up in the rank of the working class in the measure that both realize they are tugging at the same rope, and there is but one means towards satisfactory conditions for themselves and their family—the radical reformation of society that shall make human beings of them all."[11]

Insofar as Bebel considers the social source for the pervasive oppression of women, he relies on the concept of dependence. In general, he asserts, "all social dependence and oppression [have their] roots in the *economic dependence* of the oppressed upon the oppressor." Thus, woman's oppression is founded on her dependence upon men. "Economically and socially unfree" in capitalist society, for instance, woman "is bound to see in marriage her means of support; accordingly, she depends upon man and becomes a piece of property to him." If oppression has its basis in personal dependence, then liberation in the socialist future must involve the individual's independence. "The woman of future society is socially and economically independent; she is no longer subject to even a vestige of dominion and exploitation; she is free, the peer of man, mistress of her lot."[12] Apart from carrying the bewildering theoretical implication that chattel slavery systematically characterizes capitalism since every wife must be "a piece of property," statements such as these show that Bebel has lost touch with the essence of Marx's orientation. For Marx, class struggle within a specific mode of production constitutes the basis of social development, and individual oppression has its root, therefore, in a particular set of exploitative social relations that operate at the level of classes. Bebel, caught up in the reformist tendencies of his time, replaces Marx's concept of class exploitation with the vague and far less confrontational notion of dependence, particularly the dependence of the individual on others. Social well-being is measured, then, by the location of the individual on a scale ranging from dependence to independence, not by the nature of the social relations of production in a given society. Similarly, socialism is pictured largely in terms of the redistribution of goods and services already available in capitalist society to independent individuals, rather than in terms of the wholesale reorganization of production and social relations. Despite Bebel's commitment to socialism, his emphasis on the full development of the individual in future society recalls nothing so much as liberalism, the political philosophy of the nineteenth-century bourgeoisie.

It is the focus on individual dependence, viewed largely in isolation from the mechanisms governing social development as a whole, that undermines Bebel's strategic perspective. In *Woman and Social-*

ism, women's oppression is treated as an important but theoretically muddled problem, and it is hardly surprising that Bebel comes up with a variety of implicitly contradictory strategic approaches. In the first place, he often insists that the complete resolution of the problem must be postponed to the revolutionary future, when it can be fully addressed in the context of solving the social question. Nevertheless, practical work on the issue remains critical in the present. At the same time, it somehow becomes subsumed in the working-class movement's struggle against capitalism. Finally, Bebel often pictures the solution to the so-called woman question in terms of achieving equal rights to participate in society without distinction of sex. This approach fails to differentiate socialist aims from the liberal feminist goal of sex equality in capitalist society. In short, Bebel could not, despite his best socialist intentions, sufficiently specify the relationship between the liberation of women in the communist future and the struggle for equality in the capitalist present. He conceptualized the so-called woman question as an issue pertaining to woman's situation as an individual, on the one hand, and to social conditions in general, on the other, but he was unable to construct a reliable bridge between the two levels of analysis.

The popularity of *Woman and Socialism* reflected the consolidation within the Second International of a definite position on the question of women, Engels's low-key and rather ambiguous opposition in the *Origin* notwithstanding. Insofar as the socialist movement took up the problems of women's oppression, it spontaneously embraced Bebel's analysis.

In England, for example, Eleanor Marx—Marx's youngest daughter and an active participant in the British labor and socialist movements—wrote with her husband, Edward Aveling, a pamphlet entitled *The Woman Question*.[13] First published in 1886, and reprinted in 1887, the popular pamphlet took the form of a speculative review of the recently published English edition of Bebel's *Woman*. Its sixteen pages represented "an attempt to explain the position of Socialists in respect to the woman question."

Like Bebel's *Woman*, *The Woman Question* focuses on issues of love, sexuality, and human feeling, while at the same time challenging the supposedly natural character of woman's place in social relations. As for the source of women's oppression in capitalist society, the authors repeatedly insist that "the basis of the whole matter is economic," but they hardly offer any exposition of what they mean. The implication is, however, that they follow Bebel in pointing to woman's economic dependence on men as the essential problem. In a future socialist society, by contrast, "there will be equality for all, without distinction of sex," and women will therefore be independent. Equality, in the sense of equal rights, constitutes a major theme throughout *The Woman Question*. Unlike the feminists, the pamphlet claims, socialists press beyond the concept of equal rights as a "sentimental or professional" issue, for they recognize the economic basis of the woman question and the impossibility of resolving it within capitalist society.

The Woman Question strikes a new note when it openly argues that the position of women with respect to men parallels that of men with respect to capitalists. "Women are the creatures of an organised tyranny of men, as the workers are the creatures of an organised tyranny of idlers." Women "have been expropriated as to their rights as human beings, just as the labourers were expropriated as to their rights as producers." In short, both groups have been denied their freedom. With such formulations, the authors conceptualize oppression primarily in terms of lack of political rights and the presence of hierarchical relations of authority. Moreover, the idea that women's situation parallels that of workers suggests a strategy of parallel social struggles for freedom. "Both the oppressed classes, women and the immediate producers, must understand that their emancipation will come from themselves. [The] one has nothing to hope from man as a whole, and the other has nothing to hope from the middle class as a whole." Despite the pamphlet's socialist stance, its images of parallel denials of rights and parallel movements for liberation come quite close to liberal views of purely political freedoms in bourgeois society.

This explicit emphasis on the parallels between sex and class oppression takes a logical step beyond Engels's *Origin* and Bebel's *Woman*. In the *Origin*, the parallelism had remained latent in the series of dualities Engels had used to frame his arguments: family and society, domestic labor and public production, production of human beings and production of the means of existence, equal rights between the sexes and legal equality of the classes. In *Woman and Socialism*, Bebel often counterposed the woman question and the social question, ambiguously according them equal weight as either separate or, paradoxically, identical questions. Moreover, in arguing that "women should expect as little help from the men as working men do from the capitalist class," he implicitly postulated a strategy of parallel social movements.[14] The notion of a theoretical and strategic parallel between the sex and class struggles obviously had a certain currency within the Second International. While *The Woman Question* represented one of the first clear formulations of the position, socialist theorists and activists had evidently already adopted its substance, and it quickly became a staple of the socialist heritage.

Bebel's *Woman and Socialism* and the Avelings' *The Woman Question* may be taken as indicative of the dominant views within the Second International. To the extent that the late nineteenth-century socialist movement took up practical work on the issue of women's subordination, these views generally underlay the programs and tactics that were developed. All too often, the movement offered a perspective on women's oppression that combined visionary promises of individual sexual and social liberation in the distant socialist future, on the one hand, with an understanding of equal rights as an immediate but possibly bourgeois goal, on the other. In this way, the Second International left a legacy of theory and practice on the so-called woman question that tended to sever the struggle for equality from the tasks of revolutionary social transformation.

8

Toward

Revolution

As the twentieth century approached, the parties of the Second International increasingly substituted a concern with immediate practical gains for a revolutionary long view. At the theoretical level this reformism, whose origins went back to the 1870s, was dubbed revisionism because it supposedly revised many of Marx's original positions. Revisionism affected every aspect of the International's theoretical outlook, but its impact on the socialist movement's approach to the so-called woman question is hard to assess. Even in the time of Marx and Engels, socialist work on the problem of women's oppression had remained quite undeveloped, and the Second International's general underestimation of its political significance only perpetuated this state of underdevelopment. It was not entirely obvious, therefore, what constituted the orthodox revolutionary position, nor in what manner it might be subjected to revision by reformists.

Reformism did not go unopposed within the Second International. A left wing emerged, which sought to restore the movement to a revolutionary path. Although ultimately unsuccessful, the effort deepened its participants' grasp of Marxism and of virtually all the major theoretical and practical tasks facing socialists. Because of the confused history of work on the question of women, as well as the generally weak commitment to it among socialists, the problem of women's oppression did not come under explicit scrutiny in the course of this struggle. On this issue, then, the opposition to reformism within the socialist movement could only acquire rudimentary shape, most visibly within the German Social Democratic party.

106

The SPD had always been at the forefront of the socialist movement on the issue of woman's oppression, even though its theory and practice left much to be desired. It produced the major political text on the question, Bebel's *Woman and Socialism*. Within the Second International, it consistently took the strongest and most advanced positions for women's suffrage and against all types of discriminatory legislation. The portion of its membership that was female was the largest of any socialist party, reaching sixteen percent just before World War I. It supported, on paper at least, women's active involvement in party affairs, and took some steps toward developing special internal mechanisms to facilitate their participation. By the closing years of the nineteenth century, the German Social Democratic party could boast of a large, well-organized, and extremely militant socialist women's movement.

Many of these achievements bore witness to the dedicated work of German socialist women themselves. Moreover, on all major issues, women party members generally took political positions well to the left of the party as a whole. As the struggle around reformism intensified, the socialist women's movement became a stronghold of left-wing revolutionary orthodoxy.[1] While the issue of women's subordination never became a clear area of disagreement, members of the left wing put forth theoretical and practical perspectives that suggested opposition to dominant SPD positions on women.

The speeches and writings of Clara Zetkin, leader of the SPD's socialist women's movement and an early opponent of the reformism engulfing the party, offer some of the clearest statements of this implicitly left-wing approach to the problem of women's oppression. In 1896, for instance, Zetkin delivered an address on the issue at the annual party congress, which was subsequently distributed as a pamphlet.[2] The 1896 talk was an official policy statement of the German socialist movement. At the same time, its text suggested a theoretical position that implicitly countered the movement's drift toward reformism.

Zetkin opens the 1896 speech with a brief sketch of the origins of women's social subjugation. Morgan and other writers have shown that the development of private property engenders a contradiction within the family between the man as property owner and the woman as non-owner. On this basis arises the economic dependence of the entire female sex, and its lack of social rights. Quoting Engels to the effect that such lack of social rights constitutes "one of the foremost and earliest forms of class rule," Zetkin nevertheless pictures the precapitalist family household in conventionally idyllic terms. "It was the capitalist mode of production that first brought about the social transformation which raised the modern woman question: it smashed to smithereens the old family economy that in pre-capitalist times had provided the great mass of women with the sustenance and meaningful content of life."[3] To this point, Zetkin's account generally follows the lines laid down by the dominant socialist tradition. Only the remark on the specificity of the "modern woman question" in the capitalist mode of production suggests a different perspective.

Zetkin presses further in her analysis of the theoretically specific character of the question of women. Having observed its emergence as a "modern" question with the rise of capitalist society, she proceeds to dissect it in terms of class. "There is a woman question for the women of the proletariat, of the middle bourgeoisie and the intelligentsia, and of the Upper Ten Thousand; it takes various forms depending on the class situation of these strata." In the following passages, which occupy half the text of the speech, Zetkin outlines these three forms of the question, in each case specifying the source of woman's oppression, the nature of the demands for equality, and the obstacles to their adoption. While in places her discussion falters, sometimes quite seriously, the very attempt to develop such a systematic analysis constituted an implicit rebuke to the vagaries of the dominant socialist position.

Zetkin begins with the ruling-class women of the "Upper Ten Thousand." The specific woman question here involves wives' sexual and economic dependence upon men of their own class. Not work, either paid or unpaid, but property represents the core of their problem, since women of this class can employ servants to accomplish virtually all their household tasks and spousal duties. When these women "desire to give their lives serious content, they must first raise the demand for free and independent control over their property." To achieve this demand, they fight against men of their own class, much as the bourgeoisie earlier had to fight against all privileged classes. In this sense, the struggle of ruling-class women for control over their own wealth after marriage constitutes "the last stage in the emancipation of private property," and Zetkin views it as entirely consistent with bourgeois claims to liberate the individual.

The woman question presents itself in a quite different social form among women of the small and middle bourgeoisie and the bourgeois intelligentsia. These are the intermediate strata, which undergo intensifying strain with the expansion of capitalist relations of production throughout society. As a class, the small and middle bourgeoisie is increasingly driven to ruin, its small-scale enterprises unable to compete with capitalist industry. At the same time, capital requires an intelligent and skilled labor force, and encourages "overproduction in proletarian brain-workers," with the result that the bourgeois intelligentsia gradually loses its formerly secure material position and social standing. Men of the small and middle bourgeoisie and of the intelligentsia often postpone marriage, or even put it off altogether. The basis of family life in these strata becomes ever more precarious, with a growing pool of unmarried women, and Zetkin argues that "the women and daughters of these circles are thrust out into society to establish a life for themselves, not only one that provides bread but also one that can satisfy the spirit." Among these women of the small and middle bourgeoisie and the bourgeois intelligentsia, a specific woman question appears in the form of a demand for women's economic equality with men of their own class in the field of employment. Women fight for equal access to the education that will enable them to enter the liberal professions, and for the right to carry on those professions. These demands amount to nothing less than a call for capitalism to fulfill its pledge to promote free competition in every arena, this time between women and men. And, according to Zetkin, it is the fear of this competition within the liberal professions that lies behind the petty obstinacies of male resistance. The competitive battle soon drives the women of these strata to organize a women's movement and demand political rights, in order to overcome the barriers to their full economic and social participation.

In speaking of the bourgeois women's movement, Zetkin refers mainly to the organized activity of women from the small and middle bourgeoisie, and from the intelligentsia. Like women of the ruling class, these women focus on their lack of equality with men of their own class, although as earners rather than as property owners. In both cases, there is a gap between the promise of equality offered by bourgeois society and its actual absence in daily life. While the economic aspect represents the heart of the matter, Zetkin observes that the bourgeois women's movement encompasses far more than purely economic motives. "It also has a very much deeper intellectual and moral side. The bourgeois woman not only demands to earn her own bread, but she also wants to live a full life intellectually and develop her own individuality." Moreover, at all levels, "the strivings of the bourgeois women's-rightsers are entirely justified."[4]

Among the women of the proletariat, the woman question assumes yet another form. Working-class women have no need to fight for entry into capitalist economic life; they are there already. "For the proletarian woman, it is capital's need for exploitation, its unceasing search for the cheapest labor power, that has created the woman question." Moreover, Zetkin claims, the working-class woman already enjoys both equality and economic independence, although she pays for them dearly, because of her dual obligations as worker both in the factory and in the family household. "Neither as a person nor as a woman or wife does she have the possibility of living a full life as an individual. For her work as wife and mother she gets only the crumbs that are dropped from the table by capitalist production." Since capitalism has relieved her of the need to struggle for equality with the men of her own class, the working-class woman has other demands. In the immediate future, "it is a question of erecting new barriers against the exploitation of the proletarian woman; it is a question of restoring and ensuring her rights as wife and mother." Furthermore, "the end-goal of her struggle is not free competition with men but bringing about the political rule of the proletariat." Alongside the men of her own class, not in competition with them, she fights to achieve this goal. Her principal obstacle is, then, capitalism itself. At the same time, adds Zetkin, the working-class woman supports the demands of the bourgeois women's movement, "but she regards the realization of these demands only as a means to an end, so that she can get into the battle along with the workingmen and equally armed."

Obviously, a great deal of what Zetkin has to say about the three forms of the woman question departs from the realities of capitalist society. To some extent, these inaccuracies owe their existence to her failure to distinguish, within the 1896 speech, theoretical argument from empirical description, a confusion shared by most socialist writers of her day. Beyond this problem, however, Zetkin's contribution remains limited by certain theoretical weaknesses. That is, the distortions in Zetkin's consideration of the woman question appear to be largely empirical, but they have theoretical roots as well as serious political ramifications.

In the first place, along with virtually all her contemporaries, not to mention Marx and Engels, Zetkin glosses over the issue of domestic labor within the family household. She severely underestimates the contradictions that arise from the sex division of this labor in all three classes. In this way, she loses an important opportunity to strengthen her argument for the existence of specific forms of the woman question according to class. Empirically, the ruling-class wife's mediated relationship to housework bears little resemblance to the working-class woman's never-ending domestic drudgery. And at the theoretical level, the distinction stands out even more sharply, for only the unpaid domestic labor in the working-class household contributes to the reproduction of the labor power required for capitalist production.

Second, Zetkin's picture of the working-class woman constitutes an abstraction that verges on caricature. While the ability to command a wage always entails a certain level of independence, in no way could it be asserted as a fact that "the wife of the proletarian, in consequence, achieved her economic independence." In 1896, no less than now, working-class women suffered grievously from their lack of equality with men of their own class at the work place, in every possible way: pay, working conditions, access to jobs, opportunity for promotion, and so forth. Furthermore, working-class women lacked equality in the civil sphere and were oppressed as women within the working-class family. Elsewhere in the text Zetkin even cites several examples of the harmful effects of these phenomena, not only for women but for the working-class movement. By not confronting such facts theoretically, Zetkin simplifies her analysis but thereby passes over the problem of specifying the relationship between the fight for women's equality and the struggle against capitalism. Moreover, along with most socialist theorists of her period, she fails to distinguish women workers from working-class women; that is, in speaking of the proletarian woman, she always assumes that the woman participates in wage work. In this way, household members who do not engage in wage work—for example, wives, young children, the elderly, the sick—become analytically, and therefore politically, invisible. At the root of these confusions, which haunt socialist work to this day, lies the theoretical invisibility of the unpaid labor required to reproduce labor power in the working-class household.

Finally, Zetkin errs in arguing that specific woman questions arise only within those classes thrust forward by the capitalist mode of production. In a period in which peasants still made up the majority of the European oppressed masses, she, along with many other socialists, idealized the peasantry as representing a "natural economy," however "shrunken and tattered" under the impact of emergent capitalism. In general, the parties of the Second International tended to ignore the difficult theoretical and strategic problems presented by the existence of this massive peasantry alongside a growing industrial proletariat, and Zetkin, despite her political acuity, all too easily fell into line. Peasant women, she claimed, "found a meaningful content of life in productive work, . . . their lack of social rights did not impinge on their consciousness," and therefore, "we find no woman question arising in the ranks of the peasantry." Here, the reality of any peasant society, past or present, strenuously contradicts Zetkin's remarks. Among European peasants at the end of the nineteenth century, the woman question had

its own, quite specific, character, which required analysis by the socialist movement. Peasants could not, any more than women, be excluded
from a revolutionary perspective.

Having clarified, to the best of her ability, the theoretical issues
involved in the problem of women's oppression, Zetkin devotes the
rest of the 1896 speech to the current situation of the women's movement in Germany and the practical tasks to be taken up by the party. In
the long run, the goal of the bourgeois women's movement—equality
with men of one's own class—hardly threatens capitalist relations of
power; hence "bourgeois society does not take a stance of basic opposition to the demands of the bourgeois women's movement." In
Germany, however, a prejudiced and shortsighted bourgeoisie fears
any reform whatsoever, not understanding that if the reforms were
granted, nothing would change. "The proletarian woman would go
into the camp of the proletariat, the bourgeois woman into the camp of
the bourgeoisie." Zetkin also cautions against "socialistic outcroppings
in the bourgeois women's movement, which turn up only so long as
the bourgeois women feel themselves to be oppressed." In this context, the responsibility falls on the German Social Democratic party to
make good its commitment to strengthening the socialist women's
movement.

Zetkin proposes certain general guidelines for socialist work
among women. The party's main task is to arouse the working-class
woman's class consciousness and engage her in the class struggle.
Hence, "we have no special women's agitation to carry on but rather
socialist agitation among women." Zetkin warns against the tendency
to focus on "women's petty interests of the moment," and emphasizes
the importance, as well as the difficulty, of organizing women workers
into trade unions. She notes that several major obstacles, specific to
women as women, stand in the way of successfully undertaking socialist work among working-class women. Women often work in occupa-
tions that leave them isolated and hard to mobilize. Young women believe that their wage work is temporary, while married women suffer
the burden of the double shift. Finally, special laws in Germany deny
women the right to political assembly and association, and working-
class women therefore cannot organize together with men. Zetkin emphasizes that special forms of work must be devised in order to carry
out socialist work among women.

For example, a proposal that the party appoint field organizers
whose task would be to encourage working-class women to participate
in trade unions and support the socialist movement receives Zetkin's
backing. The idea had already been endorsed at the 1894 congress,

and Zetkin's comments actually represent an insistence that the party follow through on its commitment. If developed systematically, consistently, and on a large scale, she argues, the network of field organizers would draw many working-class women into the socialist movement.

Family obligations make it impossible for many women to come to meetings, and Zetkin therefore underscores the critical role of printed material. She suggests the party produce a series of pamphlets "that would bring women nearer to socialism in their capacity as workers, wives and mothers." She criticizes the party's daily press for not taking a more political approach in articles designed to speak to its female readership. And she proposes that the party undertake the systematic distribution of agitational leaflets to women: "Not the traditional leaflets which cram the whole socialist programme onto one side of a sheet together with all the erudition of the age—no, small leaflets that bring up a single practical question with a single angle, from the standpoint of the class struggle." Furthermore, these leaflets must be attractively printed, on decent paper and in large print. As good examples of agitational material for women, Zetkin cites contemporary United States and British temperance literature.[5]

Behind these comments lies more than a criticism of the party's work among women. Zetkin clearly makes a general indictment of the officialdom's bureaucratic and passive approach to socialist agitation and propaganda. Unlike the reformists, she insists that the party take "the standpoint of the class struggle: this is the main thing." When the party reaches out to women, it must treat them as political beings. In the short as well as the long run, the socialist revolution needs women's creative participation at least as much as working-class women need full liberation. Work among women "is difficult, it is laborious, it demands great devotion and great sacrifice, but this sacrifice will be rewarded and must be made. For, just as the proletariat can achieve its emancipation only if it fights together without distinction of nationality or distinction of occupation, so also it can achieve its emancipation only if it holds together without distinction of sex." Most important, she concludes, "the involvement of the great mass of proletarian women in the emancipatory struggle of the proletariat is one of the pre-conditions for the victory of the socialist idea, for the construction of a socialist society."

In sum, Zetkin's 1896 speech made an important theoretical and political contribution to the socialist movement's understanding of the problem of women's subordination. Significantly, the speech rarely mentions love, sexuality, interpersonal relations, or human feelings, subjects that represented the core of the so-called woman question for

most nineteenth-century socialists. Instead, Zetkin focuses on the theoretical issues and practical tasks that confront the socialist movement.
Only her comments on the working-class household sometimes de-
part from this businesslike and unromantic stance, even idealizing
working women as nurturant wives and mothers of the fighting—
male—proletariat. Similarly, her sketch of the socialist future recalls
Bebel's work in its depiction of the family as an isolated entity as well
as its emphasis on woman's independence. "When the family disap-
pears as an economic unit and its place is taken by the family as a
moral unit, women will develop their individuality as comrades advancing on a par with men with equal rights, an equal role in production and equal aspirations, while at the same time they are able to
fulfill their functions as wife and mother to the highest degree." From
a theoretical standpoint, such remarks retreat from the position put
forth in the body of the speech. Politically, they suggest an almost ritual
concession to the ambiguity of the socialist tradition, probably necessary to guarantee the speech's acceptance by party delegates.

The major portion of Zetkin's text attempted to build a theoretical
foundation for revolutionary strategy. More explicitly than any socialist
thinker before her, she assessed the particular theoretical character of
the problem of women's subordination in class society. Her discussion
of the specific forms taken by the so-called woman question in terms
of different modes of production, and the various classes within them,
remains, despite its problems, important. Indeed, its weaknesses,
which can be traced to inadequacies shared by the socialist movement
as a whole, actually delineate a new set of theoretical tasks. To the extent that Zetkin worked out her analysis within the framework of
Marx's theory of social reproduction, she generally avoided the theoretical quagmires—utopianism, economic determinism, and the like
—into which both Engels and Bebel had fallen. In this sense, the
thrust of Zetkin's remarks placed her in opposition to the reformist
tendency to revise Marxist theory, however undeveloped that theory
had remained on the issue of women's oppression.

Consistent with her vigorous opposition to the reformism spread-
ing throughout the socialist movement, Zetkin's strategic orientation
in the 1896 speech pushed well beyond two obstacles hindering socialist work among women. First, she questioned the Second International's tendency to identify the woman question with the general social
question, even if she did not adequately specify their actual relationship. In this way, she attempted to force the socialist movement to confront the practical problems flowing from its professed commitments.
And second, she insisted that women's active participation is central to

the socialist revolution, and therefore refused to postpone serious socialist work with women. In later years, with the hindsight afforded by several more decades of experience, Zetkin reached the conclusion that the Second International had actually been wholly incapable of providing a sound theoretical or organizational foundation for such work. Beset with reformism and "the most trivial philistine prejudices against the emancipation of women," the socialist movement had taken "no initiative in the theoretical clarification of the problems or practical carrying out of the work." In this atmosphere, Zetkin commented, "the progress achieved was essentially the work of women themselves."[6]

The eruption of World War I in 1914 forced the tension within the socialist movement between reformism and a more revolutionary outlook to the breaking point. Most parties in the Second International supported the war, taking whichever side their national bourgeoisie happened to stand on. Working-class internationalism seemed to vanish into thin air, as a narrow patriotism swept through socialist ranks. Meanwhile, individual left-wing socialists recognized they had lost the battle against reformism, and began to regroup. They opposed the war, either assuming an essentially pacifist stance or, more militantly, viewing it as an opportunity for revolutionary action. As hostilities dragged on, popular discontent replaced the initial patriotic euphoria, and important sectors of the population turned to those who sought to end the war. In consequence, the pacifist and revolutionary minorities in every socialist party grew stronger. Their antiwar perspective seemed vindicated when the Bolshevik party came to power in Russia in 1917.

The Bolshevik revolution transformed not only Russia but the international socialist movement. For the first time, revolutionaries had fought for and won the opportunity to begin the transition to a communist society, and the effort commanded the attention of socialists everywhere. The seizure of state power was only the first step, and weighty problems confronted the new society. Externally, the forces of capitalism tried, in every possible way, including military intervention, to undermine the revolution's success. And internally, the task of building a socialist society quickly proved tremendously difficult. Every question that had formerly concerned the international socialist movement now became a matter of the utmost urgency, to be resolved in concrete detail, in both theory and practice. Among these tasks loomed the problem of women's subordination, made all the more pressing because of several peculiarities of the Russian revolution. First, the majority of Russia's population consisted of peasants, half of whom lived the particularly hard life of peasant women—often working in the fields as well as the household, and brutally oppressed by feudal traditions of male supremacy. Second, women wage earners constituted a relatively new and fast-growing group, especially in the very small Russian industrial sector, where their numbers rose to include forty percent of the industrial work force during the war. Last, radical movements in Russia had traditionally attracted a large number of women activists, who often played leading roles, and the Bolshevik party was no exception. Objectively, and from the start, the question of women represented a critical issue for the future of socialism in Russia.

The history of women's situation in the Soviet Union has yet to be fully analyzed. Most accounts sketch a gloomy picture in which numerous obstacles conspire to block full liberation for women: insufficient material resources, erroneous or opportunist political priorities, wholesale ideological backwardness, a low level of theoretical attention. Although correct in its general outlines, the picture remains blurred. In particular, despite a great deal of research, it fails to situate the history of the question of women within an adequate understanding of the development of the Russian revolution, and of the international socialist and communist movements.[7] Moreover, the problem of the nature and source of the theoretical framework underpinning Soviet work on the issue of women's subordination has barely been addressed.

The rudiments of that theoretical framework were established by V. I. Lenin, the leader of the Bolshevik party and a prolific writer on questions of socialist theory and practice. Lenin's comments on women make up only a tiny portion of his work, and it is not clear to what extent they were taken up within the Bolshevik party or implemented in practice. Nonetheless, they are important for their insight into the theoretical heart of the problem of women's oppression.

Like Zetkin, Lenin took a left-wing position in the struggle against reformism. In the Russian context, however, this struggle acquired its own form, quite distinct from the public battle fought within the massive and powerful German party. Under the czars, Marxism remained an illegal movement in a backward country. Neither a strong trade union movement nor a socialist party affiliated with the Second International could be built. The major theoretical task for Russian socialists at the end of the nineteenth century was to assimilate Marxist theory in order to put it into practice in their own country, where conditions differed sharply from the industrializing nations of Western Europe and North America. Opposition to revisionism among Russian socialists therefore initially took the particular shape of an effort to grasp and defend Marxism itself.

Two tendencies within Russian radicalism stood in the way of the developing Marxist movement. First, the Russian populists, or *narodniks*, argued that the peasantry constituted the backbone of the revolutionary process, that Russia would be able to bypass the stage of industrial capitalism, and that the peasant commune provided the germ of a future communist society. Second, a group known as the "legal Marxists," so named because they wrote in a form capable of passing Russian censorship, embraced Marxism largely because it recognized the historically progressive character of capitalism. In opposition to the *narodniks*, the legal Marxists welcomed capitalism as a necessary first stage on the way to socialism; as might be expected, many of them later lost their interest in revolution and became staunch bourgeois liberals.

A central theme in Lenin's earliest writings was the defense of Marxism against attacks from the *narodniks*, on the one hand, and distortions by the legal Marxists, on the other. At the same time, he began to elaborate a Marxist analysis of the development of capitalism in Russia and of the prospects for a socialist revolution. When Russian Marxists founded the Social-Democratic Workers' party, after the turn of the century, bourgeois liberalism became yet another target of his polemics.

Lenin's first comments touching on the problem of women's oppression appear in his critique of 1894 of the *narodnik* writer N. Mikhailovsky, who had caricatured Marxist theory. The issue of women's situation arises because Mikhailovsky mocks Engels's discussion of "'the production of man himself,' i.e. procreation," in the preface to the *Origin*, castigating it as a peculiar form of "economic materialism." He suggests instead that "not only legal, but also economic relations themselves constitute a 'superstructure' on sexual and family relations." In reply, Lenin ridicules Mikhailovsky's argument that "procreation is not an economic factor," and asks sarcastically, "Where have you read in the works of Marx or Engels that they necessarily spoke of economic materialism? When they described their world outlook they called it simply materialism. Their basic idea . . . was that social relations are divided into material and ideological. . . . Mr. Mikhailovsky surely does not think that procreation relations are ideological?" The way Lenin defends Engels's statements in the preface, however questionable their theoretical status may be, is significant. He puts the major emphasis on the point that Marxism is not economic determinism. And he insists on the material core embedded in all social relations, even those involving women, the family, and sexuality.[8] This perspective, which relies far more on Marx than on later socialist theorists, became the foundation of Lenin's approach to the problem of women's subordination.

Capitalism developed in Russia on the basis of a savagely patriarchal feudal culture. In *The Development of Capitalism in Russia*, published in 1899, Lenin examined the impact of capitalist social relations on peasant life. Because of its highly socialized labor processes, capitalism "absolutely refuses to tolerate survivals of patriarchalism and personal dependence" over the long run. Lenin argues that in this sense "the drawing of women and juveniles into production is, at bottom, progressive," despite the particularly oppressive conditions these sectors often encounter under the rule of capital. In sum: "By destroying the patriarchal isolation of these categories of the population who formerly never emerged from the narrow circle of domestic, family relationships, by drawing them into direct participation in social production, large-scale machine industry stimulates their development and increases their independence, in other words, creates conditions of life that are incomparably superior to the patriarchal immobility of pre-capitalist relations." Lenin points out that any attempts "to ban the work of women and juveniles in industry, or to maintain the patriarchal manner of life that ruled out such work, would be reactionary and utopian."[9] With these remarks, Lenin has simply used Marxist theory to develop an analysis of the significance in Russia of women's and children's participation in social labor. Obvious though this approach may seem, at the time it represented a rare return to the best of Marx and Engels.

In these early decades of the Russian socialist movement, Lenin also addressed several specific problems having to do with the special oppression of women as women. He condemned prostitution, locating it in social conditions and incidentally taking swipes at liberal attempts to end it. He analyzed the class character of the birth-control movement, contrasting the psychology of the petit-bourgeois liberal to that of the class-conscious worker. At the same time he underscored the need for socialists to support the abolition of all laws limiting availability of abortion or contraception. "Freedom for medical propaganda and the protection of the elementary democratic rights of citizens, men and women, are one thing. The social theory of neomalthusianism is quite another." Most important, Lenin repeatedly denounced the peasantry's "century-old traditions of patriarchal life," and their particularly brutal implications for women.[10]

In subsequent years, Lenin began to pay special attention to the relationship between sex oppression and class cleavages. While he had always supported equality between women and men, in the traditional socialist manner, he now came up against the more difficult problem of specifying the nature of that equality. Initially, the problem appeared in the context of discussions on the so-called national question. Among socialists, questions of the equality of nations and the rights of national minorities became matters of heated debate in the early twentieth century, as nationalist feelings and political conflict intensified around the world. At the root of these developments lay the emergence of imperialism, with its chain of oppressed and oppressor nations. Hence, it was imperialism that forced Lenin to examine the nature of equality in bourgeois society, and to delineate the role of the struggle for democratic rights in the context of a revolutionary movement to overthrow capitalism.

The peculiar character of the question of democratic rights owes its existence, according to Lenin, to the fact that in capitalist society, political phenomena have a certain autonomy with respect to economic phenomena. Numerous economic evils are part of capitalism as such, so that "it is *impossible* to eliminate them economically without eliminating capitalism itself." By contrast, departures from democracy constitute political evils, and in principle can be resolved within the framework of capitalist society. Lenin cites the example of divorce, an example first used by Rosa Luxemburg in a discussion of the national question and the right to uphold national autonomy. It is perfectly possible, if rare, argues Lenin, for a capitalist state to enact laws granting the right to full freedom of divorce. Nonetheless, "in most cases the right of divorce will remain unrealizable under capitalism, for the oppressed sex is subjugated economically. No matter how much democracy there is under capitalism, the woman remains a 'domestic slave,' a slave locked up in the bedroom, nursery, kitchen. . . . The right of divorce, as *all* other democratic rights without exception, is conditional, restricted, formal, narrow and extremely difficult of realization." In sum, "capitalism combines formal equality with economic and, consequently, social inequality."[11]

If equality is so difficult to realize in capitalist society, why should socialists enter the fight to defend and extend democratic rights? Why devote energy to a seemingly useless battle on bourgeois terrain? First, because each victory represents an advance in itself, however limited, in that it provides somewhat better conditions of life for the entire population. And second, because the struggle for democratic rights enhances the ability of all to identify their enemy. As Lenin put it,

> Marxists know that democracy does *not* abolish class oppression. It only makes the class struggle more direct, wider, more open and pronounced, and that is what we need. The fuller

the freedom of divorce, the clearer will women see that the source of their "domestic slavery" is capitalism, not lack of rights. The more democratic the system of government, the clearer will the workers see that the root evil is capitalism, not lack of rights. The fuller national equality (and it is *not* complete without freedom of secession), the clearer will the workers of the oppressed nations see that the cause of their oppression is capitalism, not lack of rights, etc.[12]

In this sense, the battle for democratic rights is a means for establishing and maintaining the best framework within which to carry out the class struggle.

Lenin's work on democratic rights went well beyond earlier socialist analyses of the nature of equality. At the theoretical level, it offered serious insights into the mystery of the relationship among sex, class, and national oppression in capitalist societies. And practically, it constituted an important element in the development of revolutionary strategy with respect to national minorities, oppressed nations, and women. Here, twin dangers haunted the socialist movement. On the one hand, some denied the critical significance of these special oppressions, and refused to take them up seriously in practice, and often in theory as well. On the other, many developed reformist positions that scarcely differed, at the practical level, from bourgeois nationalism or liberal feminism. Armed with an understanding of the character of democratic rights, a socialist movement had a better chance to confront national and women's oppression without slipping into either error.

Once the bourgeois state has been overthrown in a socialist revolution, as happened in Russia in 1917, full political equality comes immediately onto the agenda. The new Soviet government began to enact legislation granting formal equality to women in many areas. Yet precisely because formal equality remains distinct from real social equality, even in the socialist transition, legislation could not be enough. Indeed, observes Lenin, "the more *thoroughly* we clear the ground of the lumber of the old, bourgeois laws and institutions, the more we realize that we have only cleared the ground to build on, but are not yet building." In the case of women, he identifies as the major barrier to further progress the material phenomenon of unpaid labor within the family household. Writing in 1919, for instance, he points out that despite "all the laws emancipating woman, she continues to be a *domestic slave*, because *petty housework* crushes, strangles, stultifies and degrades her, chains her to the kitchen and the nursery, and she wastes her labor on barbarously unproductive, petty, nerve-racking, stultify-ing and crushing drudgery."[13]

From the start, Lenin always put more weight on the problem of women's material oppression within the individual family household than on their lack of rights, their exclusion from equal social participa-tion, or their dependence upon men. Speaking of peasant and pro-letarian women, and sometimes of petit-bourgeois women as well, he repeatedly drew a picture of domestic slavery, household bondage, humiliating subjugation by the savage demands of kitchen and nursery drudgery, and the like.[14] This emphasis was unique in the Marxist liter-ature, and probably originated in Lenin's focus on the peasantry, with its traditions of patriarchal relations, as a critical element in the revolu-tionary struggle. Whatever its source, Lenin's concern with the prob-lem of domestic labor enabled him to formulate the questions of women's oppression and of the conditions for women's liberation with a clarity not previously achieved.

Lenin argues that the special oppression of women in capitalist society has a double root. In the first place, like national minorities, women suffer as a group from political inequality. And in the second, women are imprisoned in what Lenin terms domestic slavery—that is, they perform, under oppressive conditions, the unpaid labor in the household required to maintain and renew the producing classes: "The female half of the human race is doubly oppressed under capital-ism. The working woman and the peasant woman are oppressed by capital, but over and above that, even in the most democratic of the bourgeois republics, they remain, firstly, deprived of some rights be-cause the law does not give them equality with men; and secondly—and this is the main thing—they remain in 'household bondage,' they continue to be 'household slaves,' for they are overburdened with the drudgery of the most squalid and backbreaking and stultifying toil in the kitchen and the individual family household." In this passage, Lenin makes it evident that he considers the second factor—domestic slavery—to be "the main thing."[15]

Just as the source of women's oppression as women is twofold, so the basic conditions for their full liberation are also twofold. Obvi-ously, the lack of equal rights must be remedied, but this political obli-gation is only the first, and easiest, step because "even when women have full rights, they still remain downtrodden because all housework is left to them."[16] Lenin recognizes that developing the material condi-tions for ending women's historic household bondage constitutes a far more difficult task. He mentions the need "for women to participate in common productive labor" and in public life on a basis of equality, but he puts major emphasis on efforts to transform petty housekeeping into a series of large-scale socialized services: community kitchens, public dining rooms, laundries, repair shops, nurseries, kindergartens, and so forth.[17] Finally, in addition to the political and material conditions for women's liberation, Lenin points to the critical role of ideological struggle in remolding "the most deep-rooted, inveterate, hidebound and rigid" mentalities inherited from the old order.[18]

To implement its policies with respect to women, the new Soviet government faced the task of developing appropriate methods of work on several fronts. It was easy enough to pass legislation removing women's legal inequality, but to persuade people to live with it was quite another matter. Lenin addressed this issue in a speech to the hastily organized First All-Russia Congress of Working Women, held in Moscow in November 1918, where his appearance caused a sensation and seemed to offer tangible evidence of Bolshevik support for the undertaking of special work among peasant and proletarian women. Using the new marriage law as his example, Lenin stresses the importance of careful propaganda and education, for "by lending too sharp an edge to the struggle we may only arouse popular resentment; such methods of struggle tend to perpetuate the division of the people along religious lines, whereas our strength lies in unity." Similarly, the drawing of women into the labor force and the initiation of measures to begin to socialize housework and child care required the utmost sensitivity to existing conditions. Here, Lenin argues that "the emancipation of working women is a matter for the working women themselves," for it is they who will develop the new institutions. At the same time, the party had the obligation to provide guidance and devote resources to their work, and in 1919 Lenin already found its commitment wanting. "Do we in practice pay sufficient attention to this question," he asks, "which in theory every Communist considers indisputable? Of course not. Do we take proper care of the *shoots* of communism which already exist in this sphere? Again the answer is *no*. . . . We *do not nurse* these shoots of the new as we should."[19]

Women's participation in political life constituted an area of serious concern, for "you cannot draw the masses into politics without drawing the women into politics as well." Here again, Lenin regarded the timid efforts of both the international socialist movement and his own Bolshevik party as insufficient. Two major obstacles hampered the work. In the first place, many socialists feared that any attempt to do special work among women inevitably smacked of bourgeois feminism or revisionism, and therefore attacked all such activities. For this position, Lenin had nothing but scorn. While arguing that within the party itself, a separate organization of women would be factional, he insisted the realities of women's situation meant that "we must have our own groups to work among [women], special methods of agitation, and special forms of organization." Even more serious was the lack of enthusiasm among socialists when it came to providing practical support for the special work among women. In a conversation recorded by Zetkin, Lenin criticized the general passivity and backwardness of male comrades on this issue. "They regard agitation and propaganda among women and the task of rousing and revolutionizing them as of secondary importance, as the job of just the women Communists. . . . Unfortunately, we may still say of many of our comrades, 'Scratch the Communist and a philistine appears.'" Behind this view lies contempt for women. "In the final analysis, it is an underestimation of women and of their accomplishments." As evidence of the seriousness of the problem, Lenin describes how party men complacently watch their own wives take on the burdens and worries of the household, never thinking to lend a hand. Lenin concludes that special work must be done on these questions among men. "Our communist work among the masses of women, and our political work in general, involves considerable educational work among the men. We must root out the old slave-owner's point of view, both in the Party and among the masses." According to Zetkin's notes, Lenin went so far as to weight this task equally with that of forming a staff and organizations to work among women.[20]

Lenin's remarks about male chauvinism never acquired programmatic form, and the campaign against male ideological backwardness remained at most a minor theme in Bolshevik practice. Nonetheless, his observations on the problem represented an extremely rare acknowledgment of its seriousness. As for the development of special work among women, numerous socialists, almost all of them women, took it up as best they could.

On the issues of love and sexuality, Lenin, like Zetkin, said very little, and nothing that was meant for official publication. In a correspondence with Inessa Armand in 1915, he criticizes her notion of free love for its lack of clarity. While agreeing that love must be free from economic, social, and patriarchal restrictions, he cautions against a "bourgeois interpretation" that wishes to free love from interpersonal responsibility.[21] Later, in the conversation recorded by Zetkin, Lenin directs a lengthy tirade against those who give too much attention to "sex and marriage problems." He criticizes German socialist organizers who dwell on the subject in discussions with women workers. And he worries about attempts in the Soviet Union to transform the nihilist tradition of sexual radicalism into a socialist framework. "Many people call it 'revolutionary' and 'communist.' They sincerely believe that this is so. I am an old man, and I do not like it. I may be a morose ascetic, but quite often this so-called 'new sex life' of young people—and frequently of the adults too—seems to me purely bourgeois and simply an extension of the good old bourgeois brothel. All this has nothing in common with free love as we Communists understand it." For Lenin and much of the socialist tradition, it was individual sex love in socialist society that was destined to transcend the hypocritical two-sided sexual life of capitalist societies, abolishing repressive marriages on the one hand, and prostitution on the other. Individual sex love was the socialist answer to "the decay, putrescence, and filth of bourgeois marriage with its difficult dissolution, its licence for the husband and bondage for the wife, and its disgustingly false sex morality." Anything else smacked of promiscuity, and "promiscuity in sexual matters is bourgeois. It is a sign of degeneration."[22] Lenin's formulations, as remembered by Zetkin and published after his death, functioned mainly as a rationale for sexual conservatism among socialists.

In the long run, the experience of the Russian revolution raised at least as many questions about the relation of women's liberation to socialist transformation as it answered. Zetkin might have observed that here, too, history had posed a specific woman question, distinct from those thrust forward by capitalist relations of production: the question of women in the era of the transition to communism.

Given the generally undeveloped state of socialist work on the problem of women's oppression, Zetkin's and Lenin's theoretical contributions failed to make a lasting impression. With some exceptions, twentieth-century socialists and communists have adopted positions very similar to those dominant within the Second International. Yet the legacy is both incomplete and ambiguous.

Part Four

From the

Woman Question

to Women's

Liberation

9

A Dual

Legacy

As the preceding chapters demonstrate, the nineteenth- and early twentieth-century Marxist tradition provides only limited theoretical guidance on the twin problems of women's oppression and women's liberation. Marked by omissions and inconsistencies, the classical literature fails to confront the issues in a systematic manner. Much of it rests, furthermore, on an inadequate grasp of Marx's theory of social development. Despite a general commitment to Marxism, commentaries tend also to vacillate among several different critiques of bourgeois society, notably, utopian socialism, crude materialism, and liberal feminism. In short, no stable Marxist theoretical framework has been established for the consideration of the question of women by socialists.

Given the disorderly state of this theoretical work, it is not surprising that certain patterns have gone unnoticed. As it turns out, two essentially contradictory approaches to the problem of women's subordination have always coexisted within the socialist tradition, although the distinction has not been explicitly recognized, nor the positions clearly differentiated from one another. An unspoken debate between two alternatives has therefore haunted efforts to address a variety of major theoretical and practical questions concerning women's oppression and liberation. The origins of this hidden debate go back to the works of Marx and Engels themselves, and it has taken concrete shape in the ambiguous theory and practice of later socialist and communist movements. The implicit controversy has recently reappeared, transformed in significant ways, within the contemporary women's movement.

Tangled within the socialist literature, then, lie two distinct views of women's situation, corresponding to divergent theoretical positions. For convenience, the two positions may be labeled according to their starting point for the analysis of women's oppression. On the one hand is the "dual systems perspective": women's oppression derives from their situation within an autonomous system of sex divisions of labor and male supremacy. On the other is the "social reproduction perspective": women's oppression has its roots in women's differential location within social reproduction as a whole.[1] The following brief characterization of the two perspectives aims simply to suggest the theoretical underpinning and analytical consequences of each position. The social reproduction perspective is explored in more depth in the next chapters.

In essence, the dual systems perspective takes off from what appears to be obvious: divisions of labor and authority according to sex, the oppression of women, and the family. These phenomena are treated more or less as givens, analytically separable, at least in part, from the social relations in which they are embedded. The major analytical task is to examine the origin and development of the empirical correlation between sex divisions of labor and the social oppression of women. In general, it is women's involvement in the sex division of labor, and their direct relationship—of dependence and of struggle—to men, rather than their insertion in overall social reproduction, that establishes their oppression. At the same time, women's oppression and the sex division of labor are seen to be tied to the mode of production dominant in a given society, and to vary according to class. These latter factors enter the investigation as important variables which are, however, essentially external to the workings of women's oppression.

Class and sex oppression therefore appear to be autonomous phenomena from the dual systems perspective. Despite its assertions of an "inextricable relationship" between sex and class, this perspective leaves the character of that relationship unspecified. Logically speaking, however, the dual systems perspective implies that women's oppression follows a course that is essentially independent from that of class oppression. And it suggests, furthermore, that some systematic mechanism, peculiar to the sex division of labor and distinct from the class struggle characterizing a given mode of production, constitutes the main force behind women's oppression. In other words, according to the theory implicit in the dual systems perspective, two powerful motors drive the development of history: the class struggle and the sex struggle.

While the dual systems perspective begins with empirically given phenomena whose correlations are interpreted by means of a chain of plausible inferences, the social reproduction perspective starts out from a theoretical position—namely, that class struggle over the conditions of production represents the central dynamic of social development in societies characterized by exploitation. In these societies, surplus labor is appropriated by a dominant class, and an essential condition for production is the constant presence and renewal of a subordinated class of direct producers committed to the labor process. Ordinarily, generational replacement provides most of the new workers needed to replenish this class, and women's capacity to bear children therefore plays a critical role in class society.

From the point of view of social reproduction, women's oppression in class societies is rooted in their differential position with respect to generational replacement processes. Families constitute the historically specific social form through which generational replacement usually takes place. In class societies, "one cannot speak at all of the family *'as such*,'" as Marx once put it, for families have widely varying places within the social structure.[2] In propertied classes, families usually act as the carrier and transmitter of property, although they may also have other roles. Here, women's oppression flows from their role in the maintenance and inheritance of property. In subordinate classes, families usually structure the site at which direct producers are maintained and reproduced; such families may also participate directly in immediate production. Female oppression in these classes derives from women's involvement in processes that renew direct producers, as well as their involvement in production. While women's oppression in class societies is experienced at many levels, it rests, ultimately, on these material foundations. The specific working out of this oppression is a subject for historical, not theoretical, investigation.

Presented in crystallized form, the distinction between the dual systems and the social reproduction perspectives is relatively clear. Of the two the social reproduction perspective accords most closely with Marx's analysis of the workings of the capitalist mode of production, particularly as elaborated in *Capital*. The demarcation between the two perspectives has always been blurred, however, even while the presence of contradictory positions underlies much of the ambiguity marking the theoretical work produced by the socialist movement. The dual systems perspective has generally prevailed over the social reproduction perspective, despite periodic efforts to derive an analysis of the question of women from Marx's work.

Engels's *The Origin of the Family, Private Property and the State*, for example, relies heavily on the dual systems perspective. In the first place, the perspective is built into the very organization of the book. By assigning a separate chapter to the family, Engels implicitly suggests that the category of family—whose general shaping by the sex division of labor he takes as a given—can be considered virtually autonomously. Moreover, he regards the sex division of labor as biologically based and historically inflexible, whereas all other major phenomena in the *Origin* have a social foundation. In this way, Engels awards a central role to the sex division of labor in the family, but places it in a theoretical limbo. Similarly, women's oppression seems to spring from the independent nature of the sex division of labor itself. The remarks in the preface concerning the twofold character of production make these dualities explicit. The dual systems perspective takes the general form, in the *Origin*, of an emphasis on the sex division of labor and on the family as critically important phenomena which are not, however, firmly located with respect to overall social reproduction.

The *Origin*'s characterization of the single family as the "economic unit of society," with the additional implication that "modern society is a mass composed of these individual families as molecules," further illustrates its implicit dependence on the dual systems perspective. In such statements, Engels retains the separation of family from social reproduction, but peculiarly assigns a dominant constitutive role to the former. The manner in which the family unit functions within social reproduction, other than, in the case of the ruling class, to hold property, is never clearly defined. Along the same lines, Marx, as well as Engels, spoke several times of the sex division of labor in the family as a sort of representative miniature of the social division of labor in society. "The modern family contains in germ not only slavery (*servitus*) but also serfdom, since from the beginning it is related to agricultural services. It contains *in miniature* all the contradictions which later extend throughout society and its state." Engels also uses the image to describe relations between the sexes. "Within the family, [the husband] is the bourgeois, and the wife represents the proletariat." Since neither Marx nor Engels ever specifies, in any precise manner, the nature of this "representation"—that is, the relationship between the family "germ" and the social whole—these images function as simplistic parallels. At best, they are dangerous metaphors; at worst, uncritical borrowings from early bourgeois political philosophy.[3]

Finally, the *Origin*'s discussion of the family as the site of a struggle between the sexes accords with the dual systems perspective. While Engels underscores the simultaneous emergence of sex and class conflict, he never achieves a clear picture of their connection. The two developments remain historically parallel phenomena, whose theoretical relationship is best characterized as one of autonomy. For the propertied family, women's oppression has its source in the husband's need to preserve and transmit his private property. Obviously, the absence of private property should be accompanied by an absence of sex conflict. In fact, as Engels is forced to acknowledge, women occupy a subordinate place in propertyless households. Engels offers no theoretical basis for this historic oppression, although the preface's concept of systematic "production of human beings themselves" hints obliquely at a distinct mechanism.

The *Origin* does not entirely neglect the social reproduction perspective. It is implicit when Engels states that participation in public production offers the path to emancipation for the proletarian woman, when he insists that domestic work must be converted into a public industry, or when he argues that the single family must cease to be the economic unit of society. These assertions function as important insights which need, however, to be supported theoretically. Why does participation in public production offer a precondition for social equality? What does it mean to say the family's aspect as an economic unit must be abolished? In what sense is the family an economic unit? How are these issues linked to the requirement that domestic work be converted into a public industry? Unfortunately, Engels never manages to provide the explicit theoretical underpinning necessary to answer these questions properly. Marx had presented the outlines of a theory of the reproduction of labor power and the working class that could, in principle at least, have constituted the starting point. But such a serious extension of Marx's work represented an undertaking for which Engels lacked time and, perhaps, motivation. With the publication of the *Origin*, Engels's contradictory blend of the dual systems and social reproduction perspectives became, in effect, the unstable theoretical foundation for all subsequent socialist investigation of the so-called woman question.

The unrecognized gap between the two perspectives widened as the struggle between Marxism and revisionism intensified in the Second International. Whereas Engels had managed to combine both perspectives, however awkwardly, in a single text, subsequent analyses tended more clearly to emphasize one at the expense of the other. In general, the dual systems perspective dominated within the reformist wing of the socialist movement, while a rough version of the social reproduction perspective underlay the occasional efforts by opponents of reformism to address the question of women.

Behind the mass of data in August Bebel's *Woman and Socialism*, for instance, is a conceptual framework thoroughly in accord with the dual systems perspective. The book's position within the terms of the dual systems perspective is established, first of all, by Bebel's assumption that the category "woman" represents an appropriate theoretical starting point. Despite ritual assertions that the "solution of the Woman Question coincides completely with the solution of the Social Question," Bebel treats the phenomenon of women's oppression as analytically separable from social development as a whole. He argues, furthermore, that women's individual dependence on men is the source of their oppression in class society, but fails to situate that dependence within overall social reproduction. In short, Bebel's *Woman and Socialism* puts the sex division of labor and the relationship of dependence between women and men, taken as empirically obvious and ahistorical givens (at least until the advent of socialist society), at the heart of the problem of women's oppression.

Next to the theoretical and political confusion that permeates *Woman and Socialism*, Engels's analysis in the *Origin* has considerable force and clarity. Rather than zigzagging erratically between the so-called woman and social questions, he concentrates on the social phenomena that produce woman's position in a given society, and on the conditions that might lead to changes in that position. He does his best, that is, to delineate the relationships among the factors involved in women's oppression—the family, sex divisions of labor, property relations, class society, and the state—at times hinting also at the more comprehensive concept of the reproduction of labor power implicit in the social reproduction perspective. Although Engels's discussion in the *Origin* sorely lacks the powerful theoretical and political insight that Marx might have brought to the subject, it moves well beyond Bebel's effort in *Woman and Socialism*.

The Avelings' pamphlet *The Woman Question* confirms, even more clearly than Bebel's *Woman and Socialism*, the dominance of the dual systems perspective within the socialist movement. Like Bebel, the authors assert that the basis of women's oppression is economic dependence, but they fail to explain how, thus effectively severing the problem of women's subordination from its location within social development. The pamphlet's conceptualization of woman's position mainly in terms of love, sexuality, marriage, divorce, and dependence on men, reinforces this theoretical demarcation between women, the family, and the sex division of labor, on the one hand, and social reproduction, on the other. Finally, the pamphlet's explicit formulation of sex and class oppression as parallel phenomena, engendering parallel struggles whose relationship is never discussed, reveals most sharply its reliance on the dual systems perspective.

At the theoretical level, the growing strength of reformism in the Second International undoubtedly found a reflection in the consolidation of the dual systems perspective as the unspoken basis for any socialist efforts to address the question of women. Against this position, the left wing of the socialist movement presented an implicit, if all too undeveloped, challenge, which accorded with the general premises of the social reproduction perspective. Thus, in their approach to the issue of women's subordination, Clara Zetkin and Lenin, both leaders in the struggle against reformism, reject the universal categories of "woman" or "the family" as theoretical starting points. Instead, each focuses on the specificity of women's oppression in different classes in a given mode of production.

In her 1896 speech to the party congress, for example, Zetkin insists on the class-dependent character of the so-called woman question in capitalist societies. She identifies three distinct woman questions, all demanding resolution, but differentiated by the source of oppression, the nature of the demands for equality, and the obstacles to achieving the demands. Refusing to consider the woman question as a classless abstraction to be resolved in the future, she suggests a comprehensive program of organizational activity. At the practical level, Zetkin's opposition to reformism took the form of a commitment to developing socialist work among women of all classes—work that would support reforms without falling into reformism, and simultaneously keep the revolutionary goal firmly in view. In contrast to many of her contemporaries in the socialist movement, she saw the fight for changes in the relations between women and men as a task for the present, not for some indefinite socialist future.

With more theoretical precision than Zetkin, if less originality and commitment, Lenin places the issue of women's subordination in the context of the reproduction of labor power in class society. His repeated emphasis on the decisive role of domestic labor reflects an understanding, heightened by the experience of the Bolshevik revolution, of the material foundation of women's oppression. His grasp of the workings of capitalist social reproduction enables him to sketch the outlines of a theoretically coherent relationship between sex and class oppression, by means of the concept of democratic rights. These positions constitute the theoretical basis underlying Lenin's strategic clarity—never sufficiently implemented by the Bolsheviks in practice —on the importance of special work among women, on the need for mass women's organizations bringing together women of all classes, and on the problem of combatting male ideological backwardness. Taken together, Zetkin's and Lenin's observations on women offer the rudiments of a specific use of the social reproduction perspective to analyze women's oppression in capitalist society.

In the context of the modern women's movement in North America and Western Europe, specifically its socialist-feminist wing, the tension between the two perspectives has taken a new form. Whereas the socialist movement of the late nineteenth century sought mainly to differentiate its positions on the problem of women's oppression from those of liberal feminism, contemporary socialist feminism has developed as much in sympathetic response to the views of radical feminism as to the failures of both liberal feminism and the socialist tradition. It is this advanced position, in part, that has enabled the socialist-feminist movement to make its many significant contributions.

In certain ways, theoretical work produced from within the socialist-feminist framework recreates the major characteristics of the dual systems perspective. For example, socialist-feminist theorists tend, no matter what their stated intentions, to separate the question of divisions of labor and authority according to sex from social reproduction.[4] Furthermore, they remain generally unable to situate women's oppression theoretically in terms of mode of production and class. And they offer a one-sided emphasis on the family and issues of sexuality and personal dependence. Last, socialist feminists have not provided theoretical underpinning for their strategic emphasis on the integral role, in the struggle for socialism, of the autonomous organization of women from all sectors of society. In these ways, socialist feminists often reproduce the weaknesses of the dual systems perspective, but their work also points the way toward a more adequate theoretical grasp of the issue of women's oppression. In particular, they insist on the centrality of achieving a materialist understanding of woman's situation within the family—as childbearer, child rearer, and domestic laborer—as the key to the problem of the persistence of women's oppression across different modes of production and classes. It is here that socialist-feminist theorists have made especially important contributions. Those who focus on the task in terms of Marx's theory of social reproduction have renewed, furthermore, the elements of the social reproduction perspective, and have deepened it in ways never achieved either by Marx or by the socialist tradition. In sum, the political seriousness of socialist-feminist involvement in theoretical work, fueled by the continuing militance of women in social movements around the world has both reproduced and transformed the tension between the two perspectives. On the one hand, socialist feminism revives the contradictory coexistence of the two theoretical perspectives, which originated with Marx and Engels, only to disappear under the pressures of revisionism. On the other, it moves well beyond limitations established in the earlier period.

Socialist-feminist theory unknowingly recapitulates, then, certain failures of the classical socialist tradition, while also laying the basis to correct them. Like much of the socialist movement of the late nineteenth and early twentieth centuries, it has, willy-nilly, adopted some positions that are essentially at odds with its commitment to Marxism and social revolution. Unlike that movement, however, it has not closed itself off to a revolutionary perspective, and therefore has every interest in transcending the contradiction.

10

The Reproduction
of Labor Power

The argument in these pages has taken the form of a critical reading of certain socialist texts pertaining to women's oppression and women's liberation. It is time to sum up the results.

Marx, Engels, and their immediate followers contributed more to understanding the oppression of women than participants in the modern women's movement usually recognize. At the same time, the socialist tradition's approach to those issues presumed to make up the so-called woman question has been not only incomplete but seriously flawed. In the absence of any stable analytical framework, socialists have had to rely for theoretical guidance on a potpourri of notions drawn from various sources. This 100-year legacy of ambiguity still hampers work on the question of women, although recent developments suggest that the conditions now exist for resolving it, both in theory and in practice. Women today take an increasingly active role in revolutionary change around the world, thereby forcing socialist movements to acknowledge and facilitate their participation. Against this background, recent advances made by socialist-feminist theorists have a critical importance. They reflect a new impetus to develop an adequate theoretical foundation for socialist work on women. And they move beyond many of the weaknesses inherited from the socialist tradition.

Thus, objectively speaking, the concerns of socialists within the modern women's movement and of revolutionaries within the socialist movement have converged. The relationship of women's struggles to social transformation, a question that is simultaneously practical and theoretical, once again appears as a pressing matter on the revolutionary agenda.

In the theoretical sphere, the first requirement for further forward motion is to abandon the idea that the so-called woman question represents an adequate category of analysis. Despite its long history as a serious issue for socialists, the term turns out to have no coherent meaning as a scientific concept. The various notions associated with it actually conceal, as socialist feminists have pointed out, a theoretical problem of fundamental significance: the reproduction of labor power in the context of overall social reproduction. Socialist theorists have never sufficiently confronted this problem, yet the rudiments of a usable approach lie buried just below the surface of Marx's analysis of social reproduction in *Capital*.

The discussion in this and the following chapter suggests a theoretical framework that can situate the phenomenon of women's oppression in terms of social reproduction. Given the weak tradition of theoretical work on the question of women, some words of caution are in order. Theory is, of course, critical to the development of specific analyses of women's situation. Explicitly or implicitly, empirical phenomena must be organized in terms of a theoretical construct in order to be grasped conceptually. At the same time, theory is, by its very nature, severely limited. As a structure of concepts, a theoretical framework simply provides guidance for the understanding of actual societies, past and present. However indispensable this theoretical guidance may be, specific strategies, programs, or tactics for change cannot be deduced directly from theory. Nor can the phenomenon of variation in women's situation over time, and in different societies, be addressed solely by means of theory. These are matters for concrete analysis and historical investigation. By contrast, the argument in these chapters is largely theoretical, and it is therefore necessarily abstract. No attempt is made to develop detailed analyses of women's oppression in, for example, contemporary capitalist society. Such studies, and the political conclusions and tasks they imply, will be undertaken elsewhere.

The phenomenon of women's oppression is a highly individual and subjective experience, often dissected in elaborate descriptive terms, with emphasis on issues of sexuality, interpersonal relations, and ideology. As Michèle Barrett observes, "the women's liberation movement has laid great stress on the experiential aspects of oppression in marriage, in sexual relationships, and in the ideology of femininity and male dominance. In the establishment of 'sexual politics' as a central area of struggle it has succeeded in drawing back the veil on privatized relationships. This politicization of personal life . . . . is a major achievement of feminist activity and one from which Marxism has learnt a great deal." Barrett argues that such analyses are not enough, however, for they have "tended to ignore the ways in which private oppression is related to broader questions of relations of production and the class structure." In the following pages, the focus is on this latter question, in particular, on the economic, or material, aspect of women's situation. However restricted the approach may seem from the point of view of the desire for a full-blown exposition of women's oppression, it is necessary to establish these material foundations. Once laid, they will form the indispensable basis for further work. In sum, the starting point in these chapters is a theoretical perspective on social reproduction, but the ultimate goal is to confront the twin problems of women's oppression and the conditions for women's liberation.[1]

To situate women's oppression in terms of social reproduction and the reproduction of labor power, several concepts need to be specified, beginning with the concept of labor power itself. Marx defines labor power as something latent in all persons: "By labor-power or capacity for labor is to be understood the aggregate of those mental and physical capabilities existing in a human being, which he exercises whenever he produces a use-value of any description." A use-value is "a useful thing" something that "by its properties satisfies human wants of some sort or another." Use-values, and the useful labor that may go into their production, exist in every society, although the precise social form they take varies. "So far . . . as labor is a creator of use-value, is useful labor, it is a necessary condition, independent of all forms of society, for the existence of the human race." Labor power, which is simply the capacity for useful labor, is therefore also "independent of every social phase of [human] existence, or rather, is common to every such phase."[2]

Labor power is a latent capacity borne by a human being. Its potentiality is realized when labor power is put to use—consumed—in a labor process. Once having entered the labor process, the bearer of labor power contributes labor, for "labor-power in use is labor itself."[3] Labor power must therefore be distinguished from the bodily and social existence of its bearer.

Labor processes do not exist in isolation. They are inserted in determinate modes of production. Futhermore, any production is, at one and the same time, reproduction. "A society can no more cease to produce than it can cease to consume. When viewed, therefore, as a connected whole, and as flowing on with incessant renewal, every social process of production is, at the same time, a process of reproduction." Social reproduction entails, finally, the reproduction of the conditions of production. For example, in feudal society, "the product of the serf must . . . suffice to reproduce his conditions of labor, in addition to his subsistence." This is "a circumstance which remains the same under all modes of production. For it is not the result of their specific form, but a natural requisite of all continuous and reproductive labor in general, of any continuing production, which is always simultaneously reproduction, i.e., including reproduction of its own operating conditions."[4] Among other things, social reproduction requires that a supply of labor power always be available to set the labor process in motion.

The bearers of labor power are, however, mortal. Those who work suffer wear and tear. Some are too young to participate in the labor process, others too old. Eventually, every individual dies. Some process that meets the ongoing personal needs of the bearers of labor power as human individuals is therefore a condition of social reproduction, as is some process that replaces workers who have died or withdrawn from the active work force. These processes of maintenance and replacement are often imprecisely, if usefully, conflated under the term reproduction of labor power.[5]

Despite the linguistic similarity of the terms production and reproduction, the processes that make up the reproduction of labor power and those that form part of a society's production are not comparable from a theoretical point of view. Reproduction of labor power is a condition of production, for it *re*posits or *re*places the labor power necessary for production. Reproduction of labor power is not, however, itself a form of production. That is, it does not necessarily involve some determinate combination of raw materials and means of production in a labor process whose result is the product labor power. While some have argued that reproduction of labor power is a production process taking place in family households, in fact such activities represent only one possible mode of renewing the bearers of labor power. Labor camps or dormitory facilities can also be used to maintain workers, and the work force can be replenished through immigration or enslavement as well as by generational replacement of existing workers.

To give preliminary theoretical shape to the problem of reproduction of labor power, Marx introduced the concept of individual consumption (discussed in Chapter 5). Individual consumption refers to the individual direct producer's consumption of means of subsistence. Marx underscores the difference between individual consumption and the productive consumption that takes place in the social labor process. "Such productive consumption is distinguished from individual consumption by this, that the latter uses up products, as means of subsistence for the living individual; the former, as means whereby alone, labor, the labor-power of the living individual, is enabled to act. The product, therefore, of individual consumption, is the consumer himself; the result of productive consumption, is a product distinct from the consumer."[6]

As used here, the concept of individual consumption refers essentially to the daily processes that restore the direct producer and enable him or her to return to work. That is, it does not cover generational replacement of existing workers, nor the maintenance of nonlaboring individuals, such as the elderly and the sick. Neither does it pertain to the recruitment of new workers into the labor force by, for example, enslavement or immigration. Individual consumption concerns solely the maintenance of an individual direct producer already enmeshed in the production process; it permits the worker to engage, again and again, in the immediate production process.[7]

The concept of individual consumption refers, then, to the reproduction of labor power at the level of the immediate production process. At the level of total social reproduction it is not the individual direct producer but the totality of laborers that is maintained and replaced.[8] It is evident that such renewal of the labor force can be accomplished in a variety of ways. In principle, at least, the present set of laborers can be worked to death, and then replaced by an entirely new set. In the more likely case, an existing labor force is replenished both generationally and by new laborers. Children of workers grow up and enter the labor force. Women who had not previously been involved begin to participate in production. Immigrants or slaves from outside a society's boundaries enter its labor force. To the brief extent that Marx considered these questions in general terms, he spoke of laws of population. "Every special historic mode of production has its own special laws of population, historically valid within its limits alone. An abstract law of population exists for plants and animals only, and only in so far as man has not interfered with them."[9] Not all present laborers will work in a subsequent production period, moreover. Some will become sick, disabled, or too old. Others may be excluded, as when protective legislation is enacted to prohibit child labor or women's night work. In sum, at the level of total social reproduction, the concept of reproduction of labor power does not in the least imply the reproduction of a bounded unit of population.[10]

The discussion so far has not required that the gender of direct producers be specified. From a theoretical perspective, it does not yet matter whether they are women or men, so long as they are somehow available to make up the labor force. What raises the question of gender is, of course, the phenomenon of generational replacement of bearers of labor power—that is, replacement of existing workers by new workers from the next generation. If generational replacement is to happen, biological reproduction must intervene. And here, it must be admitted, human beings do not reproduce themselves by parthenogenesis. Women and men are different.

The critical theoretical import of the biological distinction between women and men with respect to childbearing appears, then, at the level of total social reproduction. While reproduction of labor power at the level of total social reproduction does not necessarily entail generational replacement, it is at this theoretical level that the issue must be located.

Before proceeding further, a popular analytical misconception should be acknowledged. People ordinarily experience the processes of generational replacement in individualized kin-based contexts, and attempts to develop a theory of the reproduction of labor power often focus on the family unit or household as a starting point. Such a procedure, however understandable, represents a serious confusion with respect to theoretical levels. As commonly understood, the family is a kin-based social structure in which take place processes contributing to the worker's daily maintenance—his or her ongoing individual consumption. Families also provide the context in which children are born and grow up, and they frequently include individuals who are not currently participating in the labor force. In most societies, families therefore act as important sites for both maintenance and generational replacement of existing and potential workers.[11] They are not, however, the only places where workers renew themselves on a daily basis. For example, many workers in South Africa live in barracks near their work, and are permitted to visit their families in outlying areas once a year. Furthermore, children do not necessarily constitute a family's only contribution to the replenishment of society's labor power. Other family members may at times enter the work force, at harvest, for instance, or during economic crises. Finally, families are not the only source of such replenishment; other possibilities, as previously mentioned, include migration and enslavement of foreign populations. These observations demonstrate that the identification of the family as the sole site of maintenance of labor power overstates its role at the level of immediate production. Simultaneously, it fetishizes the family at the level of total social reproduction, by representing generational replacement as the only source of renewal of society's labor force.

In any case, it is premature from a theoretical point of view to introduce a specific social site of reproduction of labor power, such as the family, into the discussion at this stage. Two further observations should, however, be made concerning the existence of a biological distinction between women and men in the area of childbearing. First, biological differences constitute the material precondition for the social construction of gender differences, as well as a direct material factor in the differential position of the sexes in a society.[12] Second, sex differences cannot be considered apart from their existence within a definite social system, and nothing more can be said, at this point, about their significance for the process of reproduction of labor power. The concepts pertaining to the question of reproduction of labor power have been developed so far without reference to a specific mode of production. Hence, the discussion has necessarily proceeded at an extreme level of abstraction—or, as Marx puts it, speaking of the labor process, "independently of the particular form it assumes under given social conditions."[13] Let us move, now, to a consideration of the reproduction of labor power in class society.

The appropriation of surplus labor, or exploitation, constitutes the foundation of class relations. In a class society, the ruling class appropriates surplus labor performed by an exploited class of direct producers. Marx sums up the essence of class society in an important passage:

> The specific economic form, in which unpaid surplus-labor is pumped out of direct producers, determines the relationship of rulers and ruled, as it grows directly out of production itself and, in turn, reacts upon it as a determining element. Upon this, however, is founded the entire formation of the economic community which grows up out of the production relations themselves, thereby simultaneously its specific political form. It is always the direct relationship of the owners of the conditions of production to the direct producers—a relation always naturally corresponding to a definite stage in the development of the methods of labor and thereby its social productivity—which reveals the innermost secret, the hidden basis of the entire social structure, and with it the political

form of the relation of sovereignty and dependence, in short, the corresponding specific form of the state.[14]

In a class society, the concept of labor power acquires a specific class meaning. Labor power refers to the capacity of a member of the class of direct producers to perform the surplus labor the ruling class appropriates. In other words, the bearers of labor power make up the exploited class. For a class society, the concept of reproduction of labor power pertains, strictly speaking, to the maintenance and renewal of the class of bearers of labor power subject to exploitation. While a class society must also develop some process of maintaining and replacing the individuals who make up the ruling class, it cannot be considered part of the reproduction of labor power in society. By definition, labor power in a class society is borne only by members of the class of direct producers.[15]

Marx contrasts the surplus labor performed by direct producers in a class society to their necessary labor, defining both kinds of labor in terms of the time expended by a single producer during one working day. Necessary labor is that portion of the day's work through which the producer achieves his own reproduction. The remaining portion of the day's work is surplus labor, appropriated by the exploiting class.[16] In reality, a portion of the direct producer's labor may also be devoted to securing the reproduction of other members of the exploited class. Where, for example, children, the elderly, or a wife do not themselves enter into surplus production as direct producers, a certain amount of labor time must be expended for their maintenance. Marx was never explicit about what the concepts of individual consumption and necessary labor cover. As discussed above, the concept of individual consumption has been restricted here to the direct producer's immediate maintenance. Necessary labor is used, however, to cover all labor performed in the course of the maintenance and renewal of both direct producers and members of the subordinate class not currently working as direct producers.

Necessary labor ordinarily includes several constituent processes. In the first place, it provides a certain amount of means of subsistence for individual consumption by direct producers. In a feudal society, for example, direct producers may retain a portion of the total product. In a capitalist society, wages permit the purchase of commodities in the market. In most cases, the raw means of subsistence so acquired do not themselves ensure the maintenance of the laborer. A certain amount of supplementary labor must be performed in order that the necessaries can be consumed in appropriate form: firewood must be chopped, meals cooked, garden plots tended, clothes repaired, and so forth. In addition to these labor processes facilitating the individual consumption of direct producers, two other sets of labor processes can be identified. A portion of necessary labor goes to provide means of subsistence to maintain members of the exploited classes not currently working as direct producers—the elderly, the sick, a wife. And an important series of labor processes associated with the generational replacement of labor power may also take place—that is, the bearing and raising of the children of the subordinate class. As discussed above, these various aspects of necessary labor have a certain autonomy from a theoretical point of view. Together they represent an indispensable condition for the reproduction of labor power and therefore for overall social reproduction. It should be noted that the concept of necessary labor pertains strictly to tasks associated with the reproduction of labor power in the exploited class. Individuals in the ruling class also require daily maintenance and ordinarily replace themselves through generational reproduction. Such activities do not qualify as necessary labor in Marx's sense, however, for they do not concern the renewal of exploitable labor power.

In a given class society, the circumstances and outcome of the processes of reproduction of labor power are essentially indeterminate or contingent. To maintain otherwise would be to fall into the functionalist argument that a system's needs for labor power must inevitably be fulfilled by the workings of that system. The social relations through which necessary labor is carried out therefore cannot be postulated independent of specific historical cases. In particular, the family, however defined, is not a timeless universal of human society. As with any social structure, the form kin-based relationships take always depends on social development, and is potentially a terrain of struggle.[17]

Although analytically distinct, necessary labor and surplus labor may lose their specificity and separateness when experienced in the real life of concrete labor processes. Several examples suggest the range of possibilities. First, in a feudal society in which serfs pay rent in kind, bringing the lord a share of the product, necessary labor and surplus labor interpenetrate as labor processes. In the case of labor rent, by contrast, in which serfs work the lord's fields independently from their own plot, a clear spatial and temporal demarcation divides surplus labor from necessary labor. In capitalist societies, as we shall see in Chapter 11, a distinction appears between two components of necessary labor, one carried out in conjunction with surplus labor and the other taking place outside the sphere of surplus labor appropriation. Last, consider the hypothetical example of a slave system that imports laborers from outside its boundaries, and forces them to work at a literally killing pace. Under such conditions, generational replacement might become almost impossible, and the amount of necessary labor could be reduced to nearly zero.

Of the three aspects of necessary labor—maintenance of direct producers, maintenance of nonlaboring members of the subordinate class, and generational replacement processes—only the last requires, in an absolute sense, that there be a sex division of labor of at least a minimal kind. If children are to be born, it is women who will carry and deliver them. Women belonging to the subordinate class have, therefore, a special role with respect to the generational replacement of labor power. While they may also be direct producers, it is their differential role in the reproduction of labor power that lies at the root of their oppression in class society. This differential role can be situated in theoretical terms. The paragraphs that follow, which elaborate the argument first made by Paddy Quick, offer such a theoretical framework as a basis for the analysis of women's oppression.[18]

The argument hinges on the relationship of childbearing to the appropriation of surplus labor in class society. Childbearing threatens to diminish the contribution a woman in the subordinate class can make as a direct producer and as a participant in necessary labor. Pregnancy and lactation involve, at the minimum, several months of somewhat reduced capacity to work.[19] Even when a woman continues to participate in surplus production, childbearing therefore interferes to some extent with the immediate appropriation of surplus labor. Moreover, her labor is ordinarily required for the maintenance of labor power, and pregnancy and lactation may lessen a woman's capacity in this area as well. From the ruling class's short-term point of view, then, childbearing potentially entails a costly decline in the mother's capacity to work, while at the same time requiring that she be maintained during the period of diminished contribution. In principle, some of the necessary labor that provides for her during that time might otherwise have formed part of the surplus labor appropriated by the ruling class. That is, necessary labor ordinarily has to increase somewhat to cover her maintenance during the childbearing period, implying a corresponding decrease in surplus labor. At the same time, childbearing is of benefit to the ruling class, for it must occur if the labor force is to be replenished through generational replacement. From the point of view of the dominant class, there is therefore a potential contradiction between its immediate need to appropriate surplus labor and its long-term requirement for a class to perform it.

The argument outlined in the previous paragraph analyzes the potential implications of an empirical phenomenon—women's capacity to bear children—for the processes of surplus labor appropriation. The discussion operates, it must be emphasized, at the level of theory, and it reveals a contradiction. To resolve the contradiction in an actual society, the dominant class prefers strategies that minimize necessary labor over the long term while simultaneously ensuring the reproduction of labor power. To what extent it actually succeeds in implementing such strategies is, of course, a matter of class struggle.

As one element in the historical resolution of the contradiction, actual arrangements for the reproduction of labor power usually take advantage of relationships between women and men that are based on sexuality and kinship. Other adults, ordinarily the biological father and his kin group, or male kin of the childbearing woman herself, historically have had the responsibility for making sure that the woman is provided for during the period of diminished activity associated with childbearing. Men of the subordinate class thereby acquire a special historical role with respect to the generational replacement of labor power: to ensure that means of subsistence are provided to the childbearing woman.

In principle, women's and men's differential roles in the reproduction of labor power are of finite duration. They come into play only during the woman's actual childbearing months. In reality, the roles take specific historical form in the variety of social structures known as the family. From a theoretical point of view, families in subordinate classes may be conceptualized as kin-based social units within which men have greater responsibility for the provision of means of subsistence to childbearing women during the period of their reduced working contribution. As institutionalized structures in actual class societies, the families of a subordinate class ordinarily become major social sites for the performance of the maintenance as well as the generational replacement aspects of necessary labor. Here, then, is one source for the historical division of labor according to sex that assigns women and men different roles with respect to necessary and surplus labor. Generally, women have greater responsibility for the ongoing tasks associated with necessary labor, and especially for work connected with children. Men, correspondingly, often have greater responsibility for the provision of material means of subsistence, a responsibility that is ordinarily accompanied by their disproportionately greater involvement in the performance of surplus labor.

While women have historically had greater responsibility for the ongoing tasks of necessary labor in class societies, it is not accurate to say that there is some universal domestic sphere separate from the world of public production. In class societies based on agriculture— feudalism, for example—the labor processes of necessary labor are frequently integrated with those of surplus production.[20] It is the development of capitalism, as Chapter 11 shows, that creates a sharp demarcation between the arena in which surplus labor is performed and a sphere that can properly be called domestic. To the extent that analysts assert the universality of some invariant domestic sphere, they are in fact projecting onto noncapitalist class societies a distinction that is the product of capitalist relations of production.

The exact form by which men obtain more means of subsistence than needed for their own individual consumption varies from society to society, but the arrangement is ordinarily legitimated by their domination of women and reinforced by institutionalized structures of female oppression. The ruling class, in order to stabilize the reproduction of labor power as well as to keep the amount of necessary labor at acceptable levels, encourages male supremacy within the exploited class. Quick outlines the dynamic:

> Any attempt by women to appropriate to themselves more
> than is required for their subsistence is an indirect demand
> for part of the surplus appropriated by the ruling class. Thus
> male authority over women is supported and even enforced
> by the ruling class. On the other hand, any attempt by men to
> evade their "responsibilities" for the support of women is also
> resisted, within the confines of a system which relies on male
> supremacy. Men's control of means of subsistence greater than
> needed for their own reproduction on a day-to-day level is
> "granted" to them only in order to enable them to contribute
> to the reproduction of their class.[21]

Such strategies work on behalf of the dominant class, whatever the immediate advantages of male supremacy to men.

It is the provision by men of means of subsistence to women during the childbearing period, and not the sex division of labor in itself, that forms the material basis for women's subordination in class society. The fact that women and men are differentially involved in the reproduction of labor power during pregnancy and lactation, and often for much longer, does not necessarily constitute a source of oppression. Divisions of labor exist in all societies. Even in the most egalitarian hunting and gathering society, a variety of tasks is accomplished every day, requiring a division of labor. Differences among people arising out of biological and social development also characterize every society. Some individuals may be mentally retarded or physically handicapped. Some may be heterosexual, others homosexual. Some may marry, some may not. And, of course, some may be men, and others women, with the capacity to bear children. The social significance of divisions of labor and of individual differences is constructed in the context of the actual society in which they are embedded. In class societies, women's childbearing capacity creates contradictions from the point of view of the dominant class's need to appropriate surplus labor. The oppression of women in the exploited class develops in the process of the class struggle over the resolution of these contradictions.

Women in the ruling class may also be subordinated to the men of their class. Where such subordination exists it rests, ultimately, on their special role with respect to the generational replacement of individual members of the ruling class. As the socialist tradition has argued, the issue here is property. If property comes to be held by men and bequeathed to children, female oppression becomes a handy way to ensure the paternity of those children. In a particular society, shared experiences of and cultural responses to female oppression may produce a certain degree of solidarity among women across class lines. While this solidarity has a basis in reality, and can be of serious political import, the situations of women in the dominant and exploited classes are fundamentally distinct from a theoretical perspective. Only women in the subordinate class participate in the maintenance and replacement of the indispensable force that keeps a class society going —exploitable labor power.

The existence of women's oppression in class societies is, it must be emphasized, a historical phenomenon. It can be analyzed, as here, with the guidance of a theoretical framework, but it is not itself deducible theoretically. Confusion as to the character of women's oppression has frequently generated an unproductive search for some ultimate theoretical cause or origin of women's oppression. Origins exist, of course, but they are historical, not theoretical.[22]

The argument to this point may be recapitulated as follows. Human beings have the capacity to produce more use-values than they need for their own immediate subsistence. In a class society, this potential is organized to the benefit of a ruling class, which appropriates the surplus labor of a subordinate class according to some determinate set of social relations. For this class society to survive, an exploitable labor force must always be available to perform surplus labor. Workers, however, do not live forever; they suffer "wear and tear and death, [and] must be continually replaced by, at the very least, an equal amount of fresh labor-power." Where replacement is through generational reproduction, the fact that human beings fall into two distinct biological groups, women and men, comes into play. Women's somewhat diminished capacity to work during the childbearing period potentially creates a contradiction for the ruling class. Out of the class struggle over resolving this contradiction, a wide variety of forms of reproduction of labor power has developed in the course of history. In virtually all cases, they entail men's greater responsibility for provision of material means of subsistence, women's greater responsibility for the ongoing tasks of necessary labor, and institutionalized forms of male domination over women. While exceptions exist, and may indeed offer important insights on the question of reproduction of labor power in class society, the historical legacy remains one that has been characterized, for better or worse, as patriarchal. In this sense, Joan Kelly is right to point out that "patriarchy . . . is at home at home. The private family is its proper domain."[23]

In most class societies, women of the exploited class participate to some extent in surplus production as well as in necessary labor.[24] Their specific responsibilities and subordination in the tasks of necessary labor may carry consequences for the work they do in the area of surplus production. For instance, individual responsibility for child care in capitalist society renders women exceptionally vulnerable to the oppressive conditions of home work. Conversely, involvement in surplus labor may affect the forms of women's necessary labor. On American plantations, for example, most slave women worked in the master's fields, while the tasks of cooking and child care were collectively carried out by older women and very young children.[25] At a particular juncture in the development of a given class society, the oppression of women in the exploited class is shaped not only by women's relationship to the processes of maintenance and renewal of labor power, but by the extent and character of their participation in surplus labor.

The actual working out of a specific class society's forms of reproduction of labor power is a matter for historical investigation—and, in the present, for political intervention as well. Certain tendencies can be deduced, however, from the theoretical framework just presented. In situations that minimize the importance of generational replacement of labor power, sex divisions of labor and family institutions in the exploited class may be relatively weak. If a ruling class relies on migrant labor from outside the society's boundaries, for example, it might house these workers in barracks, put women and men to work at similar jobs, encourage contraception or sterilization, and ignore the effects of heavy work on women in the last months of pregnancy. Ordinarily, generational replacement provides the major part of a society's need for the reproduction of labor power. Here, a severe labor shortage caused by war, famine, or natural catastrophe would tend to exaggerate the contradictory pressures on women workers. Depending on the historical situation, either the role of the family as the site of generational reproduction, or the importance of women's participation in surplus labor, or both, might be emphasized. During a period in which the ruling class's need to maximize surplus labor overwhelms long-range considerations, all individuals in the exploited class might be mobilized into surplus production, causing severe dislocation in its institutions of family life and male dominance. Such was the case in industrializing England during the nineteenth century, and, such, it can be argued, is again the case in the advanced capitalist countries today.

These tendencies will not proceed unopposed. Migrant workers may fight against their isolation from kin. Native-born workers may oppose the use of foreign labor. Women may refuse to stay home to bear and raise children. Men may resist the participation of women in the labor force. Workers may support legislation banning child labor. Women and men may organize to defend the existing forms of their institutions of family life. In short, the processes of reproduction of labor power in class society ordinarily constitute an important terrain of battle.

11

Beyond
Domestic Labor

The preceding chapter established some basic concepts pertaining to the reproduction of labor power, and used them to address the question of women's oppression in class society. We can now turn to the problem of women's oppression in the context of capitalist social reproduction. In capitalist societies, exploitation takes place through the appropriation of surplus value, and surplus labor appears in the form of wage labor. Labor power acquires the particular form of a commodity, bought and sold on the market. This commodity possesses the peculiarly useful property, as Marx discovered, of being a source of value. Although it is exchanged in the market, it is not a commodity like any other, for it is not produced capitalistically. Instead, some process of reproduction of the bearers of exploitable labor power continually brings labor power into being as a commodity. Such a process is a condition of existence for capital. In Marx's words, the worker "constantly produces material, objective wealth, but in the form of capital, of an alien power that dominates and exploits him; and the capitalist as constantly produces labor-power, but in the form of a subjective source of wealth, separated from the objects in and by which it can alone be realized; in short he produces the laborer, but as a wage-laborer. This incessant reproduction, this perpetuation of the laborer, is the sine qua non of capitalist production." Such dramatic statements are true in a broad sense, but they shed little light on the theoretical status of the reproduction of labor power in capitalist society, and even less on the manner in which it takes place.[1]

Capitalist reproduction demands that labor power be available as

151

a commodity for purchase in adequate quantity and quality and at an appropriate price. However imperfectly, these needs shape the processes that maintain the existing bearers of labor power, while at the same time the labor force as a whole is continually reconstituted to accord with future needs. The manner in which the sellers of labor power live out their lives is, in principle, a matter of indifference to the capitalist class. By contrast, it represents a central concern for the bearers of labor power. In this sense, the circumstances under which reproduction of labor power takes place, which include the determination of its price, are always an outcome of class struggle.

Several characteristics of the reproduction of labor power and women's oppression in capitalist society arise from the logic of capitalist accumulation itself. Perhaps most consequential is the special form taken by necessary labor. Necessary labor becomes divided into two components. One, which we can call the social component of necessary labor, is indissolubly bound with surplus labor in the capitalist production process. As Marx showed, the working day in capitalist employment includes a certain amount of time during which the worker produces value equivalent to the value of the commodities necessary for the reproduction of his or her labor power. This is, for Marx, the worker's necessary labor, for which he or she is paid. For the rest of the working day, the worker produces surplus value for the capitalist, value for which he or she is not paid. From the point of view of the worker, however, no distinction exists between necessary and surplus labor time, and the wage appears to cover both. In Marx's words, "the wage-form thus extinguishes every trace of the division of the working-day into necessary labor and surplus labor, into paid and unpaid labor. All labor appears as paid labor."[2]

Marx did not discuss a second component of necessary labor in capitalist society, one that we can call the domestic component of necessary labor—or domestic labor. Domestic labor is the portion of necessary labor that is performed outside the sphere of capitalist production. For the reproduction of labor power to take place, both the domestic and the social components of necessary labor are required. That is, wages may enable a worker to purchase commodities, but additional labor—domestic labor—must generally be performed before they are consumed. In addition, many of the labor processes associated with the generational replacement of labor power are carried out as part of domestic labor. In capitalist societies, then, the relationship between surplus and necessary labor has two aspects. On the one hand, the demarcation between surplus labor and the social component of necessary labor is obscured through the payment of wages in the capitalist labor process. On the other hand, the domestic component of necessary labor becomes dissociated from wage labor, the arena in which surplus labor is performed.

As accumulation proceeds, the opposition between wage labor and domestic labor sharpens. Capitalism's drive to increase surplus value by enhancing productivity, especially through industrialization, forces a severe spatial, temporal, and institutional separation between domestic labor and the capitalist production process. Capitalists must organize production so that more and more of it is under their direct control in workshops and factories, where wage labor is performed for specified amounts of time. Wage labor comes to have a character that is wholly distinct from the laborer's life away from the job, including his or her involvement in the domestic component of necessary labor. At the same time the wage mediates both daily maintenance and generational replacement processes, supplemented or sometimes replaced by state contributions. That is, the social component of the worker's necessary labor facilitates the reproduction of labor power indirectly, by providing money that must then be exchanged to acquire commodities. These two characteristics—the separation of wage labor from domestic labor and the payment of wages—are materialized in the development of specialized sites and social units for the performance of domestic labor. Working-class families located in private households represent the dominant form in most capitalist societies, but domestic labor also takes place in labor camps, barracks, orphanages, hospitals, prisons, and other such institutions.[3]

In capitalist societies, the burden of the domestic component of necessary labor rests disproportionately on women, while the provision of commodities tends to be disproportionately the responsibility of men, fulfillable through participation in wage labor. This differential positioning of women and men with respect to surplus labor and the two components of necessary labor, which is generally accompanied by a system of male supremacy, originates as a historical legacy from oppressive divisions of labor in earlier class societies. It is then strengthened by the particular separation between domestic and wage labor generated by the capitalist mode of production. Domestic labor increasingly takes place in specialized social units, whose isolation in space and time from wage labor is further emphasized by male supremacy. These conditions stamp domestic labor with its specific character.

Experientially, the particular nature of domestic labor in industrial capitalist society gives rise, for both women and men, to intense feelings of opposition between one's private life and some public sphere. The highly institutionalized demarcation of domestic labor from wage labor in a context of male supremacy forms the basis for a series of powerful ideological structures, which develop a forceful life of their own. Isolation of the units of domestic labor appears to be a natural separation of women from men as well. Confinement to a world that is walled off from capitalist production seems to be woman's time-honored natural setting. A series of correlated opposites embodies the seemingly universal division of life into two spheres of experience: private and public, domestic and social, family and work, women and men. Rooted in the economic workings of the capitalist mode of production, and reinforced by a system of male supremacy, this ideology of separate spheres has a force that is extremely difficult to transcend. Where some categories of male workers command wages sufficient to maintain a private household staffed by a nonworking wife, the ideology takes a particularly stubborn institutional form.

The drive for accumulation causes constant change in capitalist societies, including changes in the quantity and character of the domestic component of necessary labor. As Marx demonstrated, capitalist accumulation depends on the growth of surplus labor, appropriated in the form of absolute and relative surplus value.[4] He discussed these two forms of augmented surplus value in terms of a particular society's established working day of ten hours in capitalist production, divided into five hours each of necessary and surplus labor. If the hours of work are extended to, say, twelve hours, the capitalists appropriate two hours' worth of absolute surplus value for each worker. If the amount of necessary labor falls to, say, four hours, they appropriate an hours' worth of relative surplus value for each worker. While both processes contribute to capitalist accumulation, relative surplus value ordinarily plays a greater part, for the established working day of an individual can only be extended so far. Marx analyzed two major ways of producing relative surplus value that are available to the capitalists: introduction of machinery, technological improvements, and the like, and reduction in the costs of the means of subsistence. Together, he noted, they fuel capitalism's penetration into all sectors of social life.

Capital's need to augment surplus value implies a contradiction between domestic labor and wage labor. As a component of necessary labor, domestic labor potentially takes away from the commitment workers can make to performing surplus labor through participation in wage work. Objectively, then, it competes with capital's drive for accumulation. If one tends one's own garden plot, chops one's own firewood, cooks one's own meals, and walks six miles to work, the amount of time and energy available for wage labor is less than if one buys food in a supermarket, lives in a centrally heated apartment building, eats in restaurants, and takes public transportation to work. Similarly, if one supports another person, for example a wife, in order that she take care of domestic labor, that person is less available to participate in wage labor, while at the same time one's own wage must cover the costs of her means of consumption. To the extent that the domestic labor of a capitalist society takes place within private households, the pressure of capitalist accumulation results in a tendency to decrease the amount performed in each household. That is, the domestic component of necessary labor is severely reduced. At the same time, more household members may enter the work force, increasing the total amount of wage labor performed by the household, a phenomenon akin to intensification of a single worker's labor. In short, reduction of domestic labor potentially creates both relative and absolute surplus value.

A major way to reduce domestic labor is to socialize its tasks. Laundromats, stores selling ready-made clothing, and fast-food chains, for instance, remove domestic labor tasks to the profit-making sector, where they also provide new opportunities for capitalist entrepreneurs. Public education and health care make aspects of domestic labor the responsibility of the state, at the same time distributing the costs of reproduction of labor power more widely through contributions and taxes. A society's total domestic labor can also be reduced by employing institutionalized populations (prison labor, army labor), and by importing migrant labor from outside national boundaries. Over time, the tendency to reduce domestic labor affects the units in which it is performed in numerous ways, many of which have been documented by scholars in terms of changes in the family and in the relationship between work and the family. The history of the tendency's impact on sites of reproduction of labor power that are not based on kin relations (prisons, dormitories, migrant labor camps) is less well studied.

The domestic component of necessary labor cannot be completely socialized in capitalist society. The main barrier is economic, for the costs are extremely high in such areas as child rearing and household maintenance.[5] Profitable chains of day-care centers have yet to be developed, for example, and housecleaning services have not been able to reduce costs to a level that makes them available to working-class households. Political and ideological barriers to the socialization of domestic labor also play a role. Socialization of work formerly done in the home may be experienced as an attack on established working-class life-styles, as when the introduction of public education encountered opposition among some working-class militants fearful of capitalist indoctrination. The recent expansion of nursing home care for the elderly has sometimes been opposed as part of a general decline in so-called traditional family values. Working-class families in capitalist societies have generally welcomed advances in the socialization of domestic labor, however. In so doing they register their appreciation of the labor saved, as well as of the potential qualitative enhancement of social experience.[6] A different type of political barrier to the socialization of domestic labor exists in the case of migrant workers housed in dormitories or labor camps. Such arrangements reduce domestic labor and cheapen the cost of renewal, but, as recent events in South Africa show, they also represent a political threat to the ruling class by facilitating organization. An ultimate barrier to the socialization of domestic labor is constituted by biology. While domestic labor might conceivably be reduced to a minimum through the socialization of most of its tasks, the basic physiological process of childbearing will continue to be the province of women.[7]

The tendency for domestic labor to be reduced in capitalist society remains, of course, no more than a general trend. Actual arrangements develop out of and depend on the history of a particular society, and are affected by class conflict within it. It is in this context that such phenomena as the family wage, female labor-force participation, discrimination against women in the labor market, protective legislation, and child labor laws must be analyzed. Generally speaking, the specific amounts and kinds of domestic labor performed in a particular society are an outcome of the struggle between contending classes at several levels. Domestic labor has, in fact, a highly contradictory role within capitalist social reproduction. On the one hand, it forms an essential condition for capitalism. If capitalist production is to take place, it must have labor power, and if labor power is to be available, domestic labor must be performed. On the other hand, domestic labor stands in the way of capitalism's drive for profit, for it also limits the availability of labor power. From the point of view of capital, domestic labor is simultaneously indispensable and an obstacle to accumulation. Over the long term, the capitalist class seeks to stabilize the reproduction of labor power at a low cost and with a minimum of domestic labor. At the same time, the working class, either as a united force or fragmented into competing sectors, strives to win the best conditions possible for its own renewal, which may include a particular level and type of domestic labor.

Domestic labor takes as its raw material a certain quantity and quality of commodities bought with the wages workers obtain by selling labor power on the market. How are wages determined?

In Marx's view, the value of labor power is determined by the amount of socially necessary labor incorporated in the means of subsistence needed to maintain and replace the laborer. That is, the value of labor power equals the value of the commodities the worker requires. Marx cautions, however, that into the determination of this value enters a "historical and moral element." Two other factors also affect the determination of the value of labor power: first, the costs of developing labor power with the appropriate skills; and second, "its natural diversity, the difference between the labor power of men and women, of children and adults," a fact that "makes a great difference in the cost of maintaining the family of the laborer, and in the value of the labor power of the adult male." Throughout most of his argument, Marx makes the simplifying assumption that the effect of these various factors can be excluded.[8]

Recent work on the value of labor power, particularly that developed in the context of socialist feminism, has pointed to ambiguities in Marx's formulation. Of special interest here is the discussion centered on the role of nonworking women and other dependents supported by the worker's wage. The question of the contribution, if any, made by domestic labor to the determination of the value of labor power has given rise to a prolonged controversy known as the domestic labor debate (reviewed in Chapter 2). The most satisfactory answer to this question was first proposed by Ira Gerstein and developed in more rigorous fashion by Paul Smith. Both argue that domestic labor, as concrete, useful labor, simply transfers the value of the commodities purchased with the wage to the labor power borne by the worker. The norm of the family wage—a wage paid to a single male worker sufficient to cover the consumption of his entire family—represents, for Gerstein, a specific instance of how the "historical and moral element" affects the determination of the value of labor power.[9] That is, wage norms not only include a certain quantity and quality of commodities, they also imply a certain quantity and quality of domestic labor.

The wage of a worker corresponds, then, to the total value of the commodities required for his or her maintenance and replacement in particular, historically established, conditions. These conditions may or may not include such nonworking dependents as wives, children, aged parents, and so forth. Existence of the family wage for some male workers has prompted discussion concerning the proper interpretation of the "historical and moral element" in this case. Some claim that the family wage represents a higher standard of living and therefore a victory for the working class in its battle with capital. The family wage has been available, however, only to certain sectors within the working class; most working-class households in capitalist societies cannot manage on one income. Other commentators therefore argue that the family wage functions as a concession made by capital to certain sectors of the working class in return for a political stability based on male supremacy. In this view, the family wage constitutes not a victory but a privilege offered to a subgroup of male workers. This controversy cannot be resolved in the abstract. The significance of the demand for and achievement of the family wage must be ascertained through concrete analysis, not logical deduction. It should be clear, however, that the presence of a nonworking wife does not lower the value of male labor power, and therefore is not of inevitable benefit to the capitalist class. Quite the contrary: to have a wife not in the labor force requires a male wage large enough to cover the consumption of two adults. The capitalist class will evaluate such a wage level very carefully, weighing economic costs against political and ideological benefits and pressures.[10]

Socialists have sometimes endorsed the family wage as part of a general strategy to defend the working-class family, meaning a heterosexual nuclear unit with a single male wage earner. Defense of the working class's right to the best conditions for its own renewal in no way entails a particular fixed social form, however. In some situations, the demand for a family wage may actually distort the legitimate fight for the best conditions possible for the reproduction of the working class as bearers of labor power. For example, where female-headed households make up a large sector of the population, demand for a family wage will most likely threaten women's position in the labor market and deepen divisions already existing within the working class. In short, the specific content of socialist demands in the area of reproduction of labor power (as elsewhere) must flow from a concrete analysis. As a first condition for developing such an analysis, socialists need to discard rigid ideological notions about the working-class family as invariant, as the sole social unit in which labor power is maintained and replaced, and as the always deserving recipient of a family wage.

Viewed from the perspective of overall social reproduction, the reproduction of labor power is not, it must be recalled, a bounded process of renewal of a fixed unit of population. Capitalist reproduction requires only that a more or less adequate labor force be available to set the production process in motion. In principle, capitalists may work the present labor force to death, so long as they have some means of recruiting a new one. In practice, they generally adopt other alternatives. Ordinarily, a society's active labor force is made up of some mix of established and new workers—the latter including children of established workers, members of the industrial reserve army, and immigrants.

At this level, reproduction of labor power becomes a question of the reproduction of the working class as a whole. The term working class is sometimes interpreted as referring solely to wage workers. In this usage, for instance, only women workers would be considered working-class women. Such categorization abandons all those not in the labor force—children, the elderly, and the disabled, as well as nonworking wives—to a theoretical limbo outside the class structure. Here, the working class will be viewed as consisting of a society's past, present, and potential wage labor force, together with all those whose maintenance depends on the wage but who do not or cannot themselves enter wage labor. At any given moment, it comprises the active labor force, the industrial reserve army, and that portion of the relative surplus population not incorporated in the industrial reserve army. The history of capitalism demonstrates that this last category has at times included very few persons, aside from infants and toddlers. Even those seriously handicapped from birth have sometimes been forced into the labor market, and have therefore belonged, however tenuously, to the industrial reserve army.

In order to place women theoretically in terms of the working class, some analysts have assigned them as a group to the industrial reserve army. Women, they argue, form a reserve, which can easily be called upon during periods of expansion and returned to the home when no longer needed. Women not only participate in this cyclical movement, they represent an increasingly important element of the contemporary floating, latent, and stagnant layers within the industrial reserve army. Most such discussions suggest, finally, that women's entry into the ranks of the industrial reserve army is rather recent, and leave unanswered the question of their previous location within the working class. While this analysis of women in terms of their position in the industrial reserve army is suggestive, a more adequate view would acknowledge that major sectors of the female population have been present in the industrial reserve army for decades, even if, in Engels's words, "it is only at times of exceptionally good trade that they realize [it]." Those working-class women not in the industrial reserve army would form part of the relative surplus population.[11]

The question of women's position with respect to the industrial reserve army is not, in fact, a theoretical one, but a matter for concrete analysis. Which groups of women in a given society move more actively between the industrial reserve army and wage labor? How large are the numbers and how intense the participation in the various sectors? Which groups of women remain locked in the relative surplus population outside the industrial reserve army, and why? What are the political and ideological obstacles to certain women's entry into wage labor? What are the determinants of any movement that can be observed? In a particular capitalist society, for example, unmarried daughters living in their father's households may work until marriage. Elsewhere, daughters from rural areas may migrate to industrial concentrations, where they become the major support of families left behind. Women in immigrant, but not in native, households, or black, but not white, mothers of school-age children, may enter wage labor. Wives may normally hold jobs until children are born, or after children enter school, or after they leave home. In periods of intensifying labor exploitation, mothers of preschool children may engage in wage labor. As Veronica Beechey points out, "the question of who constitutes the preferred sources of the industrial reserve army in any given historical situation must be concretely investigated. It cannot be derived from the logic of capitalism, but is determined by the class struggle—by the strategies employed by individual capitals, by trade union practices, and by state policies which are themselves a product of class struggle."[12] Beechey argues that married women in Britain have been an important sector of the industrial reserve army since World War II. To which it must be added that the general trend in the advanced capitalist countries is toward equalization of participation rates among different categories of women, in the direction of increased commitment of all women to wage labor. In the United States, for example, labor-force participation rates among different groups of women have been converging. As many white as black wives are in the work force, more mothers of very young children are now working, and so forth.

Equalization of female labor-force participation is a particular manifestation of the structural tendency in capitalist society toward free availability of all labor power. Like the tendency toward the reduction of domestic labor, this tendency embodies the forward drive of capitalist accumulation. Marx discussed it explicitly in the context of his analysis of competition among individual capitals. Capital moves from sectors of relatively low profit rate into sectors of high profit rate, thereby contributing to the equalization of the rate of profit in different branches of production and among different individual capitals. The more mobile capital and labor power can be, the more easily and quickly can competition work its effects in establishing an average rate of profit. In principle, then, capitalist accumulation demands perfect mobility of labor power and hence, in Marx's words, "the abolition of all laws preventing the laborers from transferring from one sphere of production to another and from one local center of production to another; indifference of the laborer to the nature of his labor; the greatest possible reduction of labor in all spheres of production to simple labor; the elimination of all vocational prejudices among laborers; and last but not least, a subjugation of the laborer to the capitalist mode of production." Where barriers to mobility exist, the force of capitalist expansion attempts to push them aside. If certain obstacles remain in place, they may in part reflect the contradictory position of the capitalist class, caught within the conflicting pressures of its long-term economic demand for perfect mobility, its short-term requirements for different categories of workers, and its need to maintain political and ideological hegemony over a divided working class. To the extent that women remain segregated within and without the labor force, such conflicting factors play an important role.[13]

As those primarily responsible for domestic labor, women contribute heavily to the maintenance and renewal of the relative surplus population, as well as the active labor force. Traditionally, as Marx observes, "society in its fractional parts undertakes for Mr. Capitalist the business of keeping his virtual instrument of labor—its wear and tear—intact as reserve for later use."[14] The working class pays for most of the upkeep of the surplus population, and working-class women do most of the domestic tasks required. To the extent, however, that women enter wage labor, they become less able to take care of members of the household not presently in the work force. In a particular situation, the advantages to capital of increased female labor-force participation may outweigh the inroads into women's capacity to perform domestic labor. State intervention of various kinds may then become more important in the maintenance of the relative surplus population. In the United States today, for example, elderly and disabled persons increasingly become the direct responsibility of governmental agencies.

To this point, the concept of reproduction of labor power in capitalist society has been developed as an economic phenomenon. Political and ideological issues have entered the discussion mainly in the course of describing the way structural tendencies located at the economic level take specific form in actual societies. There is, however, an important political phenomenon that has its root in the economic workings of the capitalist mode of production. The tendency toward equality of all human beings, a fundamental political feature of bourgeois society, has a basis in the articulation within the economic level of production and circulation. (This is not to say that equality of persons, even in formal terms, is an inevitable accompaniment of capitalist relations of production. As it turns out, numerous obstacles get in the way of the development of this tendency. The extent to which the tendency toward equality of persons becomes a reality in a specific society depends on its historical development, and in particular on the strength of popular social movements in the subordinate classes.)

As Marx showed, the idea of equality takes different forms in different societies, only attaining a firm foundation with the capitalist mode of production. "Equality and freedom presuppose relations of production as yet unrealized in the ancient world and in the Middle Ages."[15] Two aspects of equality in capitalist society are of interest for the analysis of women's oppression: first, the manner in which the phenomenon of equality of persons is embedded in the economic workings of the capitalist mode of production itself; and second, the transformations of this phenomenon with the evolution of capitalism.

The particular form taken by equality in capitalist society derives, ultimately, from the special character of commodities. A commodity is a product of labor that possesses both value and use-value. In the opening pages of Volume 1 of *Capital*, Marx analyzes the nature of commodities with great care, showing that value arises in a process of equalization of human labor. The exchange of commodities puts the great variety of concrete useful labor that produces them on an equal footing. Through the exchange of these commodities, "the private useful labor of each producer ranks on an equality with that of all others." Commodities can be exchanged because they each embody a certain amount of the same thing: human labor in the abstract, that is, value. "The equality of all sorts of human labor is expressed objectively by their products all being equally values." The existence of value requires that differences among various types of labor be disregarded. "The equalization of the most different kinds of labor can be the result only of an abstraction from their inequalities, or of reducing them to their common denominator, viz., expenditure of human labor-power or human labor in the abstract." In sum, equalization of differences in human labor is a fundamental characteristic of the capitalist mode of production, providing the basis for the formation of value.[16] Expansion of capitalism brings with it, furthermore, increasing equalization of labor. Accumulation demands that human labor more and more take the form of undifferentiated abstract labor.

The very labor power that, when put to use, releases labor is itself a commodity, albeit a somewhat peculiar one. Like all commodities, labor power has both value and use-value. Its value, as we have seen, consists of the sum of the values of the commodities required for the maintenance and replacement of its human bearer, taking into account the particular "historical and moral" circumstances. Its use-value, from the point of view of the capitalist, is its ability in production to contribute more value than it has itself, thereby yielding surplus value. As a commodity, labor power is bought and sold on the market. The worker enters the market bearing his or her commodity—labor power—and looking for a buyer. Similarly, the capitalist comes to the market, carrying his commodity—money—and seeking to purchase labor power. Each is an owner, desiring to sell a mass of abstract human labor congealed in a commodity. As commodity owners, they are equal traders who meet in the market to contract an exchange—the wage bargain. Their transaction follows the laws of commodity exchange. To buy the worker's labor power, the capitalist must offer a wage that is equivalent to its value. Marx devoted considerable effort to showing that this exchange of equivalents "on the basis of equal rights" of buyer and seller goes hand and hand with the exploitation characteristic of capitalist production.[17] In the sphere of circulation, paradoxically, the requirements of the capitalist mode of production itself decree that equality must reign.

In order for capitalists to buy labor power, its bearers must be able to sell it. That is, the bearers of labor power have to enter the market as independent traders, seeking an exchange of equivalents. In Marx's ironic words, wage laborers must be "free in the double sense." First, they have to be the free owners of their labor power, able to dispose of it as they wish. They cannot, for example, be enmeshed in feudal restrictions, personally dependent and incapable of autonomous action. Second, they must be free of any other way to put their labor power to use for their own account. Those who have other sources of subsistence will not easily submit to the capitalist's demands. It is precisely this double freedom that forces workers onto the market to sell their labor power.[18]

Equality of persons is situated in the sphere of circulation, where labor power is bought and sold. "To be sure," Marx observes, "the matter looks quite different if we consider capitalist production in the uninterrupted flow of its renewal, and if, in place of the individual capitalist and the individual worker, we view in their totality, the capitalist class and the working class confronting each other. But in so doing we should be applying standards entirely foreign to [the wage bargain]."[19] Class relations are rooted in the process of capitalist production, not in the sphere of circulation where the individual wage bargain is concluded. It is in the production process that the labor power bought on the market is consumed and surplus value produced. In the sphere of production, the rules of exploitation and economic power, rather than political equality, govern relations between capitalists and workers.

Powerful forces of class oppression therefore lurk behind the tendency toward equality of persons established in the sphere of circulation. The phenomenon of individual freedom is not, however, an illusory projection of capitalist social relations. Rather, it is a real tendency, bound to class exploitation by the very logic of capitalist reproduction. Capitalism couples political freedom with economic constraint in a tension that is characteristic of bourgeois society. It is this contradiction that Lenin analyzed in terms of the concept of democratic rights.

Equality of persons is not, then, simply an abstract political principle or a false ideology. It is a complex phenomenon with material roots in capitalist relations of production. As capitalism develops, more and more social processes come under capital's domination, with accompanying tendencies toward increasing equalization of human labor and, potentially, increasing equality of persons. In reality, these tendencies meet a variety of obstacles, and history shows that capitalism is in fact compatible with a stratified labor market as well as with highly undemocratic political arrangements. Even in those societies with a relatively continuous history of democracy, the phenomenon of equality of persons undergoes significant transformation over time.

In the early stages of capitalist society, the phenomenon of equality of persons emerged against a background of feudal restrictions on property and person. Early capitalism extended an inspiring pledge of freedom from such restrictions to all individuals, regardless of personal differences. Slave, serf, or free, propertied or propertyless, man or woman—to each capitalism offered hope of equality, freedom, and liberation. While the pledge of equality was fulfilled for some, large categories of the population ordinarily remained unfree, or at least excluded from full civil and political equality. The Declaration of Independence declared, for example, that it is "self-evident" that all persons are "created equal, that they are endowed by their Creator with certain unalienable Rights, that among these are Life, Liberty, and the Pursuit of Happiness." Nonetheless, the United States Constitution excluded slaves, women, and the propertyless from equal status as citizens. Much of the history of the last century reflects struggles to achieve the basic freedom to dispose of one's person and property denied to these groups.[20]

Two hundred years after the beginnings of industrial capitalism, gross civil and political inequalities have largely disappeared. Bourgeois society's promise of equality remains in force, however, and campaigns to make it even more of a reality continue. Today, the kinds of personal differences that demand to be equalized are far more subtle. In the United States, for example, blacks and women pursue struggles started long ago, but now with a more finely drawn interpretation of discrimination. In addition, every ethnic or racial group that has a distinct history organizes to eradicate its particular heritage of inequality. And numerous other sectors that have been identified as collectively different—homosexuals, the elderly, the disabled, ex-mental patients, even the obese—document their discrimination and fight for their rights.

Demands for equality in the late twentieth century in part reflect the trend toward the perfection of the conditions for the free sale of labor power. At the same time, they embody the high degree of equalization of human labor that occurs with the extension of the sphere of value in advanced capitalism. Subjectively, they reveal an intensification of desire for the freedom promised by capitalism but never consistently delivered. Indeed, even as people struggle for it, the goal of equality within bourgeois society no longer seems so compelling, for it is increasingly losing its connotations of personal freedom and human liberation. In the closing decades of the twentieth century, capitalism's wonderful promises of equality and individual fulfillment clash more openly than ever with its brutal realities. An old question persists, now posed with new energy: Why sell one's labor power—whether on a basis of equality or not—at all? Promising freedom from exploitation itself, socialist movements throughout the world suggest an answer.

Given the contradictory character of equality in capitalist society, struggles for democratic rights potentially have serious revolutionary import. To fight for equality means, in the first place, to demand and defend the best conditions possible for people within capitalist society. By their very nature, however, these conditions are severely limited. As Lenin puts it, "capitalism combines formal equality with economic and, consequently, social inequality."[21] The tendency to increasing equality has, therefore, a highly contradictory outcome. The more democratic rights are extended to all persons, the more the oppressive economic and social character of capitalism stands revealed. The struggle for equality threatens the dominance of capitalist social relations on two fronts. It promises to reduce divisions within and among oppressed classes, as well as between these classes and other sectors, by placing all persons on a more equal footing. Simultaneously, it exposes the foundation of bourgeois society to be class exploitation, not individual equality. Far from a useless exercise in bourgeois reformism, the battle for democratic rights can point beyond capitalism.

Many groups of varying makeup and character are denied equal rights within capitalist society. Some, like those comprised of persons of African or native American origin in the United States, have specific histories as oppressed peoples. Their members' lack of equality derives from a history of oppression that relentlessly passes from generation to generation, stamping each person's experience from cradle to grave. Other groups, like homosexuals, the disabled, or the elderly, are made up of individuals with particular characteristics acquired more or less accidentally, and not necessarily shared by kin. These characteristics, which may or may not be permanent, form a basis for discrimination and denial of rights. Women in capitalist societies are neither an oppressed people with a distinct history nor a collection of individuals with certain characteristics. They are, rather, the fifty-one percent of human beings who have the capacity to bear children, which if done may replenish capital's supply of labor power. Their lack of equality has, in other words, a specific character that distinguishes it from the denial of democratic rights to other groups. It is a specific character rooted in women's differential place within capitalist social reproduction. Correspondingly, the obstacles to the achievement of real social equality for women have their own character, separable from those blocking equality for other groups.

The discussion in this chapter has established a theoretical framework for analyzing women's oppression in the context of capitalist social reproduction. Women's special position in capitalist society has two defining aspects. In the first place, as in all class societies, women and men are differentially located with respect to important material aspects of social reproduction. In the second place, women, like many other groups in capitalist society, lack full democratic rights.

The differential location of women and men with respect to social reproduction varies according to class. Working-class women have disproportionate responsibility for the domestic component of necessary labor, that is, for the ongoing tasks involved in the maintenance and replacement of labor power. Correspondingly, working-class men have disproportionate responsibility for the social component of necessary labor, that is, for provision of the means of subsistence that take the form of commodities, a responsibility they can only hope to fulfill by entering into wage labor. In the capitalist class, women may have disproportionate responsibility for the processes involved in the generational replacement of individual class members, while men may be disproportionately involved in maintaining the processes of capitalist accumulation. (The analysis of just which women in contemporary capitalist society fall into the category of working class is not attempted here. It properly forms part of the much debated and still confused Marxist investigation into the contemporary class structure. Insofar as this problem remains unresolved, the movement for women's liberation lacks necessary theoretical guidance.)

While only certain women perform domestic labor in capitalist society—namely, working-class women, whose efforts maintain and renew exploitable labor power—all women suffer from a lack of equality under capitalism, at least in principle. Women's lack of equality constitutes a specific feature of women's oppression in capitalist, as opposed to other class, societies. Discriminatory conventions that survive from earlier class societies are supplemented and strengthened by newly developed mechanisms of bourgeois political discrimination. Both the legal system and an array of informal social practices support the oppression and inequality of women. At the same time, capitalism promises equality to all persons, and where it fails to deliver in the case of women, the lack is strongly felt. Like other groups denied equal rights, women struggle to achieve them. In the past, the feminist movement focused on the gross inequalities in civil society, especially those embedded in legal codes. In the advanced capitalist countries today, the battle for equality continues, and reaches into areas never dreamed of by nineteenth-century feminists. Women fight for equal rights in the so-called private sphere, formerly regarded as largely outside the scope of legal and social redress. For example, they focus on equality in the household, freedom of sexual choice, and the right to bear or not bear children. In the area of paid work, women push the issue of equality beyond demands for equal pay and equal opportunity, by calling as well for equal compensation for work of comparable worth. In essence, recent demands for equality often pose the question of the meaning of formal equality in a society based on real inequity. Advanced capitalist countries have become, furthermore, the first class societies in which differences between women and men sometimes appear to outweigh differences between classes. In these countries, expansion of the middle layers of the class structure and development of a homogenized consumerist life-style combine with the still powerful demarcation between "women's sphere" of domestic labor and "men's sphere" of wage labor to provide a context in which lack of equality with respect to men may seem to be the most consequential social factor in many women's lives. It is all too easy to overlook the fundamental distinction between the working class and other sectors of society. Socialist feminists insist that Jacqueline Kennedy Onassis is not, in any real sense, a sister, but other distinctions tend to fade.

The specific character of women's oppression in capitalist societies is established, in short, by women's particular dual position with respect to domestic labor and equal rights. At the same time, women's special status constitutes an obstacle to certain trends inherent in capitalist accumulation. Thus, barriers to female labor-force participation and isolation in a private household inhibit the tendencies toward reduction of domestic labor and free availability of labor power. Over time, most capitalist societies in fact experience a reduction of women's isolation as well as an increase in female participation in wage labor. To the extent that the special status of women continues, it permits discrimination against them that may work in capital's favor. For example, wages for "women's" jobs remain notoriously low. At the political level, women's lack of rights comes into increasing contradiction with the tendency to widen the scope of equality in advanced capitalist countries. In the twentieth century, the barriers to equality for women have been enormously reduced, revealing the underlying tension between formal and substantive equality. For many women, as for most members of other oppressed groups in capitalist society, bourgeois equality now shows itself as sharply distinct from liberation in a just society.

Lack of equality as a group constitutes the basis for women's movements that unite women from different classes and sectors. These movements will differ according to their interpretation, explicit or implicit, of the meaning of equality. Some may, for example, view equality of women and men within bourgeois society as an essentially satisfactory goal. Such movements would quite properly be called bourgeois women's movements. The contradictions of late capitalism make it likely, however, that women's movements will have at least some insight into the difference between bourgeois equality and real social equality. This could form a basis for the development of a women's movement oriented toward socialism. Over the past twenty years, women's movements in the advanced capitalist countries have often shown such potential. Unfortunately, the left has rarely been capable of intervening constructively. Its weakness has resulted, in part, from the lack of an adequate theory of women's oppression.

The position advanced here—which analyzes women's oppression in terms of domestic labor and equal rights—differs greatly from much socialist and socialist-feminist analysis. Socialist-feminist writings often locate women's oppression in capitalist society in their dual position as domestic workers and wage laborers. In a typical formulation, Margaret Coulson, Branka Magas, and Hilary Wainwright assert, for example, that "the central feature of women's position under capitalism is the fact that they are *both* domestic and wage labourers, that the two aspects of their existence are by no means harmoniously related and that this dual and contradictory role generates the specific dynamic of their oppression." Jean Gardiner has elaborated the same distinction in terms of women's "dual relationship to the class structure," directly as wage laborers, and indirectly as family members dependent on men and responsible for domestic labor.[22] This argument, which often appears in contemporary socialist as well as socialist-feminist work focuses solely on economic phenomena. It fails to account for the oppression of women not in the working class, and cannot explain the potential for building progressive women's organizations that cross class divisions, nor the possible obstacles to uniting women from distinct racial or national groups into a single women's movement. Put another way, the claim that women's oppression rests on their dual position with respect to domestic and wage labor is economistic. Despite the socialist-feminist movement's commitment to the liberation of all women, to organizational autonomy, and to the importance of subjective experience, it has paradoxically embraced a view of women's oppression quite similar to the economism of much of the socialist tradition. By contrast, the argument that women's oppression is rooted in their dual position with respect to domestic labor and equal rights provides a framework for both understanding women's position in wage labor and analyzing how a broad-based women's liberation movement may represent an essential component in the fight for socialism.

Although many changes in the character of domestic labor and the status of equal rights have taken place in the era of capitalist domination, women's oppression remains a fixture of capitalist society. As it does in every class society, the ruling class manages, one way or another, to stabilize the reproduction of labor power with a historically established minimum of necessary labor. The current constellation of domestic labor, women's rights, and female oppression represents the outcome of specific struggles over the reproduction of labor power.

So long as capitalism survives, domestic labor will be required for its reproduction, disproportionately performed by women and most likely accompanied by a system of male supremacy.

It is now possible to situate, in theoretical terms, the working-class family in the context of capitalist social reproduction. In essence, the working-class family is a kin-based site for the reproduction of labor power. Like most units for domestic labor in capitalist society, it is socially isolated from the realm of wage labor. Ordinarily, the site takes the form of a household, or a series of households linked by networks of mutual obligation. For example, a working-class family may include several generations of adults, with their children, living in adjacent rental units. Or it may consist of two persons, with or without children, living in their own home. In the case of migrant labor, a single worker may participate in two households. One will be in his or her place of origin, and include dependent kin; the other will be at work, and may take the form of dormitory quarters, lodgings, and the like. In most capitalist societies, working-class family households have the major responsibility for the processes that maintain and renew the bearers of labor power.

Performance of the domestic component of necessary labor constitutes the material pivot of the working-class family household. Given that this task has historically been carried out primarily by women, in a context usually characterized by male supremacy, the working-class family becomes a highly institutionalized repository of women's oppression. As domestic laborers in the private household, women seem to devote much of their time to performing unpaid services for wage-earning men, a situation that can give rise to antagonistic relationships between the sexes. In addition, women's political and social inequality, and their struggle to acquire rights, provide another potential source of conflict between the sexes. In this atmosphere of chronic tension within private family households, women's oppression may appear to be solely an oppression by men, rooted in a transhistorically antagonistic sex division of labor and embodied in the family. Nonetheless, it is responsibility for the domestic labor necessary to capitalist social reproduction—and not the sex division of labor or the family per se—that materially underpins the perpetuation of women's oppression and inequality in capitalist society.

These comments provide, it must be emphasized, only a sketch of the material foundation for the working-class family. Its actual form and character vary widely, according to the specific historical development of a given capitalist society. Ordinarily, working-class family experience reflects the contradictory role in capitalist social reproduction of domestic labor and the reproduction of labor power. On the one hand, family life in capitalist society is generally characterized by male supremacy and women's oppression, producing tensions and conflict that may further fragment an already divided working class. On the other hand, families constitute important supportive institutions within working-class communities, offering meaning and warmth to their members, and potentially providing a base for opposition to attempts by the capitalist class to enforce or extend its economic, political, or ideological domination. In other words, the family is neither wholly a pillar of defense and solidarity for the working class, as some socialists would have it, nor an institution so torn by internal struggle and male domination that it must be abolished, as some socialist feminists might argue. Instead, working-class families generally embody elements of both support and conflict, bound together in a dynamic combination that is not necessarily fixed. Concrete investigation will reveal whether the supportive or the conflictual aspects dominate in a particular situation. In a successful strike, for example, solidarity within and among working-class families may be a major factor, although this defensive aspect of working-class family life may recede after the conclusion of the battle. Elsewhere, a strike of male workers may be lost in part because organizers fail to involve dependent wives and children in support, thereby heightening already existing tensions in the family. Contention over the family wage, or the sex-segregation of the occupational structure, also has roots in the contradictory experience of working-class family life. Indeed, nineteenth- and twentieth-century social history abounds with case studies demonstrating the key and contradictory role of the working-class family: a haven for its members against the onslaughts of capitalist accumulation, yet simultaneously a concentrated locus of patriarchal relations.[23]

In the late twentieth century, the success of working-class and popular struggles has become increasingly dependent on the mobilization of women as well as men. Male chauvinism and women's oppression in working-class families represent, therefore, a greater obstacle to the achievement of socialist goals than ever before. A socialist movement that uncritically supports existing forms of working-class family life, or only perfunctorily addresses the problem of female subordination, risks alienating more than half its activists and allies. Conversely, popular movements that vigorously confront male chauvinism and oppose women's oppression have the potential to lay the groundwork for a future society in which the real social equality of women and men can be built.

So long as a society is dominated by the capitalist mode of production, an opposition between surplus labor and necessary labor, and between wage labor and domestic labor, will exist. While it is conceivable that the tendency and struggle for equal rights might reduce sex differences in the performance of the domestic component of necessary labor to a minimum, that minimum would still assign disproportionate responsibility to women in their capacity as childbearers, and potentially provide the material foundation for a system of male supremacy. Extension of democracy, no matter how wide, can never abolish capitalist exploitation, nor can it liberate women.

In a society not characterized by class exploitation, the relationship between the processes of surplus production and reproduction of labor power is qualitatively distinct from that characterizing societies in which exploitation dominates. In the former society, according to Marx, surplus labor is identified by the nature of its contribution to social reproduction, not by the fact that it is privately appropriated. Surplus labor produces that portion of the total social product that is surplus in several senses. Some of it is reserved for replacing depleted means of production, future expansion, insurance against catastrophe, administration costs, and so on. The surplus product also provides for the collective satisfaction of such needs as education and health care. And it serves to maintain those individuals who for reasons of age, infirmity, etc., are currently not participating in production. For Marx, necessary labor in such a society seems to be simply that labor "whose product is directly consumed individually by the producers and their families." The labor that contributes to the reproduction of labor power is not in antagonistic contradiction, furthermore, with the production of a surplus.[24] Anthropologists have examined this phenomenon in early human society, arguing that "domestic, or 'family' production in such a society *is* public production."[25] For socialists, a classless, or "communist" society, in which all labor, whether necessary or surplus, forms part of social production, represents the ultimate goal of socialist revolution. To arrive at the goal of communism, society must go through a long period of transition.

What becomes of domestic labor, the family, and the oppression of women in the course of the socialist transition? The question can, of course, only find adequate answers in the reality of an actual society's experience. Some general features of the transition period are, however, clear.

An opposition between two components of necessary labor—the one social, or public, and the other domestic, or private—continues in force during the socialist transition. Production cannot be organized all at once on a communist basis. Let us keep the term domestic labor to designate the necessary labor involved in the reproduction of labor power performed outside the realm of public production. Evidently, domestic labor plays an important role during the socialist transition. At the same time, it begins a long process of transformation into an integral component of social production in a communist society.

As in capitalist society, a tendency exists to reduce the amount of domestic labor carried out in individual households. Rather than embodying the capitalist drive for accumulation, however, it represents the socialist tendency for all labor to become part of social production in a communist society. While reduction of this domestic labor contributes to the development of the productive forces, it does not result from blind tendencies at the economic level. In principle, socialist society lessens the burdens of domestic labor carried out in individual households in a planned and conscious manner, corresponding to the needs of the people as a whole.

A major political characteristic of the socialist transition is the transformation of democracy. In capitalist society, democracy always remains severely limited. Only male members of the propertied classes effectively possess the rights bourgeois society promises to all persons. To achieve real social equality, socialist society must eliminate the many restrictions that limit democracy to a small minority. With respect to women, democracy for the majority in socialist society entails, in the first place, equal rights. Here, it is immediately obvious that laws alone are not sufficient. As an obstacle to effective equality for women, domestic labor has a stubborn material presence that no legislation, by itself, can overcome. A major index of socialist society is, then, progressive reduction of the disproportionate burden on women of domestic labor. Two paths toward this goal are available. First, domestic labor itself can be reduced through the socialization of its tasks. Second, the domestic labor that remains to be done outside public production can be shared among women, men, and, in appropriate proportion, children. Because domestic labor cannot be substantially reduced, much less eliminated, overnight, socialist society must take both paths in order to assure women of real social equality.

Kin-based sites for the reproduction of labor power—that is, families—have a definite role in social reproduction during the socialist transition. In principle, they differ on several important counts from working-class families in capitalist society. To an increasing extent, all family members take part in public production and political life as equal individuals. At the same time, domestic labor within the family household is progressively reduced. What domestic labor remains is shared on a more and more equitable basis.

Existing socialist societies have made important advances in the area of women's equal participation in public production and political life. On the whole they have been unable, however, to confront the problems of domestic labor and women's subordination in a systematic way. To some extent, efforts have been made to socialize domestic labor, but the oppressive division of labor within the family household remains largely untouched. As a result, socialist feminists sometimes argue that the drawing of women into public production in socialist societies represents not liberation but the imposition of a burdensome double shift. Only since the 1970s has the question of sharing housework and child-care responsibilities been considered in a few socialist countries. How adequate the concrete steps taken in this area are is a question that requires serious investigation.[26]

In the long run, the establishment of effective social equality between women and men in socialist society meets an obstacle in the real differences between them, particularly in the area of childbearing. As a transformation of the contradictions inherent in capitalist society, equality in socialist society has itself a contradictory character. In Marx's words, "*equal* right [in socialist society] is an unequal right for unequal labor." That is, differences between people mean that equal remuneration for equal amounts of work in socialist society will most likely result in an unequal outcome. "One worker is married, another not; one has more children than another and so on and so forth. Thus with an equal output, and hence an equal share in the social consumption fund, one will in fact receive more than another, one will be richer than another, and so on. To avoid all these defects, right, instead of being equal, would have to be unequal."[27] Similarly, real social equality for women will actually require unequal treatment at certain times: maternity leaves, lighter work during the later months of pregnancy, rest periods when necessary for menstruating women, and so on. In this way, the material conditions for women's full participation in all areas of social life—production, politics, culture, personal relations, and so forth—can be developed.

Socialist society does not, it is clear, abolish the family in the sense of doing away with individual social units in which domestic labor is performed. Neither does it eliminate the sex division of labor. What it does do is undermine the foundation for the oppression of women within the individual household and in society. The extension of democracy, the drawing of women into public production, and the

progressive transformation of domestic labor during the socialist transition open up the possibility for what Marx calls "a higher form of the
family and of relations between the sexes." The exact form such relations will take cannot be predicted in advance. As Engels argues, "what
we can now conjecture about the way in which sexual relations will be
ordered after the impending overthrow of capitalist production is
mainly of a negative character, limited for the most part to what will
disappear." It is up to future generations to determine how they wish
to live. "When these people are in the world, they will care precious
little what anybody today thinks they ought to do; they will make their
own practice and their corresponding public opinion about the practice of each individual—and that will be the end of it."[28]

Confronted with the terrible reality of women's oppression, nineteenth-century utopian socialists called for the abolition of the family.
Their drastic demand continues to find advocates among socialists
even today. In its place, however, historical materialism poses the difficult question of simultaneously reducing and redistributing domestic
labor in the course of transforming it into an integral component of
social production in communist society. Just as in the socialist transition "the state is not 'abolished,' *it withers away*," so too, domestic
labor must wither away.[29] The proper management of domestic labor
and women's work during the transition to communism is therefore a
critical problem for socialist society, for only on this basis can the economic, political, and ideological conditions for women's true liberation be established and maintained. In the process, the family
in its particular historical form as a kin-based social unit for the reproduction of exploitable labor power in class society will also wither
away—and with it both patriarchal family relations and the oppression
of women.

Notes

Works Cited

Index

Notes

Preface

1. Karl Marx and Frederick Engels, *Selected Works in One Volume*, p. 29. Lise Vogel, "The Earthly Family." This text was in fact an 1888 revision by Engels of Marx's 1845 notes. For discussion, as well as a more accurate translation of the 1888 version, see note 5 of Chapter 4.

2. Juliet Mitchell, *Woman's Estate*, pp. 93–94.

3. Lillian Robinson, "The Question," *Robinson on the Woman Question.*

Chapter 1   Introduction

1. Red Apple Collective, "Socialist-Feminist Women's Unions," p. 39. While socialism and Marxism are of course not synonymous, I use the terms socialist feminism and Marxist feminism interchangeably, following ordinary practice within the contemporary women's movement in the United States. Socialist feminism is not, moreover, the exclusive province of women: the New American Movement called itself a socialist-feminist organization.

2. Important landmarks in the early sixties include the following: In 1961, President Kennedy established the President's Commission on the Status of Women, whose final report appeared in 1963. Friedan's *The Feminine Mystique* was published in 1963, heralded by magazine articles and media interviews. As the book quickly became a bestseller, a series of more scholarly reconsiderations of woman's place—led off in 1964 by a special issue of *Daedalus*, the magazine of the American Academy of Arts and Sciences—signaled a new turn in liberal ideology. Meanwhile, legislation and executive orders had begun to create a governmental policy structure in support of women's equality: the 1963 Equal Pay Act, Title VII of the 1964 Civil Rights Act, and executive orders in 1962 and 1965 prohibiting discrimination in federal employment. For NOW's statement of purpose, see Judith Hole and Ellen Levine, *Rebirth of Feminism*, p. 85.

3. For differing accounts of the history of second-wave feminism, see: Barbara Deckard, *The Women's Movement*; Marlene Dixon, "Where Are We Going?"; idem, "Why Women's Liberation—2?"; Barbara Easton, "Feminism and the Contemporary Family"; Barbara Epstein, "Thoughts on Socialist Feminism in 1980"; Sara Evans, "The Origins of the Women's Liberation Movement"; idem, *Personal Politics*; Jo Freeman, "The Origins of the Women's Liberation Movement"; idem, "The Women's Liberation Movement"; "The National Conference on Socialist-Feminism"; Red Apple Collective, "Socialist-Feminist Women's Unions." For the development of feminist consciousness and movements for women's liberation in the third world, see: Norma Stoltz Chinchilla, "Mobilizing Women"; idem, "Working-Class Feminism"; Gail Omvedt, *We Will Smash This Prison!*; idem, "Women and Rural Revolt in India"; Stephanie Urdang, *Fighting Two Colonialisms.*

4. "National Conference on Socialist-Feminism," p. 87.

5. I use the plural—sex divisions of labor—because in most societies there are, in fact, distinct divisions of labor according to sex in different areas of work and for different classes, age groups, and so forth. While the singular term— the sex division of labor—can be taken to include these variations, it tends also to merge them into an abstract unity. For a similar conceptualization, if not terminology, see Christopher Middleton, "The Sexual Division of Labour in Feudal England." See also Lourdes Benería, "Reproduction, Production and the Sexual Division of Labour."

Chapter 2   A Decade of Debate

1. Red Apple Collective, "Socialist-Feminist Women's Unions," p. 43.

2. Juliet Mitchell, "Women: The Longest Revolution"; idem, *Woman's Estate*.

3. Mitchell, "Longest Revolution," pp. 15, 16.

4. Ibid., pp. 34, 35; idem, *Woman's Estate*, p. 150.

5. Mitchell, "Longest Revolution," p. 34.

6. Ibid.

7. Murdock argued that the universal nuclear family incorporates the "four functions fundamental to human social life—the sexual, the economic, the reproductive, and the educational [i.e., that pertaining to socialization]." George Murdock, *Social Structure*, p. 10. For critiques of Mitchell's functionalism, see also: Joan Landes, "Women, Labor and Family Life"; Christopher Middleton, "Sexual Inequality and Stratification Theory." On the family in functionalist theory, see: Veronica Beechey, "Women and Production"; D. H. J. Morgan, *Social Theory and the Family*; Lise Vogel, "The Contested Domain"; idem, "Women, Work, and Family."

8. Mitchell, *Woman's Estate*, p. 86.

9. Margaret Benston's article circulated under the title "What Defines Women?" and was published as "The Political Economy of Women's Liberation." Peggy Morton's original essay, "A Woman's Work Is Never Done, or: The Production, Maintenance and Reproduction of Labor Power," was abridged in *Leviathan* in May 1970 and then revised for publication as "A Woman's Work Is Never Done."

10. Benston, "Political Economy," pp. 16, 20, 22.

11. Morton, "A Woman's Work," pp. 214, 215–216.

12. For early critiques of Benston, see: Morton, "A Woman's Work"; Mickey Rowntree and John Rowntree, "Notes on the Political Economy of Women's Liberation"; Roberta Salper, "The Development of the American Women's Liberation Movement, 1967–1971."

13. Mariarosa Dalla Costa's article, "Women and the Subversion of the Community," was published in Italian in 1972, and appeared simultaneously in English in *Radical America*. A corrected translation is found in *The Power of Women and the Subversion of the Community*.

14. Dalla Costa, "Women and Subversion," p. 19.

15.   Ibid., p. 52, n. 12; p. 39.

16.   Ibid., pp. 34, 47.

17.   For a fine analysis of the campaign for wages for housework, see Ellen Malos, "Housework and the Politics of Women's Liberation."

18.   For useful recent summaries and critiques of the domestic labor debate, see Nancy Holmstrom, "'Women's Work,' The Family, and Capitalism," and Maxine Molyneux, "Beyond the Domestic Labour Debate." Important early critiques include: Caroline Freeman, "When Is a Wage Not a Wage?" and Ira Gerstein, "Domestic Work and Capitalism."

19.   See Paul Smith, "Domestic Labour and Marx's Theory of Value," as well as Holmstrom, "'Women's Work,'" and Molyneux, "Domestic Labour Debate." For a recent revival of interest in the issues raised by the domestic labor debate, see the essays collected in Bonnie Fox, ed., *Hidden in the Household*.

20.   Mitchell, *Woman's Estate*, p. 99; Heidi Hartmann, "The Unhappy Marriage of Marxism and Feminism,". p. 22.

21.   Shulamith Firestone, *The Dialectic of Sex*, pp. 4, 12; Kate Millett, *Sexual Politics*, p. 169.

22.   Zillah Eisenstein, ed., *Capitalist Patriarchy and the Case for Socialist Feminism*, p. 6. For Mitchell's critique of radical feminism, see *Woman's Estate*, pp. 82–96.

23.   Heidi Hartmann and Amy Bridges, "The Unhappy Marriage of Marxism and Feminism," p. 14; Sheila Rowbotham, *Woman's Consciousness, Man's World*, p. 117. On dissolving the hyphen: Rosalind Petchesky, "Dissolving the Hyphen." Early and influential socialist-feminist discussions of patriarchy include: Hartmann and Bridges, "Unhappy Marriage"; Joan Kelly-Gadol, "The Social Relation of the Sexes"; Gayle Rubin, "The Traffic in Women."

24.   Renate Bridenthal, "The Dialectics of Production and Reproduction," p. 5. Mitchell used the concept of a mode of reproduction as early as 1966. Juliet Mitchell, "Longest Revolution," p. 21. For other examples, see: Jean Gardiner, "The Political Economy of Domestic Labour in Capitalist Society"; John Harrison, "The Political Economy of Housework"; Isabel Larguia, "The Economic Basis of the Status of Women"; Bridget O'Laughlin, "Marxist Approaches in Anthropology," pp. 365–366. In the context of the study of imperialism, a notion of the mode of reproduction is implicit in: Mina Davis Caulfield, "Imperialism, the Family, and Cultures of Resistance"; Carmen Diana Deere, "Rural Women's Subsistence Production in the Capitalist Periphery"; Heleieth Saffioti, "Women, Mode of Production, and Social Formations." The anthropologist Claude Meillassoux has put forth the concept of families as perpetual sources of cheap labor power, notably in *Femmes, greniers et capitaux*. Important reviews of Meillassoux, which discuss the concept of reproduction, include: Maureen Mackintosh, "Reproduction and Patriarchy"; Bridget O'Laughlin, "Production and Reproduction"; Rayna Rapp, "Review of Claude Meillassoux, *Femmes, greniers et capitaux*."

25.   Veronica Beechey, "On Patriarchy"; Val Burris, "The Dialectic of Women's Oppression"; Roisin McDonough and Rachel Harrison, "Patriarchy and Relations

of Production"; Iris Young, "Beyond the Unhappy Marriage"; idem, "Socialist Feminism and the Limits of Dual Systems Theory." See also Michèle Barrett, *Women's Oppression Today*, pp. 10–38, 126–128, 131–138.

26. Felicity Edholm, Olivia Harris, and Kate Young, "Conceptualising Women."

27. Young, "Social Feminism," pp. 170, 173–174; Beechey, "On Patriarchy," p. 78.

Chapter 3   Socialist Feminism and the Woman Question

1. Frederick Engels, *The Origin of the Family, Private Property and the State*, pp. 71–72.

2. See, for example, the following collections: Zillah Eisenstein, ed., *Capitalist Patriarchy and the Case for Socialist Feminism*; Annette Kuhn and Annemarie Wolpe, eds., *Feminism and Materialism*; Lydia Sargent, ed., *Women and Revolution*; "Women's Issue." Important recent articles include: Michèle Barrett and Mary McIntosh, "The 'Family Wage'"; Veronica Beechey, "On Patriarchy"; idem, "Some Notes on Female Wage Labour in Capitalist Production"; Lourdes Benería, "Reproduction, Production and the Sexual Division of Labour"; Emily Blumenfeld and Susan Mann, "Domestic Labour and the Reproduction of Labour Power"; Janet Bujra, "Female Solidarity and the Sexual Division of Labour"; Norma Stoltz Chinchilla, "Ideologies of Feminism"; Felicity Edholm, Olivia Harris, and Kate Young, "Conceptualising Women"; Nancy Holmstrom, "'Women's Work,' The Family, and Capitalism"; Jane Humphries, "Class Struggle and the Persistence of the Working-Class Family"; Joan Kelly, "The Doubled Vision of Feminist Theory"; Mary McIntosh, "The Welfare State and the Needs of the Dependent Family"; Maureen Mackintosh, "Domestic Labour and the Household"; Maxine Molyneux, "Beyond the Domestic Labour Debate"; Bridget O'Laughlin, "Production and Reproduction"; Paddy Quick, "The Class Nature of Women's Oppression"; idem, "Why Women Work for Wages"; Iris Young, "Beyond the Unhappy Marriage"; idem, "Socialist Feminism and the Limits of Dual Systems Theory."

3. Lise Vogel, "Questions on the Woman Question."

4. Mark Poster, *Critical Theory of the Family*, pp. 42–43. Poster also declares that with the exception of Juliet Mitchell, "feminists have in general not shed much light on family theory"; pp. xvii–xviii. Richard Evans, *The Feminists*, p. 156. Meyer claims that "The German Ideology" was "virtually the last pronouncement either Engels or Marx made about male-female relationships for four decades, except for the brief statements made in the *Principles of Communism* and the *Communist Manifesto*, both written in 1847, and the occasional references to the plight of female workers in *Capital*." Indeed, "the relative neglect of the 'woman question' was built into Marxist theory." Alfred Meyer, "Marxism and the Women's Movement," pp. 89–90, 99. Even Eisenstein suggests that "Marx never questioned the hierarchical sexual ordering of society" Eisenstein, *Capitalist Patriarchy*, p. 9.

5. Marlene Dixon, "The Centrality of Women in Proletarian Revolution," pp. 35–41.

6. Charnie Guettel, *Marxism and Feminism*, p. 15.

7. Juliet Mitchell, *Woman's Estate*, pp. 78, 80.

Chapter 4   Early Views

1. Karl Marx and Frederick Engels, *Collected Works*, 3: 172, 295–296, 297.

2. Ibid., 4: 196. Marx claims he is quoting Fourier, yet in fact he very freely renders a passage in which Fourier makes a quite different point, arguing that "the extension of the privileges of women is the fundamental cause of all social progress." In other words, for Fourier the condition of women is the cause, not the index, of social progress. Jonathan Beecher and Richard Bienvenu, eds., *The Utopian Vision of Charles Fourier*, pp. 195–196. Alfred Meyer also notes the distinction between Fourier's statements and Marx's paraphrase in "Marxism and the Women's Movement," p. 86, n. 2. See also Susan Moller Okin, *Women in Western Political Thought*, p. 8.

3. Marx and Engels, *Collected Works*, 4: 195.

4. Frederick Engels, *Ludwig Feuerbach and the Outcome of Classical German Philosophy*, p. 8.

5. Marx and Engels, *Collected Works*, 5: 4. In the 1888 publication, Engels modified Marx's wording of the second two sentences: "The latter must itself, therefore, first be understood in its contradiction and then, by the removal of the contradiction, revolutionized in practice. Thus, for instance, once the earthly family is discovered to be the secret of the holy family, the former must then itself be criticized in theory and transformed in practice." Ibid., p. 7. Rather than a "softening" of Marx's version, as Draper suggests, the change represents an attempt to indicate more clearly what Marx and Engels later saw to be the relationship between theory and practice. Hal Draper, "Marx and Engels on Women's Liberation," p. 89, n. 19.

6. Friedrich Engels, *The Condition of the Working Class in England*, pp. 182, 161, 184, 226. This translation has been the subject of much criticism; see, for example, Steven Marcus, *Engels, Manchester, and the Working Class*, pp. xi–xiii, 28–29. In the interest of readability, I follow Marcus in citing it nonetheless. For the authorized translation by Florence Kelley Wischnewetzky, see Marx and Engels, *Collected Works*, 4: 295–596.

7. Engels, *Condition*, pp. 166, 134. More generally, see pp. 124–129, 166–168.

8. Marx and Engels, *Collected Works*, 3: 295n.

9. Ibid., 4: 166–176.

10. Engels, *Condition*, p. 144.

11. Ibid., pp. 145, 160, 161, 225.

12. Ibid., pp. 160, 161, 163, 236.

13. Ibid., pp. 164–165. Engels also briefly discusses the dissolution of the family under the impact of the factory system in his *Outlines of a Critique of Political Economy* (1843–1844); see Marx and Engels, *Collected Works*, 3: 423–424.

14. Engels, *Condition*, pp. 363–364.

15. Ibid., p. 90.

16. Ibid., pp. 90–92. In 1885, Engels observed that "the thesis that the 'natural,' i.e.,

normal, price of labour power coincides with the minimum wage, i.e., with the equivalent in value of the means of subsistence absolutely indispensable for the life and procreation of the worker, was first put forward" in his *Outlines of a Critique of Political Economy* (1843–1844) and in *Condition*. Still, he adds, the "thesis is nevertheless incorrect. . . . In *Capital* Marx has put the above thesis right." Note to the 1885 German edition of *Poverty of Philosophy*; Marx and Engels, *Collected Works*, 6: 125. For the *Outlines*, see ibid., 3: 441.

17. Engels, *Condition*, pp. 92–98; see also pp. 320–324.

18. Karl Marx, *A Contribution to the Critique of Political Economy*, p. 22.

19. Marx and Engels, *Collected Works*, 5: 180–181. Marx and Engels do not say why they think the proletarian family has been abolished. Presumably, the statement rests on the absence of property and on observations of the type made by Engels in *Condition*. In a review appearing in 1850 of a book by Georg Friedrich Daumer, Marx and Engels make a similar argument against viewing women in abstraction from their social situation. *Collected Works*, 10: 244–246.

20. Marx and Engels, *Collected Works*, 5: 41–43.

21. Ibid., pp. 33, 43, 44, 46.

22. Ibid., pp. 75–76.

23. Marx to P. V. Annenkov, December 28, 1846; in Karl Marx and Frederick Engels, *Selected Correspondence*, p. 35.

24. Engels to Marx, November 23–24, 1847; in Marx and Engels, *Selected Correspondence*, p. 45.

25. Marx and Engels, *Collected Works*, 6: 102–103, 501, 494, 487.

26. Ibid., pp. 354, 502. Sheila Rowbotham, *Women, Resistance and Revolution*, p. 65.

27. Marx and Engels, *Collected Works*, 6: 502, 501, 102, 354.

28. Ibid., pp. 491, 502.

29. In a notebook labeled "Wages" kept at the same time, Marx also noted that the supposed minimum wage "is different in different countries" and "has a historical movement." Indeed, at times it includes "a little tea, or rum, or sugar and meat." These comments echo Engels's on the "level of culture" discussed above, as well as foreshadowing Marx's own more developed theory. Ibid., pp. 425–426, 436.

Chapter 5   Marx: The Mature Years

1. Karl Marx, *A Contribution to the Critique of Political Economy*, p. 23.

2. Karl Marx, *Grundrisse*, p. 717n.

3. Ibid., p. 283.

4. Ibid., pp. 282–283, 287, 325, 283.

5. Ibid., p. 323.

6. Ibid., pp. 604–608; quotations on p. 607.

7. Ibid., pp. 608–610.

8. Ibid., p. 401.

9. Ibid., pp. 472, 475; see also pp. 473, 484, 495. On the sources, see the introduction by Eric Hobsbawm in Karl Marx, *Pre-Capitalist Economic Formations*, pp. 20–27.

10. For a clear summary of the publishing history of the manuscripts, see the Vintage Books edition of Karl Marx, *Capital*, 1: 26–28. See also idem, *Grundrisse*, pp. 11–12.

11. Karl Marx, *Capital*, 1: 372–379. (Unless stated otherwise, all citations to *Capital* refer to the Progress Publishers edition.)

12. Ibid., pp. 434–435. Marx then proceeds to a series of examples, pp. 435–442; see also pp. 455–456, 612–666. Other evidence appears in the discussions of unregulated branches of industry, the shift system, and the struggle for a normal working day; pp. 233–238, 246–251, 264–281.

13. Ibid., p. 428; see also pp. 384, 421–446, 457, and Karl Marx, "Results of the Immediate Process of Production," p. 1061. On domestic servants, see idem, *Capital*, 1: 420–421.

14. Marx, *Capital*, 1: 460.

15. Ibid., 3: 790–791, 796, 807, 795; see also p. 877, and 1: 82.

16. Ibid., 1: 82, 396, 264; see also pp. 384, 595.

17. Ibid., p. 332.

18. Marx, "Results," p. 1083.

19. Karl Marx and Frederick Engels, *Collected Works*, 5: 46.

20. Karl Marx, *The First International and After*, p. 88. Idem, *Capital*, 1: 373; see also p. 285.

21. Marx and Engels, *Collected Works*, 6: 501.

22. For reviews of this literature, see Jane Atkinson, "Anthropology," and Rayna Rapp, "Anthropology." See also the works cited in notes 12 and 22 of Chapter 10.

23. Marx, *Capital*, 1: 346, 379; see also pp. 380, 384.

24. Ibid., p. 399.

25. Ibid., p. 459; see also p. 285.

26. Ibid., p. 283; see also p. 268.

27. Ibid., p. 179.

28. Ibid., p. 536.

29. Marx, "Results," p. 984; idem, *Capital*, 1: 536–537.

30. Marx, *Capital*, 1: 168, 537. See also pp. 538, 541–542; 2: 356, 385, 396; and idem, *Grundrisse*, pp. 458, 676–677.

31. Marx, *Capital*, 1: 164.

32. Ibid., pp. 167, 168; see also pp. 486, 524.

33. Karl Marx, *Wages, Price and Profit*, pp. 72–73; idem, *Capital*, 1: 168. See also idem, "Results," pp. 1067–1069.

34. Marx, *Capital*, 1: 579; see also pp. 580–581, and idem, "Results," pp. 1032, 1068. For the fluctuation of a commodity's price around its value, see idem, *Capital*, 1: 98–106.

35. Marx, *Capital*, 1: 373; see also 3: 233.

36. Marx, *Wages, Price and Profit*, p. 68; see also idem, *Capital*, 1: 509.

37. Marx, *Capital*, 1: 603.

38. Ibid., pp. 576, 592.

39. Ibid., p. 603.

40. Ibid., pp. 575–576. On laws of population, see pp. 591–592.

41. Ibid., 3: 236–237. See also the section entitled "Excess Capital and Excess Population," pp. 250–259.

42. Marx would perhaps have taken on the task of resolving these contradictions and gaps in the future, never developed, "special study of wage labor." *Capital*, 1: 508. Whether or not he would have addressed the question of women's oppression directly in the study is, of course, another issue. Rosdolsky's argument that Marx entirely abandoned the plan for the separate book on wage labor is unconvincing. Roman Rosdolsky, *The Making of Marx's 'Capital,'* pp. 57–62. Molyneux suggests that the reproduction of labor power constitutes a condition of existence for capitalism, but cannot itself be placed theoretically within the concept of the capitalist mode of production; hence, she claims, it was proper for Marx to exclude it from the discussion in *Capital*. Maxine Molyneux, "Beyond the Domestic Labour Debate," p. 20. For the author's view, see Chapters 10 and 11.

43. Marx, *Capital*, 1: 460.

44. *International Workingmen's Association, General Council. Minutes*, 2: 232.

45. Marx, *Capital*, 1: 285.

46. Karl Marx, *Critique of the Gotha Programme*, p. 22. See also idem, *First International*, p. 88: "[Women are to] be rigorously excluded from all *nightwork whatever*, and all sort of work hurtful to the delicacy of the sex, or exposing their bodies to poisonous and otherwise deleterious agencies."

47. Marx, *First International*, p. 88.

48. *International Workingmen's Association, Minutes*, 2: 232. Marx to Dr. Kugelmann, December 12, 1868; Karl Marx, *Letters to Dr. Kugelmann*, p. 83 (translation slightly modified to accord with the German original; Karl Marx and Friedrich Engels, *Werke*, 32: 582–583).

49. *International Workingmen's Association, Minutes*, 4: 442, 460. Like Marx, Engels supported, at least in principle, equal participation by women in political life; see Engels to Ida Pauli, February 14, 1877, cited in Alfred Meyer, "Marxism and the Women's Movement," p. 93.

50. For the program, see Jules Guesde, *Textes choisis, 1867–1882*, p. 117. The translation in Marx, *First International*, p. 376, made, unaccountably, from a German version, misleadingly gives "mankind" for "êtres humaines." Marx's later comment is in a letter to F. A. Sorge, November 5, 1880; Karl Marx and Frederick Engels, *Selected Correspondence*, p. 332. See also Engels to E. Bernstein, October 25, 1881; Marx and Engels, *Selected Correspondence*, p. 344.

Chapter 6   Engels: A Defective Formulation

1. Frederick Engels, *Anti-Dühring*, p. 308. For Marx's paraphrase of Fourier, see note 2 of Chapter 4.

2. Ibid., pp. 243–245, 304, 310, 325–328.

3. Ibid., pp. 118, 214, 215, 319, 322.

4. Ibid., p. 377. The question of changes in the organization of domestic labor had, of course, long been a concern among utopian thinkers; see, for example, Dolores Hayden, *The Grand Domestic Revolution*.

5. Engels to Kautsky, February 16 and April 26, 1884; Karl Marx and Frederick Engels, *Selected Correspondence*, pp. 368, 372. See also Lawrence Krader, ed., *The Ethnological Notebooks of Karl Marx*, pp. 388–390.

6. For the publication history and a critique of August Bebel's *Woman and Socialism*, see Chapter 7.

7. Frederick Engels, *The Origin of the Family, Private Property and the State*, p. 71. Important critical evaluations of the *Origin* include: Beverly Brown, "Natural and Social Division of Labour"; Liz Brown, "The Family and Its Genealogies"; Rosalind Delmar, "Looking Again at Engels' *Origin of the Family, Private Property and the State*"; Hal Draper, "Marx and Engels on Women's Liberation"; Barry Hindess and Paul Hirst, *Pre-Capitalist Modes of Production*, pp. 28–29, 58–59; Krader, *Ethnological Notebooks*; Ann Lane, "Women in Society"; Eleanor Leacock, Introduction to the *Origin*; Karen Sacks, "Engels Revisited"; U. Santamaria, "Review Article"; Bernhard Stern, "Engels on the Family."

8. Lewis Morgan, *Ancient Society*. Of many subsequent reprint editions, the most useful is that published by World Publishing Co. of Cleveland in 1963, with an introduction by Eleanor Leacock. Krader, *Ethnological Notebooks*.

9. Morgan, *Ancient Society*, p. 348.

10. Ibid., p. 355.

11. Ibid., p. 481.

12. Ibid., pp. 360, 398–400, 474–475, 477–478, 480–488, 499.

13. Ibid., pp. 561–562.

14. The starting point for any evaluation of Morgan's *Ancient Society* must be Leacock's introduction to *Ancient Society*.

15. Morgan, *Ancient Society*, pp. vii, 3, 8.

16. Ibid., pp. 511–512, 263, vii; see also pp. 5–6.

17. Krader, *Ethnological Notebooks*, pp. 11 and 365, n. 21. See also the review of Krader in Santamaria, "Review Article."

18. Engels, *Origin*, p. 93.

19. Ibid., pp. 101–110.

20. Ibid., p. 117.

21. Ibid., pp. 119–120.

22. Ibid., pp. 120–121.

23. Ibid., p. 128.

24. Ibid., pp. 128, 129.

25. Ibid., pp. 132, 135.

26. Ibid., pp. 135–138.

27. Ibid., p. 137.

28. Ibid.

29. Ibid., pp. 138–146.

30. Ibid., p. 145. The subjects of love and sexuality are covered at even greater length by Bebel in *Woman and Socialism*.

31. Engels, *Origin*, p. 139.

32. Ibid., p. 171.

33. Marx to J. D. Schweitzer, January 24, 1865; Marx and Engels, *Selected Correspondence*, p. 153. Karl Marx, *Capital*, 1: 115–116, 165–167.

34. Engels, *Origin*, p. 217.

35. Ibid., pp. 218–225.

36. Ibid., pp. 223, 224, 235; see also pp. 119, 161.

37. Ibid., p. 221.

38. Engels to Gertrude Guillaume-Schak, July 5, 1885; Marx and Engels, *Selected Correspondence*, p. 386.

39. Engels, *Origin*, pp. 71–72; text of passage cited in Chapter 3. Karl Marx and Frederick Engels, *Collected Works*, 5: 43.

40. Karl Marx and Friedrich Engels, *Werke*, 36: 33–34; see also pp. 39, 41, and 54, and Engels, *Origin*, p. 129. For "The German Ideology," see Chapter 4. On the textual similarity, see also H. Kent Geiger, *The Family in Soviet Russia*, pp. 30–32.

41. Marx and Engels, *Collected Works*, 5: 33, 46; Engels, *Origin*, pp. 121, 134, 137.

42. Marx and Engels, *Collected Works*, 5: 46; Engels, *Origin*, pp. 121–122, 129, 131, 137.

43. On the turn-of-the-century socialists, see Geiger, *Family in Soviet Russia*, pp. 31–32; similar opinions have been expressed more recently in Hindess and Hirst, *Pre-Capitalist Modes*, pp. 58–59. On the Soviet view, see Stern, "Engels on the Family," p. 48, n. 10. For other critiques of the dualism implicit in the

Origin, see L. Brown, "Family and Genealogies" and Bridget O'Laughlin, "Production and Reproduction," pp. 5–7.

44. Engels, *Origin*, p. 71.

Chapter 7   The Second International

1. On the popularity of Bebel's book as a vision of socialism, see Hans-Josef Steinberg, "Workers' Libraries in Germany before 1914."

2. Jean Quataert, "Unequal Partners in an Uneasy Alliance," p. 120.

3. For Zetkin's remark, see Hal Draper and Anne Lipow, "Marxist Women versus Bourgeois Feminism," pp. 197–198.

4. The correspondence between Bebel and Engels appears in Werner Blumenberg, ed., *August Bebels Briefwechsel mit Friedrich Engels*, nos. 58, 59, 62, 80, 157, 280, 298. Engels's letters to other correspondents are listed in Lawrence Krader, *The Ethnological Notebooks of Karl Marx*, pp. 388–390. See also the discussion of Engels's *Origin* in Chapter 6.

5. For the history of the early editions of *Woman and Socialism*, see Bebel's "Vorrede zur neunten Auflage," dated December 24, 1890, in *Die Frau und der Sozialismus*. The following discussion cites the easily available English translations of the second and thirty-third editions to stand for, respectively, the early version and the classic text of *Woman and Socialism*. The second edition is August Bebel, *Woman in the Past, Present and Future*, the thirty-third, idem, *Woman under Socialism*, cited hereafter as *Woman*. Citations in this paragraph are from Bebel, *Woman in the Past*, p. 18, and *Woman*, p. 10. For a useful evaluation of Bebel's work, see Richard Evans, *The Feminists*, pp. 156–159.

6. Bebel, *Woman*, pp. 85, 86, 146.

7. Ibid., pp. 192, 187, 79.

8. Ibid., pp. 343, 338–339. On kitchenless houses, see Dolores Hayden, *The Grand Domestic Revolution*.

9. Bebel, *Woman*, p. 79; see also pp. 79–88, 182–215.

10. Ibid., pp. 1, 4, 5.

11. Ibid., p. 115; see also pp. 89–90 and 233.

12. Ibid., pp. 9, 120, 343.

13. Edward Aveling and Eleanor Marx Aveling, *The Woman Question*. For the pamphlet's publication history, see Yvonne Kapp, *Eleanor Marx: II. The Crowded Years, 1884–1898*, pp. 82–85.

14. Bebel, *Woman*, p. 121.

Chapter 8   Toward Revolution

1. For discussions of the achievements and limitations of the SPD's work on women, see: Richard Evans, "Bourgeois Feminists and Women Socialists in Germany 1894–1914"; idem, *The Feminists*, pp. 159–165; Karen Honeycutt, "Socialism and Feminism in Imperial Germany"; Molly Nolan, "Proletarischer Anti-

Feminismus"; Jean Quataert, *Reluctant Feminists in German Social Democracy,
1885–1917*.

2. Clara Zetkin, "Nur mit der proletarischen Frau wird der Sozialismus siegen!"
English translation, with slight cuts, in Hal Draper and Anne Lipow, "Marxist Women versus Bourgeois Feminism," pp. 192–201. According to Karen
Honeycutt, some changes and deletions have been made in the 1957 publication of the 1896 speech; "Clara Zetkin: A Left-Wing Socialist and Feminist in
Wilhelmian Germany," chap. 5, nn. 106, 129. While only a single text can be
analyzed here, the full range of Zetkin's theoretical and practical contributions
should not be underestimated. For the period up to 1914, see Honeycutt, "Clara
Zetkin."

3. Zetkin, "Nur mit der proletarischen Frau," p. 95; Draper and Lipow, "Marxist
Women," p. 192. Honeycutt notes that both Bebel and Liebknecht wanted Zetkin
to eliminate references to the class rule of men over women in the 1896
speech, but Zetkin argued successfully that the concept could be found in Engels's *Origin*; Draper and Lipow excise the sentence without comment or ellip-
sis. Honeycutt, "Clara Zetkin," p. 193. Earlier, Zetkin had clung even more
closely to Bebel's work. For example, in a speech delivered in 1889 to the
founding conference of the Second International, she stressed women's economic dependence and maintained that "in the same way that the worker is
enslaved by capital, so is the woman by the man; and she will remain enslaved
so long as she is not economically independent." Clara Zetkin, "Für die Befreiung der Frau!," p. 4; Honeycutt, "Clara Zetkin," p. 90.

4. The term "women's rightsers" is as awkward in German as it is in English, and
was employed polemically within the socialist movement. See Draper and
Lipow, "Marxist Women," p. 180.

5. For these recommendations, see Zetkin, "Nur mit der proletarischen Frau,"
p. 109; the details are omitted in the translation by Draper and Lipow, "Marxist
Women."

6. Clara Zetkin, "Surrender of the Second International in the Emancipation of
Women," pp. 373, 375, 376. I would like to thank Charlotte Todes Stern of New
York City for bringing this article to my attention.

7. Important recent studies on women in Russia include: Anne Bobroff, "The Bol-
sheviks and Working Women, 1905–1920"; Barbara Evans Clements, "Working-
Class and Peasant Women in the Russian Revolution, 1917–1923"; Rose Glick-
man, "The Russian Factory Woman, 1880–1914"; Carol Eubanks Hayden, "The
Zhenotdel and the Bolshevik Party"; Alena Heitlinger, *Women and State So-
cialism*; Gail Warshofsky Lapidus, "Sexual Equality in Soviet Policy"; Gregory
Massell, *The Surrogate Proletariat*; Richard Stites, *The Women's Liberation
Movement in Russia*.

8. V. I. Lenin, *Collected Works*, 1: 148–152. For an analysis of the preface to Engels's *Origin*, see Chapter 6.

9. V. I. Lenin, *The Development of Capitalism in Russia*, p. 552.

10. V. I. Lenin, *The Emancipation of Women*, p. 30; idem, *Development of Capitalism*, p. 546. On abortion, see also idem, *Emancipation of Women*, pp. 28–29.
On the peasantry, see also ibid., pp. 33–35, 60, and the section entitled "Social-

ism" in Lenin's article "Karl Marx," *Collected Works*, 21: 71–74. On prostitution, see Lenin, *Emancipation of Women*, pp. 26, 31–32. The relatively high number of articles published in 1913 undoubtedly had to do with the revival of a Russian socialist women's movement in 1912–1914, and the first celebration of International Women's Day in Russia in 1913; see Stites, *Women's Liberation*, pp. 253–258.

11. Lenin, *Emancipation of Women*, pp. 42–44, 80.

12. Ibid., p. 43.

13. Ibid., pp. 63–64.

14. Ibid., pp. 25, 26, 43, 60, 63–64.

15. Ibid., pp. 83–84.

16. Ibid., p. 69; see also pp. 59–60, 63, 66–68, 80–81, 84, 88, 116.

17. On women in social production, see ibid., p. 69; see also pp. 64, 81. On socialized services, see ibid., pp. 64, 69–70, 84, 115–116.

18. Ibid., p. 84.

19. Ibid., pp. 60, 70, 64. On the 1918 congress, see the account in Stites, *Women's Liberation*, pp. 329–331. For an overview of the obstacles faced by the Bolsheviks, see Clements, "Working-Class and Peasant Women."

20. Lenin, *Emancipation of Women*, pp. 83, 114–115. It must be remembered that virtually no socialist in this period seriously challenged the sex division of domestic labor, not even Alexandra Kollontai; see Jacqueline Heinen, "Kollontai and the History of Women's Oppression."

21. Lenin, *Emancipation of Women*, pp. 36–41.

22. Ibid., pp. 101, 105–107. On nihilist sexual radicalism, and on the issue of sexuality in the Russian socialist movement, see Stites, *Women's Liberation*, pp. 89–99, 258–269, 346–391.

Chapter 9   A Dual Legacy

1. This terminology revises that used in Lise Vogel, "Questions on the Woman Question," which opposed the "family argument" to the "social production argument." The term dual systems perspective is adopted from Iris Young, "Socialist Feminism and the Limits of Dual Systems Theory." I am grateful to Nancy Holmstrom for a discussion that clarified both the terminology and the analysis in this chapter. For an interesting parallel, see the discussion of two positions on the so-called national question in James Blaut, "Nationalism as an Autonomous Force."

2. Karl Marx and Frederick Engels, *Collected Works*, 5: 180.

3. On the family as the "economic unit of society" see Frederick Engels, *The Origin of the Family, Private Property and the State*, pp. 138, 139, 223, 235, 236n. On the family as the "cellular form of civilized society" see ibid., pp. 121–122, 129, 131, 137; see also Marx and Engels, *Collected Works*, 5: 46, and Karl Marx, *Grundrisse*, p. 484. For a similar analysis, see Beverly Brown, "Natural and Social Division of Labour," esp. pp. 38–41.

4. More recently, for example, Young intelligently demolishes the dualism of much of socialist-feminist theory, but then suggests an emphasis on "gender division of labor analysis" that threatens to recreate the very dualism she wishes to avoid. Iris Young, "Beyond the Unhappy Marriage."

Chapter 10   The Reproduction of Labor Power

1. Michèle Barrett, *Women's Oppression Today*, p. 79. I would like to thank Ira Gerstein for his many perceptive comments on the theoretical arguments in this and the following chapter.

2. Karl Marx, *Capital*, 1: 164, 43, 50, 179.

3. Ibid., p. 173.

4. Ibid., p. 531; 3: 790.

5. The term reproduction of labor power has also been used in a variety of other ways. It is sometimes employed to designate processes associated with the development of skills and the maintenance of ideological hegemony. For example, the educational system in capitalist society plays an important part in social reproduction and has been analyzed in terms of its role in the so-called reproduction of labor power. Still another use of the term refers to the labor involved in the production and distribution of means of subsistence. Workers in restaurants and clothing factories in capitalist society are said, for instance, to contribute to the reproduction of labor power. While these various uses of the term reproduction of labor power are suggestive, they disregard the special character of labor that is socially organized into an economy as opposed to labor that is not. See also the comments in Barry Hindess and Paul Hirst, *Pre-Capitalist Modes of Production*, chap. 1.

6. Marx, *Capital*, 1: 179.

7. Marx was not at all consistent in his discussion of the concept of individual consumption. At times he clearly restricts it to the daily maintenance of the individual direct producer. Elsewhere, he slips into formulations that imply it covers the maintenance and renewal of the worker "and his family." Socialist feminists have pointed to these inconsistencies as evidence of the inadequacies of the Marxist tradition. The difficulty lies not only with the remarks, but with the absence of any sustained examination of wage labor in the other volumes of *Capital*, which consider social reproduction as a whole. Had Marx completed his original plan, which projected a separate volume on wage labor, some of the problems might have been rectified. On the plans for *Capital*, see note 42 of Chapter 5.

8. For the question of theoretical levels, see Roger Establet, "Presentation du plan du Capital," and Ira Gerstein, "Production, Circulation and Value." The wording "total social reproduction" is used here to refer to the theoretical level at which Volume 3 of *Capital* operates, or, in Gerstein's terms, to "the complex unity of production and circulation." Gerstein, "Production, Circulation and Value," p. 265; see also pp. 253–256.

9. Marx, *Capital*, 1: 592.

10. The distinction of theoretical levels makes it clear that the domestic labor debate discussed in Chapter 2 properly concerns the problem of individual consumption at the level of the immediate production process in the capitalist mode of production—and not, as it seemed to some at the time, the reproduction of labor power in general.

11. For a sensible discussion of commonsense meanings of the term family, see Rayna Rapp, "Family and Class in Contemporary America."

12. On the social construction of sex differences, see: Barrett, *Women's Oppression Today*, pp. 74–77; Lourdes Benería, "Reproduction, Production, and the Sexual Division of Labour"; Beverly Brown, "Natural and Social Division of Labour"; Felicity Edholm, Olivia Harris, and Kate Young, "Conceptualising Women"; Maxine Molyneux, "Androcentrism in Marxist Anthropology." For a fine critique of this literature, see Janet Sayers, *Biological Politics*. See also the works cited in note 22, this chapter.

13. Marx, *Capital*, 1: 173.

14. Ibid., 3: 791; see also 1: 209.

15. Socialist-feminist discussions of reproduction of labor power sometimes stretch the term, implicitly if not explicitly, to include the renewal of individuals in the ruling class. In so doing, they not only produce conceptual confusion, they do away with the essential distinction between classes—that between exploiters and exploited.

16. Marx, *Capital*, 1: 208–209, 226–229.

17. Bridget O'Laughlin, "Production and Reproduction," pp. 6–7; Rayna Rapp, "Review of Claude Meillassoux, *Femmes, greniers et capitaux*," pp. 319, 321–322; Lise Vogel, "The Contested Domain." For discussions of functionalism in socialist-feminist theory, see Barrett, *Women's Oppression Today*, pp. 93–96, and Sayers, *Biological Politics*, p. 202.

18. Paddy Quick, "The Class Nature of Women's Oppression." In addition to her consideration of women's oppression in class society, Quick develops a contrast between class and nonclass societies, arguing that "it is only in class society that the involvement of women in child-bearing results in the oppression of women"; p. 45. Along similar lines, she makes the radical suggestion that "'the family' . . . is a term applicable only to class societies, in which production (and reproduction) have a meaning distinct from the organization of production in the interests of society as a whole (i.e., communist societies, both primitive and advanced)"; p. 47.

19. For discussions of the relationship between biology, sex divisions of labor, and women's oppression, see Barrett, *Women's Oppression Today*, pp. 72–77, 195–199, and Sayers, *Biological Politics*. Cousins claims that the biological distinction of sex cannot be addressed by Marxism, for "the capitalist and the labourer are personifications [that are] abstract to and indifferent to the problem of sexual difference." Mark Cousins, "Material Arguments and Feminism," p. 63. By contrast, Marx did not disregard the role of biology in social reproduction. He insisted, for example, that the mortality of direct producers neces-

sitates their maintenance and replacement, thereby making the problem of the reproduction of labor power critical to the social reproduction of class society. In the case of capitalism, "reproduction of labor-power forms, in fact, an essential of the reproduction of capital itself." Marx, *Capital*, 1: 575–576. If the biological fact of mortality is central to Marxist analysis, why not the biological fact of sexual dimorphism as well!

20. See, for example, Christopher Middleton, "The Sexual Division of Labour in Feudal England."

21. Quick, "Women's Oppression," p. 47.

22. For discussion of the historical origins of women's oppression, see Sally Alexander, "Women's Work in Nineteenth-Century London"; Benería, "Reproduction, Production"; Mina Davis Caulfield, "Equality, Sex and Mode of Production"; Penelope Ciancanelli, "Exchange, Reproduction and Sex Subordination among the Kikuyu of East Africa"; Carmen Diana Deere and Magdalena Léon de Leal, "Peasant Production, Proletarianization, and the Sexual Division of Labor in the Andes"; Maurice Godelier, "The Origins of Male Domination"; Middleton, "Sexual Division of Labour"; Iris Young, "Beyond the Unhappy Marriage."

23. Marx, *Capital*, 1: 168. Joan Kelly-Gadol, "The Social Relation of the Sexes," p. 821.

24. Similarly, men ordinarily participate, to some extent, in the immediate tasks of necessary labor. It is important to recognize that personal maintenance tasks (washing oneself, brushing one's teeth, etc.) constitute necessary labor, as does the work involved in getting to the site of production (walking six miles to the mill, commuting to the office by train, etc.).

25. Alexander, "Women's Work"; Angela Davis, "Reflections on the Black Woman's Role in the Community of Slaves."

Chapter 11   Beyond Domestic Labor

1. Karl Marx, *Capital*, 1: 535–536; similar statements appear on pp. 533, 537, 538, and 542, as well as in Karl Marx, *Grundrisse*, pp. 458, 676–677, 717n. Marx's famous comments that the laborer "belongs to himself, and performs his necessary vital functions outside the process of production," a performance "the capitalist may safely leave . . . to the laborer's instincts of self-preservation and of propagation," implicitly recognize reproduction of labor power as a process that must remain external to capitalist commodity production. His unfortunate phrasing, quite rightly the object of feminist criticism, appears to exempt the process from theoretical examination, however, and conceals the kernel of genuine theoretical insight. *Capital*, 1: 536–537. Molyneux argues that "domestic labour, as privatised individual labour not subject to the law of value, *lies outside the theory of the capitalist mode of production*," but she does not deny the importance of developing a Marxist analysis of domestic labor in capitalist society. Maxine Molyneux, "Beyond the Domestic Labour Debate," p. 20.

2. Marx, *Capital*, 1: 505.

3. The units for the performance of the domestic component of necessary labor

can be analyzed in terms of what has been called the double "separation" of the direct producer, who neither "owns" nor "possesses" the means and conditions of capitalist production. The payment of wages and the isolated domestic labor site embody this double separation. Wage laborers cannot appropriate, or own, surplus value. Neither can they activate, or possess, the concrete labor process. In this sense, the payment of wages corresponds to the worker's lack of ownership of any property, save his or her own labor power. Spatial, temporal, and institutional separation of the site of domestic labor from that of wage labor reflects the worker's inability to set the instruments of social labor in motion. In sum, the bearers of labor power are in a state of nonownership and nonpossession of the means and conditions of production. From this point of view, the units for the performance of domestic labor constitute a special subset of social units in capitalist society. They are concrete forms taken by the relation between the working class's nonownership and nonpossession of the means and conditions of production. (Cf. Poulantzas's characterization of the enterprise as "the concrete form of the relation between an economic ownership and a possession that both belong to capital." Nicos Poulantzas, *Classes in Contemporary Capitalism*, p. 123. See also Louis Althusser and Etienne Balibar, *Reading Capital*, and Charles Bettelheim, *Economic Calculation and Forms of Property*.) Because these social units materialize a definite relationship to the means and conditions of production—namely, nonownership and nonpossession on the part of the bearers of labor power—they cannot be viewed as private enclaves developing in relative isolation from the processes of capitalist production. The form, composition, and internal structure of the special set of social units acting as sites for domestic labor are, in fact, directly affected by the course of capitalist accumulation.

In a limited sense, the social units in which the domestic component of necessary labor takes place are the counterparts of capitalist enterprises. From this point of view, Bettelheim's discussion of the "displacement of the limits" of the enterprise with the rise of monopoly capitalism suggests a similar conceptualization of the development of family households in capitalist society. The removal of certain functions from the private household, for example, and the development of collective consumption, represent analogous displacements of limits. It must be emphasized that to speak of the units of domestic labor as counterparts to those of capitalist production implies no simple parallelism.

4. Marx, *Capital*, 1: chaps. 12, 16.

5. Emily Blumenfeld and Susan Mann, "Domestic Labour and the Reproduction of Labour Power"; Nancy Holmstrom, "'Women's Work,' the Family, and Capitalism."

6. The liberating potential inherent in the socialization of domestic labor was especially evident in the nineteenth and early twentieth centuries; see Dolores Hayden, *The Grand Domestic Revolution*.

7. In their desire for equality and liberation, feminists have sometimes tried to abolish the role of biology. For example, Firestone calls for "the freeing of women from the tyranny of their biology by any means available," including artificial reproduction outside the womb. Shulamith Firestone, *The Dialectic of Sex*, p. 206. See Janet Sayers, *Biological Politics*, for discussion of the contradictory and antimaterialist character of such positions.

8. Marx, *Capital*, 1: 168, 486. For a more detailed exposition of Marx's discussion of the value and price of labor power, and of wages, see Chapter 5.

9. Ira Gerstein, "Domestic Work and Capitalism"; Paul Smith, "Domestic Labour and Marx's Theory of Value." Smith does not address the question of the destination of the value contained in the means of subsistence consumed by non-working household members, and says nothing about the family wage. The implication is that persons not engaged in wage labor somehow fall outside the capitalist mode of production.

10. For the controversy over the interpretation of the family wage, see Michèle Barrett and Mary McIntosh, "The 'Family Wage.'" For clear discussions of how a dependent wife not in the labor force raises (rather than lowers) the value of labor power, see Holmstrom, "'Women's Work,'" or Molyneux, "Domestic Labour Debate."

11. Friedrich Engels, *The Condition of the Working Class in England*, p. 98. For a summary of the recent discussion about women and the industrial reserve army, see Margaret Simeral, "Women and the Reserve Army of Labor." See also: Flora Anthias, "Women and the Reserve Army of Labour"; Michèle Barrett, *Women's Oppression Today*, pp. 24–27, 158–162; Irene Bruegel, "Women as a Reserve Army of Labour."

12. Veronica Beechey, "Some Notes on Female Wage Labour in Capitalist Production," p. 58.

13. Marx, *Capital*, 3: 196. Gaudemar has developed the concept of the tendency toward perfect mobility of labor power. Not once, however, does he consider the barrier formed by the existence of domestic labor and the family household. Jean-Paul de Gaudemar, *Mobilité du travail et accumulation du capital*.

14. Karl Marx, *Grundrisse*, pp. 609–610.

15. Ibid., p. 245. See also Frederick Engels, *Anti-Dühring*, pp. 124–129.

16. Marx, *Capital*, 1: 78, 76–77, 78. See also: ibid., chap. 1, secs. 1, 2, 4; idem, *A Contribution to the Critique of Political Economy*, chap. 1; Isaak Illich Rubin, *Essays on Marx's Theory of Value*, chaps. 10–14.

17. Marx, *Capital*, 1: 165. See also ibid., pp. 156–157, 164–166, 172, 188, 547–550. On the laws of exchange of commodities, see ibid., pp. 88–96, 106–115.

18. Ibid., pp. 164–167. This "double freedom" embodies the double separation discussed in note 3, this chapter.

19. Ibid., p. 550. See also the citations in note 16, this chapter.

20. For good discussions of the nature of equality in the United States in the eighteenth and nineteenth centuries, see: Alan Dawley, *Class and Community*, pp. 1–10, 60–68, 207–211; Ellen Carol DuBois, *Feminism and Suffrage*, pp. 40–47; W. E. B. Du Bois, *Black Reconstruction in America 1860–1880*, chaps. 1–2.

21. V. I. Lenin, *The Emancipation of Women*, p. 80.

22. Margaret Coulsen, Branka Magas, and Hilary Wainwright, "'The Housewife and

Her Labour under Capitalism,'" p. 65; Jean Gardiner, "Women in the Labour Process and Class Structure," p. 159.

23. Rayna Rapp summarizes the literature on these variations in "Family and Class in Contemporary America."

24. Marx, *Capital*, 3: 877. For the nonantagonistic relationship between surplus production and the reproduction of labor power, see also: idem, *Critique of the Gotha Programme*; idem, *Capital*, 1: 82–83, 496, and 3: 818–820, 847, 878. Although I follow Marx's usage, his retention of the terms necessary and surplus labor for analysis of nonexploitative systems may be more confusing than helpful, as he himself suggests when he comments that "a part of what is now surplus labor, would then count as necessary labor; I mean the labor of forming a fund for reserve and accumulation." *Capital*, 1: 496.

25. Mina Davis Caulfield, "Equality, Sex and Mode of Production," p. 213. See also Eleanor Leacock, "Women in Egalitarian Society."

26. Cuba initiated discussion of sharing housework and child-care responsibilities around 1973, as did China, and the topic was considered in Albania as early as 1967. The Soviet Union has not yet given official support to equalizing domestic responsibilities. For thoughtful studies on women in the socialist transition, see: Elisabeth Croll, *Feminism and Socialism in China*; idem, "Women in Rural Production and Reproduction in the Soviet Union, China, Cuba, and Tanzania"; Maxine Molyneux, "Socialist Societies Old and New"; Judith Stacey, *Patriarchy and Socialist Revolution in China*; as well as the works on the Soviet Union cited in note 7 of Chapter 8. In addition to documenting women's inequality in the household in socialist countries, these studies survey the persistence of a sex division of labor in the areas of public production and political life that likewise disadvantages women. On Albania, see "On the Liberation of Women in Albania," esp. pp. 25–26.

27. Marx, *Gotha Programme*, pp. 9–10.

28. Marx, *Capital*, 1: 460; Frederick Engels, *The Origin of the Family, Private Property and the State*, p. 145.

29. Engels, *Anti-Dühring*, p. 333; see also p. 338.

Works Cited

Alexander, Sally. "Women's Work in Nineteenth-Century London: A Study of the Years 1820–1850." In *The Rights and Wrongs of Women*, edited by Juliet Mitchell and Ann Oakley, pp. 59–111. Harmondsworth: Penguin Books, 1976.

Althusser, Louis, and Balibar, Etienne. *Reading Capital*. London: NLB, 1970.

Anthias, Floya. "Women and the Reserve Army of Labour: A Critique of Veronica Beechey." *Capital and Class*, no. 10 (Spring 1980): 50–63.

Atkinson, Jane. "Anthropology." *Signs* 8 (1982–1983): 236–258.

Aveling, Edward, and Aveling, Eleanor Marx. *The Woman Question*. London: Sonnenschein, 1886. Reprinted (with subtitles added) in *Marxism Today* 16, no. 3 (March 1972): 80–88.

Barrett, Michèle. *Women's Oppression Today: Problems in Marxist Feminist Analysis*. London: Verso Editions, 1980.

Barrett, Michèle, and McIntosh, Mary. "The 'Family Wage': Some Problems for Socialists and Feminists." *Capital and Class*, no. 11 (Summer 1980): 51–72.

Bebel, August. *Die Frau und der Sozialismus*. Stuttgart: Dietz Verlag, 1891.

———. *Woman in the Past, Present and Future*. 1885. Reprint. New York: AMS Press, 1976.

———. *Woman under Socialism*. Translated by Daniel De Leon. 1904. Reprint. New York: Schocken Books, 1971.

Beecher, Jonathan, and Bienvenu, Richard, eds. *The Utopian Vision of Charles Fourier*. Boston: Beacon Press, 1971.

Beechey, Veronica. "On Patriarchy." *Feminist Review*, no. 3 (1979): 66–82.

———. "Some Notes on Female Wage Labour in Capitalist Production." *Capital and Class*, no. 3 (Autumn 1977): 45–66.

———. "Women and Production: A Critical Analysis of Some Sociological Theories of Women's Work." In *Feminism and Materialism: Women and Modes of Production*, edited by Annette Kuhn and Annemarie Wolpe, pp. 155–197. Boston: Routledge and Kegan Paul, 1978.

Benería, Lourdes. "Reproduction, Production and the Sexual Division of Labour." *Cambridge Journal of Economics* 3 (1979): 203–225.

Benston, Margaret. "The Political Economy of Women's Liberation." *Monthly Review* 21, no. 4 (September 1969): 13–27.

Bettelheim, Charles. *Economic Calculation and Forms of Property*. New York: Monthly Review Press, 1975.

Blaut, James. "Nationalism as an Autonomous Force." *Science and Society* 46 (1982): 1–23.

Blumenberg, Werner, ed. *August Bebels Briefwechsel mit Friedrich Engels*. The Hague: Mouton Publishing Co., 1965.

Blumenfeld, Emily, and Mann, Susan. "Domestic Labour and the Reproduction of Labour Power: Towards an Analysis of Women, the Family, and Class." In *Hidden in the Household: Women's Domestic Labour under Capitalism*, edited by Bonnie Fox, pp. 267–307. Toronto: Women's Press, 1980.

Bobroff, Anne. "The Bolsheviks and Working Women, 1905–1920." *Soviet Studies* 26 (1974): 540–567.

Bridenthal, Renate. "The Dialectics of Production and Reproduction in History." *Radical America* 10, no. 2 (March–April 1976): 3–11.

Brown, Beverly. "Natural and Social Division of Labour: Engels and the Domestic Labour Debate." *m/f*, no. 1 (1978): 25–47.

Brown, Liz. "The Family and Its Genealogies: A Discussion of Engels' 'Origin of the Family.'" *m/f*, no. 3 (1979): 5–34.

Bruegel, Irene. "Women as a Reserve Army of Labour: A Note on Recent British Experience." *Feminist Review*, no. 3 (1979): 12–23.

Bujra, Janet. "Female Solidarity and the Sexual Division of Labour." In *Women United, Women Divided*, edited by Patricia Caplan and Janet Bujra, pp. 13–45. London: Tavistock Publications, 1978.

Burris, Val. "The Dialectic of Women's Oppression: Notes on the Relation between Capitalism and Patriarchy." *Berkeley Journal of Sociology* 27 (1982): 51–74.

Caulfield, Mina Davis. "Equality, Sex and Mode of Production." In *Social Inequality: Comparative and Developmental Approaches*, edited by Gerald Berreman, pp. 201–220. New York: Academic Press, 1981.

———. "Imperialism, the Family, and Cultures of Resistance." *Socialist Revolution*, no. 20 (October 1974): 67–85.

Chinchilla, Norma Stoltz. "Ideologies of Feminism: Liberal, Radical, Marxist." Social Sciences Research Reports, no. 61. School of Social Sciences, University of California at Irvine, February 1980.

———. "Mobilizing Women: Revolution in the Revolution." *Latin American Perspectives* 4, no. 4 (Fall 1977): 83–102.

———. "Working-Class Feminism: Domitila and the Housewives Committee." *Latin American Perspectives* 6, no. 3 (Summer 1979): 87–92.

Ciancanelli, Penelope. "Exchange, Reproduction and Sex Subordination among the Kikuyu of East Africa." *Review of Radical Political Economics* 12, no. 2 (Summer 1980): 25–36.

Clements, Barbara Evans. "Working-Class and Peasant Women in the Russian Revolution, 1917–1923." *Signs* 8 (1982–1983): 215–235.

Coulsen, Margaret; Magas, Branka; and Wainwright, Hilary. "'The Housewife and Her Labour under Capitalism': A Critique." *New Left Review*, no. 89 (January–February 1975): 59–71.

Cousins, Mark. "Material Arguments and Feminism." *m/f*, no. 2 (1978): 62–70.

Croll, Elisabeth. *Feminism and Socialism in China*. London: Routledge and Kegan Paul, 1978.

——— "Women in Rural Production and Reproduction in the Soviet Union, China, Cuba, and Tanzania." *Signs* 7 (1981–1982): 361–399.

Dalla Costa, Mariarosa. "Women and the Subversion of the Community." In *The Power of Women and the Subversion of the Community*, pp. 19–54. Bristol: Falling Wall Press, 1973.

Davis, Angela. "Reflections on the Black Woman's Role in the Community of Slaves." *Black Scholar* 3, no. 4 (December 1971): 3–15.

Dawley, Alan. *Class and Community: The Industrial Revolution in Lynn*. Cambridge, Mass.: Harvard University Press, 1976.

Deckard, Barbara Sinclair. *The Women's Movement: Political, Socioeconomic, and Psychological Issues*. New York: Harper and Row, 1978.

Deere, Carmen Diana. "Rural Women's Subsistence Production in the Capitalist Periphery." *Review of Radical Political Economics* 8, no. 1 (Spring 1976): 9–17.

Deere, Carmen Diana, and Léon de Leal, Magdalena. "Peasant Production, Proletarianization, and the Sexual Division of Labor in the Andes." *Signs* 7 (1981–1982): 338–360.

Delmar, Rosalind. "Looking Again at Engels' *Origin of the Family, Private Property and the State*." In *The Rights and Wrongs of Women*, edited by Juliet Mitchell and Ann Oakley, pp. 271–287. Harmondsworth: Penguin Books, 1976.

Dixon, Marlene. "The Centrality of Women in Proletarian Revolution." *Synthesis* 1, no. 4 (Spring 1977).

———. "Where Are We Going?" *Radical America* 4, no. 2 (February 1970): 26–35.

———. "Why Women's Liberation—2?" In *Female Liberation: History and Current Politics*, edited by Roberta Salper, pp. 184–200. New York: Alfred A. Knopf, 1972.

Draper, Hal. "Marx and Engels on Women's Liberation." In *Female Liberation: History and Current Politics*, edited by Roberta Salper, pp. 83–107. New York: Alfred A. Knopf, 1972.

Draper, Hal, and Lipow, Anne. "Marxist Women versus Bourgeois Feminism." In *Socialist Register 1976*, edited by Ralph Miliband and John Saville, pp. 179–226. London: Merlin Press, 1976.

DuBois, Ellen Carol. *Feminism and Suffrage: The Emergence of an Independent Women's Movement in America 1848–1869*. Ithaca: Cornell University Press, 1978.

Du Bois, W. E. B. *Black Reconstruction in America 1860–1880*. 1935. Reprint. New York: Atheneum Publishers, 1971.

Easton, Barbara. "Feminism and the Contemporary Family." *Socialist Review*, no. 39 (May–June 1978): 11–36.

Edholm, Felicity; Harris, Olivia; and Young, Kate. "Conceptualising Women." *Critique of Anthropology*, nos. 9–10 (1977): 101–130.

Eisenstein, Zillah, ed. *Capitalist Patriarchy and the Case for Socialist Feminism*. New York: Monthly Review Press, 1978.

Engels, Frederick. *Anti-Dühring*. Moscow: Progress Publishers, 1947.

———. *Ludwig Feuerbach and the Outcome of Classical German Philosophy*. New York: International Publishers, 1967.

———. *The Origin of the Family, Private Property and the State*. New York: International Publishers, 1972.

Engels, Friedrich. *The Condition of the Working Class in England*. Translated and edited by W. O. Henderson and W. H. Chaloner. Stanford: Stanford University Press, 1968.

Epstein, Barbara. "Thoughts on Socialist Feminism in 1980." *New Political Science* 1, no. 4 (Fall 1980): 25–35.

Establet, Roger. "Presentation du plan du Capital." In *Lire le Capital*, vol. 4, edited by Roger Establet and Pierre Macherey, pp. 47–109. Paris: François Maspero, 1973.

Evans, Richard. "Bourgeois Feminists and Women Socialists in Germany 1894–1914: Lost Opportunity or Inevitable Conflict?" *Women's Studies International Quarterly* 3 (1980): 355–376.

———. *The Feminists: Women's Emancipation Movements in Europe, America and Australasia 1840–1920*. New York: Barnes and Noble, 1977.

Evans, Sara. "The Origins of the Women's Liberation Movement." *Radical America* 9, no. 2 (March–April 1975): 1–12.

———. *Personal Politics: The Roots of Women's Liberation in the Civil Rights Movement and the New Left*. New York: Alfred A. Knopf, 1979.

Firestone, Shulamith. *The Dialectic of Sex: The Case for Feminist Revolution*. New York: William Morrow and Co., 1970.

Fox, Bonnie, ed. *Hidden in the Household: Women's Domestic Labour under Capitalism*. Toronto: Women's Press, 1980.

Freeman, Caroline. "When Is a Wage Not a Wage?" *Red Rag*, no. 5 (1973). Reprinted in *The Politics of Housework*, edited by Ellen Malos, pp. 202–209. London: Allison and Busby, 1980.

Freeman, Jo. "The Origins of the Women's Liberation Movement." *American Journal of Sociology* 78 (1973): 792–811.

———. "The Women's Liberation Movement: Its Origins, Structures, and Ideas." In *Family, Marriage, and the Struggle of the Sexes*, edited by H. P. Dreitzel, pp. 201–216. New York: Macmillan Co., 1972.

Gardiner, Jean. "The Political Economy of Domestic Labour in Capitalist Society." In *Dependence and Exploitation in Work and Marriage*, edited by Diana Leonard Barker and Sheila Allen, pp. 109–120. New York: Longman, 1976.

———. "Women in the Labour Process and Class Structure." In *Class and Class Structure*, edited by Alan Hunt, pp. 155–163. London: Lawrence and Wishart, 1977.

Gaudemar, Jean-Paul de. *Mobilité du travail et accumulation du capital*. Paris: François Maspero, 1976.

Geiger, H. Kent. *The Family in Soviet Russia*. Cambridge, Mass.: Harvard University Press, 1968.

Gerstein, Ira. "Domestic Work and Capitalism." *Radical America* 7, nos. 4–5 (July–October 1973): 101–128.

————. "Production, Circulation and Value." *Economy and Society* 5 (1976): 243–291.

Glickman, Rose. "The Russian Factory Woman, 1880–1914." In *Women in Russia*, edited by Dorothy Atkinson, Alexander Dallin, and Gail Warshofsky Lapidus, pp. 63–83. Stanford: Stanford University Press, 1977.

Godelier, Maurice. "The Origins of Male Domination." *New Left Review*, no. 127 (May–June 1981): 3–17.

Guesde, Jules. *Textes choisis, 1867–1882*. Edited by Claude Willard. Paris: Editions sociales, 1959.

Guettel, Charnie. *Marxism and Feminism*. Toronto: Women's Press, 1974.

Harrison, John. "The Political Economy of Housework." *Bulletin of the Conference of Socialist Economists*, no. 7 (Winter 1973).

Hartmann, Heidi. "The Unhappy Marriage of Marxism and Feminism: Towards a More Progressive Union." *Capital and Class*, no. 8 (Summer 1979): 1–33.

Hartmann, Heidi, and Bridges, Amy. "The Unhappy Marriage of Marxism and Feminism." Working draft. July 1975.

Hayden, Carol Eubanks. "The Zhenotdel and the Bolshevik Party." *Russian History* 3 (1976): 150–173.

Hayden, Dolores. *The Grand Domestic Revolution: A History of Feminist Designs for American Homes, Neighborhoods, and Cities*. Cambridge, Mass.: M.I.T. Press, 1981.

Heinen, Jacqueline. "Kollontai and the History of Women's Oppression." *New Left Review*, no. 110 (July–August 1978): 43–63.

Heitlinger, Alena. *Women and State Socialism: Sex Inequality in the Soviet Union and Czechoslovakia*. London: Macmillan and Co., 1979.

Hindess, Barry, and Hirst, Paul. *Pre-Capitalist Modes of Production*. London: Routledge and Kegan Paul, 1975.

Hole, Judith, and Levine, Ellen. *Rebirth of Feminism*. New York: Quadrangle Books, 1971.

Holmstrom, Nancy. "'Women's Work,' The Family, and Capitalism." *Science and Society* 45 (1981): 186–211.

Honeycutt, Karen. "Clara Zetkin: A Left-Wing Socialist and Feminist in Wilhelmian Germany." Ph.D. dissertation, Columbia University, 1975.

————. "Socialism and Feminism in Imperial Germany." *Signs* 5 (1979–1980): 30–41.

Humphries, Jane. "Class Struggle and the Persistence of the Working-Class Family." *Cambridge Journal of Economics* 1 (1977): 241–258.

International Workingmen's Association, General Council. Minutes. 4 vols. Moscow: Progress Publishers, n.d. [1964?].

Kapp, Yvonne. *Eleanor Marx: II. The Crowded Years, 1884–1898.* London: Lawrence and Wishart, 1976.

Kelly, Joan. "The Doubled Vision of Feminist Theory." *Feminist Studies* 5 (1979): 216–227.

Kelly-Gadol, Joan. "The Social Relation of the Sexes: Methodological Implications of Women's History." *Signs* 1 (1975–1976): 809–823.

Krader, Lawrence, ed. *The Ethnological Notebooks of Karl Marx.* Assen: Van Gorcum, 1972.

Kuhn, Annette, and Wolpe, Annemarie, eds. *Feminism and Materialism: Women and Modes of Production.* Boston: Routledge and Kegan Paul, 1978.

Landes, Joan. "Women, Labor and Family Life: A Theoretical Perspective." *Science and Society* 41 (1977–1978): 386–409.

Lane, Ann. "Women in Society: A Critique of Frederick Engels." In *Liberating Women's History*, edited by Berenice Carroll, pp. 4–25. Urbana: University of Illinois Press, 1976.

Lapidus, Gail Warshofsky. "Sexual Equality in Soviet Policy: A Developmental Perspective." In *Women in Russia*, edited by Dorothy Atkinson, Alexander Dallin, and Gail Warshofsky Lapidus, pp. 115–138. Stanford: Stanford University Press, 1977.

Larguia, Isabel. "The Economic Basis of the Status of Women." In *Women Cross-Culturally: Change and Challenge*, edited by Ruby Rohrlich-Leavitt, pp. 281–295. The Hague: Mouton, 1975.

Leacock, Eleanor. Introduction to *Ancient Society*, by Lewis Morgan. Cleveland: World Publishing Co., 1963.

————. Introduction to *The Origin of the Family, Private Property and the State*, by Frederick Engels. New York: International Publishers, 1972.

————. "Women in Egalitarian Society." In *Becoming Visible: Women in European Society*, edited by Renate Bridenthal and Claudia Koonz, pp. 11–35. Boston: Houghton Mifflin Co., 1977.

Lenin, V. I. *Collected Works.* 45 vols. Moscow: Progress Publishers, 1960–1970.

―――. *The Development of Capitalism in Russia*. Moscow: Progress Publishers, 1974.

―――. *The Emancipation of Women*. New York: International Publishers, 1966.

McDonough, Rosin, and Harrison, Rachel. "Patriarchy and Relations of Production." In *Feminism and Materialism: Women and Modes of Production*, edited by Annette Kuhn and Annemarie Wolpe, pp. 11–41. Boston: Routledge and Kegan Paul, 1978.

McIntosh, Mary. "The Welfare State and the Needs of the Dependent Family." In *Fit Work for Women*, edited by Sandra Burman, pp. 153–172. London: Croom Helm, 1979.

Mackintosh, Maureen. "Domestic Labour and the Household." In *Fit Work for Women*, edited by Sandra Burman, pp. 173–191. London: Croom Helm, 1979.

―――. "Reproduction and Patriarchy: A Critique of Claude Meillassoux, 'Femmes, greniers et capitaux.'" *Capital and Class*, no. 2 (Summer 1977): 119–127.

Malos, Ellen. "Housework and the Politics of Women's Liberation." *Socialist Review*, no. 37 (January–February 1978): 41–71.

Marcus, Steven. *Engels, Manchester, and the Working Class*. New York: Random House, 1974.

Marx, Karl. *Capital*. 3 vols. Moscow: Progress Publishers, n.d.–1971.

―――. *Capital*. Vol. 1. New York: Vintage Books, 1977.

―――. *A Contribution to the Critique of Political Economy*. Moscow: Progress Publishers, 1970.

―――. *Critique of the Gotha Programme*. New York: International Publishers, 1970.

―――. *The First International and After*. Edited by David Fernbach. New York: Vintage Books, 1974.

―――. *Grundrisse*. Baltimore: Penguin Books, 1973.

―――. *Letters to Dr. Kugelmann*. New York: International Publishers, 1934.

―――. *Pre-Capitalist Economic Formations*. New York: International Publishers, 1965.

―――. "Results of the Immediate Process of Production." In *Capital*, 1: 949–1084. New York: Vintage Books, 1977.

―――. *Wages, Price and Profit*. Peking: Foreign Languages Press, 1973.

Marx, Karl, and Engels, Frederick. *Collected Works*. New York: International Publishers, 1975–.

————. *Selected Correspondence*. 2d ed. Moscow: Progress Publishers, 1965.

————. *Selected Works in One Volume*. New York: International Publishers, 1968.

Marx, Karl, and Engels, Friedrich. *Werke*. 39 vols. Berlin: Dietz Verlag, 1956–1968.

Massell, Gregory. *The Surrogate Proletariat: Moslem Women and Revolutionary Strategies in Soviet Central Asia, 1919–1929*. Princeton: Princeton University Press, 1972.

Meillassoux, Claude. *Femmes, greniers et capitaux*. Paris: François Maspero, 1975.

Meyer, Alfred. "Marxism and the Women's Movement." In *Women in Russia*, edited by Dorothy Atkinson, Alexander Dallin, and Gail Warshofsky Lapidus, pp. 85–112. Stanford: Stanford University Press, 1977.

Middleton, Christopher. "The Sexual Division of Labour in Feudal England." *New Left Review*, nos. 113–114 (January–April 1979): 147–168.

————. "Sexual Inequality and Stratification Theory." In *The Social Analysis of Class Structure*, edited by Frank Parkin, pp. 179–203. London: Tavistock Publications, 1974.

Millett, Kate. *Sexual Politics*. New York: Doubleday and Co., 1970.

Mitchell, Juliet. *Woman's Estate*. Baltimore: Penguin Books, 1971.

————. "Women: The Longest Revolution." *New Left Review*, no. 40 (November–December 1966): 11–37.

Molyneux, Maxine. "Androcentrism in Marxist Anthropology." *Critique of Anthropology*, nos. 9–10 (1977): 55–81.

————. "Beyond the Domestic Labour Debate." *New Left Review*, no. 116 (July–August 1979): 3–27.

————. "Socialist Societies Old and New: Progress Towards Women's Emancipation." *Monthly Review* 34, no. 3 (July–August 1982): 56–100.

Morgan, D. H. J. *Social Theory and the Family*. London: Routledge and Kegan Paul, 1975.

Morgan, Lewis. *Ancient Society*. New York: Holt, 1877.

Morton, Peggy. "A Woman's Work Is Never Done." In *From Feminism to Liberation*, edited by Edith Altbach, pp. 211–227. Cambridge, Mass.: Schenkman Publishing Co., 1971.

Murdock, George. *Social Structure*. New York: Macmillan Co., 1949.

"The National Conference on Socialist-Feminism." *Socialist Revolution*, no. 26 (October–December 1975): 85–116.

Nolan, Molly. "Proletarischer Anti-Feminismus: Dargestellt am Beispiel der SPD-Ortsgruppe Duesseldorf, 1890 bis 1914." In *Frauen und Wissenschaft*, pp. 356–377. Berlin: Courage, 1977.

Okin, Susan Moller. *Women in Western Political Thought*. Princeton: Princeton University Press, 1979.

O'Laughlin, Bridget. "Marxist Approaches in Anthropology." *Annual Review of Anthropology* 4 (1975): 341–370.

———. "Production and Reproduction: Meillassoux's *Femmes, greniers et capitaux*." *Critique of Anthropology*, no. 8 (Spring 1977): 3–32.

Omvedt, Gail. *We Will Smash This Prison! Indian Women in Struggle*. London: Zed Press, 1980.

———. "Women and Rural Revolt in India." *Journal of Peasant Studies* 5 (1978): 370–403.

"On the Liberation of Women in Albania." New York: Gamma Publishing Co., 1975.

Petchesky, Rosalind. "Dissolving the Hyphen: A Report on Marxist-Feminist Groups 1–5." In *Capitalist Patriarchy and the Case for Socialist Feminism*, edited by Zillah Eisenstein, pp. 373–389. New York: Monthly Review Press, 1978.

Poster, Mark. *Critical Theory of the Family*. New York: Seabury Press, 1978.

Poulantzas, Nicos. *Classes in Contemporary Capitalism*. London: New Left Books, 1975.,

The Power of Women and the Subversion of the Community. Bristol: Falling Wall Press, 1973.

Quataert, Jean. *Reluctant Feminists in German Social Democracy, 1885–1917*. Princeton: Princeton University Press, 1979.

———. "Unequal Partners in an Uneasy Alliance: Women and the Working Class in Imperial Germany." In *Socialist Women: European Socialist Feminism in the Nineteenth and Early Twentieth Centuries*, edited by Marilyn Boxer and Jean Quataert, pp. 112–145. New York: Elsevier, 1978.

Quick, Paddy. "The Class Nature of Women's Oppression." *Review of Radical Political Economics* 9, no. 3 (Fall 1977): 42–53.

———. "Why Women Work for Wages." *New Political Science* 1, no. 4 (Fall 1980): 43–48.

Rapp, Rayna. "Anthropology." *Signs* 4 (1978–1979): 497–513.

————. "Family and Class in Contemporary America: Notes Toward an Understanding of Ideology." *Science and Society* 42 (1978): 278–300.

————. "Review of Claude Meillassoux, *Femmes, greniers et capitaux.*" *Dialectical Anthropology* 2 (1977): 317–323.

Red Apple Collective. "Socialist-Feminist Women's Unions: Past and Present." *Socialist Review*, no. 38 (March–April 1978): 37–57.

Robinson, Lillian. *Robinson on the Woman Question.* Buffalo: Earth's Daughters, 1975.

Rosdolsky, Roman. *The Making of Marx's "Capital."* London: Pluto Press, 1977.

Rowbotham, Sheila. *Woman's Consciousness, Man's World.* Baltimore: Penguin Books, 1973.

————. *Women, Resistance and Revolution: A History of Women and Revolution in the Modern World.* New York: Pantheon Books, 1972.

Rowntree, Mickey, and Rowntree, John. "Notes on the Political Economy of Women's Liberation." *Monthly Review* 21, no. 7 (December 1969): 26–32.

Rubin, Gayle. "The Traffic in Women: Notes on the 'Political Economy' of Sex." In *Toward an Anthropology of Women*, edited by Rayna R. Reiter, pp. 157–210. New York: Monthly Review Press, 1975.

Rubin, Isaak Illich. *Essays on Marx's Theory of Value.* Detroit: Black and Red, 1972.

Sacks, Karen. "Engels Revisited: Women, the Organization of Production, and Private Property." In *Toward an Anthropology of Women*, edited by Rayna R. Reiter, pp. 211–234. New York: Monthly Review Press, 1975.

Saffioti, Heleieth. "Women, Mode of Production, and Social Formations." *Latin American Perspectives* 4, nos. 1–2 (Winter–Spring 1977): 27–37.

Salper, Roberta. "The Development of the American Women's Liberation Movement, 1967–1971." In *Female Liberation*, edited by Roberta Salper, pp. 169–184. New York: Alfred A. Knopf, 1972.

Santamaria, U. "Review Article: The Ethnological Notebooks of Karl Marx, ed. by L. Krader." *Critique of Anthropology*, nos. 4–5 (Autumn 1975): 156–164.

Sargent, Lydia, ed. *Women and Revolution: A Discussion of the Unhappy Marriage of Marxism and Feminism.* Boston: South End Press, 1981.

Sayers, Janet. *Biological Politics: Feminist and Anti-Feminist Perspectives.* London: Tavistock Publications, 1982.

Simeral, Margaret. "Women and the Reserve Army of Labor." *Insurgent Sociologist* 8, nos. 2–3 (Fall 1978): 164–179.

Smith, Paul. "Domestic Labour and Marx's Theory of Value." In *Feminism and Materialism: Women and Modes of Production,* edited by Annette Kuhn and Annemarie Wolpe, pp. 198–219. Boston: Routledge and Kegan Paul, 1978.

Stacey, Judith. *Patriarchy and Socialist Revolution in China.* Berkeley: University of California Press, in press.

Steinberg, Hans-Josef. "Workers' Libraries in Germany before 1914." *History Workshop* 1 (1976): 166–180.

Stern, Bernhard. "Engels on the Family." *Science and Society* 12 (1948): 42–64.

Stites, Richard. *The Women's Liberation Movement in Russia: Feminism, Nihilism, and Bolshevism, 1860–1930.* Princeton: Princeton University Press, 1978.

Urdang, Stephanie. *Fighting Two Colonialisms: Women in Guinea-Bissau.* New York: Monthly Review Press, 1979.

Vogel, Lise. "The Contested Domain: A Note on the Family in the Transition to Capitalism." *Marxist Perspectives* 1, no. 1 (Spring 1978): 50–73.

———. "The Earthly Family." *Radical America* 7, nos. 4–5 (July–October 1973): 9–50.

———. "Questions on the Woman Question." *Monthly Review* 31, no. 2 (June 1979): 39–59.

———. "Women, Work, and Family: Some Theoretical Issues." Paper presented at the annual meetings of the Society for the Study of Social Problems, New York City, August 1980.

"Women's Issue." *Critique of Anthropology,* nos. 9–10 (1977).

Young, Iris. "Beyond the Unhappy Marriage: A Critique of the Dual Systems Theory." In *Women and Revolution,* edited by Lydia Sargent, pp. 43–70. Boston: South End Press, 1981.

————. "Socialist Feminism and the Limits of Dual Systems Theory." *Socialist Review*, nos. 50–51 (March–June 1980): 169–188.

Zetkin, Clara. "Für die Befreiung der Frau!" In *Ausgewählte Reden und Schriften*, 1: 3–11. Berlin: Dietz Verlag, 1957.
————. "Nur mit der proletarischen Frau wird der Sozialismus siegen!" In *Ausgewählte Reden und Schriften*, 1: 95–111. Berlin: Dietz Verlag, 1957. Translated by Hal Draper and Anne Lipow in *Socialist Register 1976*, edited by Ralph Miliband and John Saville, pp. 192–201. London: Merlin Press, 1976.
————. "Surrender of the Second International in the Emancipation of Women." *The Communist International* 6 (1929): 371–382.

Index